Participatory Action Research for Educational Leadership

This book is dedicated to the educators in the Colorado PAR project who started us on this journey and to our family and friends who continue to support us through all the projects in our lives.

Participatory Action Research for *Educational Leadership*

Using Data-Driven Decision Making to Improve Schools

E. Alana James
Jones International University

Margaret T. Milenkiewicz

Alan Bucknam
Notchcode Creative

SAGE Publications
Los Angeles • London • New Delhi • Singapore

Copyright © 2008 by Sage Publications, Inc.

All rights reserved. No part of this book may be reproduced or utilized in any form or by any means, electronic or mechanical, including photocopying, recording, or by any information storage and retrieval system, without permission in writing from the publisher.

For information:

Sage Publications, Inc.
2455 Teller Road
Thousand Oaks, California 91320
E-mail: order@sagepub.com

Sage Publications Ltd.
1 Oliver's Yard
55 City Road
London, EC1Y 1SP
United Kingdom

Sage Publications India Pvt. Ltd.
B 1/I 1 Mohan Cooperative
Industrial Area
Mathura Road, New Delhi 110 044
India

Sage Publications Asia-Pacific Pte. Ltd.
33 Pekin Street #02-01
Far East Square
Singapore 048763

Printed in the United States of America

Library of Congress Cataloging-in-Publication Data

James, E. Alana.
Participatory action research for educational leadership : using data-driven decision making to improve schools/E. Alana James, Margaret T. Milenkiewicz, Alan Bucknam.
p. cm.
Includes bibliographical references and index.
ISBN 978-1-4129-3777-1 (pbk.)
1. Action research in education. 2. Educational leadership. I. Milenkiewicz, Margaret T. II. Bucknam, Alan. III. Title.

LB1028.24.J36 2008
370.7′2—dc22 2007004814

This book is printed on acid-free paper.

07 08 09 10 11 10 9 8 7 6 5 4 3 2 1

Acquiring Editor: Diane McDaniel
Editorial Assistant: Ashley Plummer
Copy Editor: Barbara Coster
Typesetter: C&M Digitals (P) Ltd.
Proofreader: Anne Rogers
Indexer: Julie Sherman Grayson
Cover Designer: Bryan Fishman
Marketing Manager: Nichole Angress

Contents

Acknowledgments

To those who reviewed this book in process, we thank you for pressing us to sort out the forest from the trees. This book improved greatly due to your efforts on its behalf.

Judith Adkison, University of North Texas

Gary L. Anderson, New York University

Mary Brydon-Miller, University of Cincinnati

Teresa T. Field, Johns Hopkins University

Emma Fuentes, University of San Francisco

Elizabeth Grassi, Regis University

Marjorie Hall Haley, George Mason University

Leanne R. Ketterlin-Geller, University of Oregon

Scott Peters, Cornell University

Barbara A. Storms, California State University, East Bay

Patricia Weaver, Henderson State University

Brent G. Wilson, University of Colorado at Denver

Robert E. Yager, University of Iowa

Introduction

The participatory action research (PAR) process, as outlined in this text, represents the next stage of evolution for action research (AR) and practitioner research as practiced in education. This text marries participatory research, incorporating the voice of the public affected by the research, to traditional scientific methods. While some elements of this marriage may seem awkward at first to academics who grew up on either the AR or scientific research side of the fence, our continued work with educational leaders who study disadvantaged students leads us to believe that this "and/both" approach ultimately produces the results school leaders seek and appreciate.

WELCOME TO PAR FOR EDUCATIONAL LEADERS

As the authors of this book, we welcome you to the exciting and rewarding practice of PAR. Having supported a variety of people through PAR projects, we believe that this process is one of the best possible ways to improve school and individual educational practices in local communities.

PAR evolved as a tool for educational leadership by incorporating the best of organizational development (Argyris & Schön, 1974; Coghlan & Brannick, 2001) and systems theory (Senge, 1994) into a useful tool for educators that synthesizes program development and evaluation (Dick, 1998a). It is precisely this evolution that creates the need for this textbook—especially in the United States—as educational leaders are held to high standards for both data-driven decisions and community involvement.

PAR incorporates the highest values and principles for human justice and democracy:

- The belief in human capacity
- The unyielding commitment to social justice and equity
- The value of collaborative work both to individual educators and to their schools
- The norms of professional and public accountability
- Mutual inquiry as a means to honor others, empower ourselves, and adapt to a changing educational environment

The chapters draw on our direct experiences with PAR, as well as other researchers' experiences and relevant theorizing. We owe much—as do all who engage in PAR or its AR cousins—to the work of Kemmis and McTaggart (1988, 1990). Nevertheless, we have modified the older way of discussing the steps (Plan, Action, Observe, and Reflect) to Diagnose, Act, Measure, and Reflect. This book builds a foundation for the pragmatic (practical, based on actual occurrences) use of data to make decisions and to develop new programs and/or structures within a school, classroom, or community-based program. Rather than requiring hours in laboratories or setting up random control trials, these outcomes evolve from the everyday work of educators. Perhaps it is idiosyncratic to research based in the United States, but in our opinion, these modifications align PAR more closely with changes frequently implemented in schools, such as data-driven learning communities, and PAR encourages the implementation of standard research methods as integral to the foundation of educational leadership.

OUR APPROACH TO PAR

It is important to the educators who devote a great deal of time to PAR studies that they produce valid, credible, and reliable results. This research process becomes alive in the hands of the people who are affected by its results. The methodology wrestles the definition of research from the scientific research communities' rigid interpretations and expands the term to a realm where inquiry studies become fluid, as people work together to solve locally identified problems. A broader definition goes hand in hand with our reinterpretation of the PAR steps as we have seen PAR evolve. We view PAR, an appropriate tool to use in a complex environment, as being both rigorous and flexible, obtaining measurements and influencing programmatic outcomes in schools, giving practitioners a logical linear process to work from, and encouraging personalized self-reflection as the motivator for next steps.

We know PAR is a supportive and growth-producing tool in multiple venues. When employed by school leaders, PAR methodology provides an environment through which to support long-range school reform. Educators who work alone, in small groups, or in learning communities can also utilize PAR as a tool for professional development. This structure supports the movement from localized solutions to complex conditions in individual school settings and heightens the potential for all students to experience academic success.

We apply a broad definition to the concept of participatory research, relative to the studies undertaken by educational leaders in communities. As discussed in this book, a participatory research group—also referred to as a project team—is a group of people in different roles who are willing to work together in a collaboratory environment without hierarchy. These participatory groups select and study an educational issue of local pertinence. Consequently, participatory groups, in our definition, may need (but not necessarily include) participation by students, their families, or others. We use this definition to encourage PAR use by collaborative leadership teams within schools such as professional learning communities or communities of practice. Educators benefit from specific, designated times to work together across their normal roles and geographic boundaries. Many former teams have drawn upon their local PAR studies to encourage the development of national communities of practice-related educational topics. On the other hand, we highly encourage the participation of students and families in PAR teams *whenever* possible and appropriate, and we heartily promote environments that are able to embrace this level of diversity. Nevertheless, the participation of educators across the boundaries from which they usually work is sufficient to be labeled as a PAR project.

OUR READERS

While it is true that authors can never control, nor would want to control, who reads their work, books are written from certain assumptions. We are writing this textbook for master's-level students in the field of education working out of a university. Departments of educational leadership, English language acquisition, literacy, science or math concentrations, and special education employ PAR methods to ensure inclusive educational leadership for future decades. At the same time, we believe PAR will aid school administrators, teachers, and support staff currently working in schools. If our reader is a doctoral student, then this is a good book as a basic overview for the process, but other texts, geared to establishing greater academic rigor, should also be consulted.

Although we strongly encourage PAR teams, individual researchers may also select this book. We have included tasks written for both audiences. We trust that our adult readers will massage the other examples and tasks to best suit their needs. We encourage individual readers to recruit a few friends who will challenge their assumptions as they move through the process. This is discussed at length during the book as part of the conversation about participatory groups as critical friends.

We assume that our readers want a book that is clear but also contains key points and specificity to draw upon as a reference throughout a school change process. To that end, we outline PAR as a linear process, although we also know that a study may not progress as such (see Chapter 8). We also assume that educators enjoy exploring some theoretical and historical background, but that limited time does not allow reading a full academic treatise on these subjects. We have attempted to respect these constraints.

If the primary goal for our readership is to improve education for specific groups of students, we see PAR being primarily used to describe the selected population of a single school. Therefore, most statistical processes applicable to quantitative research will not apply to PAR investigations. We refer readers whose work requires a statistical base to their local university library, which should contain a variety of beneficial statistics texts.

FEATURES

This text

- Introduces a step-by-step process in the hopes of easing the reader into a process that becomes iterative and recursive.
- Contains the steps and processes of both PAR and pragmatic research techniques.
- Provides a conceptual basis for the use of PAR as a tool for educational leadership.
- Helps make the most of easily available data.
- Illustrates how educators can complete research studies despite being overwhelmed and "having no time."
- Has culled the tools most likely to be of immediate value.
- Focuses on qualitative data collection.
- Covers the basics of descriptive studies.
- Describes all mathematics in the most simple of terms.

This text does not

- Go into specific details of approval issues of the research review board.
- Supplant comprehensive texts on educational research methodology.
- Cover case studies in depth.
- Provide a course in statistics.
- Discuss quasi-experimental or experimental designs or control groups.
- Discuss statistical power or the null hypothesis.
- Include inferential statistics.

HOW TO USE THIS BOOK

PAR is the marriage between a linear and a reflective process. Therefore, this text encourages reflection in two ways. Readers are asked to begin a reflective journal early in the process, and the text discusses reflection as a method of collecting data. Thereafter, each section heading in each chapter is preceded by reflective questions. Reflective journals are not only an invaluable source of information when writing a final report, but the journals also affirm many reasons to celebrate the growth and development that takes place along the way.

Adult learners will use this text as it suits them. To allow for easy access we have geared our chapter/section headings to be as informative as possible. In addition, each chapter ends with a conclusion through which readers can establish whether and to what extent the basic material in a particular chapter is relevant to address the issues they currently face.

Readers are encouraged to examine the analysis sections in Chapter 9 directly after completing what may be their first full cycle of research. This step will enable a heightened understanding of valid, credible, and reliable results needed for final reports.

PAR teams can divide the work involved in this project by assigning chapters to individual members who will then be responsible for reporting on the material and guiding the group through the tasks involved. Individuals completing PAR projects without the participatory element are encouraged to recruit one or more critical friends with whom they share the steps they undertake throughout the inquiry. These people are asked to challenge all assumptions they hear the PAR practitioner make. Critical friends can also read and edit final reports as well as support the data collection process through brainstorming.

FINAL NOTES

PAR adds a participatory demand on a methodology that otherwise might include teachers working alone in their classrooms or principals running their schools without the benefit of critical friendships or other stakeholders. This participatory element adds, rather than detracts, to the potential of AR. Because PAR is not as widely practiced in schools, we have freely co-opted studies and results from projects whose classification and methodology might not possess the level of collegial involvement we recommend. We look forward to a future edition of this book where PAR studies abound and a growing wealth of examples supports an expanded, more efficacious form of this research methodology. Should readers complete studies they would like to see referenced in this manner, we encourage the studies to be sent to ajames@faculty.jiu.edu.

We acknowledge and are grateful for the work of the authors in the fields of AR and research methods as well as for the many K–12 educators we have had the privilege of working with in the past 5 years. Equally, we gained inspiration and clarity throughout our writing process from the work of authors who write for students working on dissertations or theses. Their work is cited throughout and referenced at the end of the book.

We recognize PAR and action researchers in the field of education, especially those we have had the privilege to work with as they studied areas of extreme disadvantage in the United States. If we bring to light the heart and soul of what you have taught us about the beauty of this work to the field of education, then we have accomplished our mission.

To the academic research community, you have seen the purpose of PAR and have furthered its evolution to the conglomerate it is today, meeting both the needs of the educators and their communities with data-driven methods. The evolution of research in education has swayed back and forth on a pendulum. Many diverse concerned voices are needed if educational research is to settle where both the local and national perspectives are held in balance.

To the next generation of educational leaders who employ PAR to improve educational practices, we look to you to show us where the next growth will come.

CHAPTER 1

The Participatory Action Research Model

Participatory action research (PAR) is a dynamic process for personal and professional development. This tool, in the hands of attentive school administrators, teachers, and their communities, often produces emancipatory results, engaging many partners in the process of school development and reform. This book will help guide readers through the process of PAR and discuss its connection to the world of educational leadership.

Concerned educators in today's schools focus on continuous academic improvement. Their initial inquiries may start with "I wonder if . . . ?" "How can we . . . ?" "Why don't I . . . ?" or "Will it be effective to . . . ?" PAR, as a change process, requires educators to work with others to build data-driven decisions into the core of their practice. As a result, they work for the betterment of students and the welfare of their local school communities.

In a "growing rural town in the southwestern United States," a middle school of 650 students, 12% of whom were identified special needs, used PAR in a yearlong school project to improve educational practices in inclusion classes (Saurino et al., 1996). The outcome of the project included three policy-level suggestions to include special needs students in classrooms during the morning hours, with a student ratio that was comprised of enough above-average students to act as peer mentors and as few inclusion students as practical. In a tertiary outcome of the project, staff reported a greater understanding of the diverse opinions among their colleagues. The awareness led to a more unified approach to a key issue. The efficacy of PAR as a tool for professional development was studied by independent researchers who concluded that PAR "served as a form of self reflective questions which enabled practitioners to better understand and solve problems of interest to them in their own education setting" (Saurino et al., 1996).

The **action research (AR)** portion of PAR is defined as a multistage type of research designed to yield practical results capable of improving a specific aspect of practice and made public to enable scrutiny and testing. This iterative process is bolstered through the strategic use of standard research methods—but AR differs from scientific research practices in a number of ways. The traditional view of scientific research sees research as a distinct and measurable construct in which scientists must remain neutral, without directly influencing the results of their experiments. PAR blends **participatory research**, defined as research conducted in circumstances where diverse practitioners work together to achieve reliable results. In local context this implies groups of citizens who have an equal say in all the aspects of the study. PAR offers a practical and effective approach for educators to study, assess, and improve their own practices, because PAR researchers intentionally make positive changes through the action cycle as they progress with the project. While the scientific view insists on absolute quantifiability, the PAR view appreciates subjective reflection as a form of data, giving credence and respect to intuitively driven moments and epiphanies.

We are particularly enthusiastic about this methodology because it includes collaborative participation and increased involvement of multiple factions within the school community as part of the problem-solving effort. In an example from a national project that we facilitate—an initiative focused on the improvement of education for students experiencing homelessness or high levels of mobility (H&HM)—Lowry Elementary School in Denver, Colorado, hosted a PAR project during the 2005–2006 school year. Involved in the PAR study were the principal, four teachers, and a woman who worked for Colorado's Coalition for the Homeless. While six different projects emerged from the PAR team, most efforts centered on improving aspects of the homework process for students experiencing transience. The community person developed a program for parents who have recently been homeless to help their children with homework. This program was aided by teachers from Lowry Elementary. The teachers in the group focused on either improving homework in their classes or ensuring that notices from school were translated for Spanish-speaking families to promote their involvement. The principal in this study focused on developing protocols within the school that welcomed families midyear and aided their participation in their children's education.

REFLECTIVE QUESTIONS

As mentioned in the Introduction, throughout this book each section will begin with reflective questions aimed at initiating the thought process about the topics within the particular section. PAR practitioners may choose to use these reflections to assist them in recording their process in a reflective journal. These reflections can later be used as qualitative data as appropriate to the practitioners' final projects.

- What concerns do you have about your school community?
- What process would you use to address these issues?
- How would you gather data to measure the problem and your solutions to it?
- How would you keep track of your process and outcomes?

SECTION 1: PAR—A TOOL FOR CHANGE

The history of PAR started in the early 20th century with the work of Kurt Lewin (Coghlan & Brannick, 2001). Lewin's work, called AR, was concerned with iterative cycles of investigation to improve the efficiencies of organizations. In the United States, it fell out of favor for a few decades because of the predominant focus on quantitative studies. Rediscovered in the 1970s (McKernan, 1996), PAR is practiced worldwide for both professional and organizational development. It has demonstrated itself to be particularly efficacious in the realm of curricular development (Elliott, 1991; McKernan, 1996; Zuber-Skerritt, 1992). While there are several subcategories of AR, the participatory model stressed in this text employs the strength of learning communities (Bray, Lee, Smith, & Yorks, 2000; Shapiro & Levine, 1999) related to group learning and data-driven decision making. A pioneer of AR, when writing about the field of education, stated:

> We shall only teach better if we learn intelligently from the experience of shortfall; both in our grasp of the knowledge we offer and our knowledge of how to offer it. That is the case for research as the basis for teaching. (Stenhouse, 1983)

PAR as a Tool for Educational Leadership

PAR, on the other hand, has a long history of use outside the United States (Africa, Latin America, Canada). One strand of this tradition has become focused on teachers and other educational practitioners, some of whom work individually on AR or practitioner research projects, while some participate as teams. Although these variations are similar, and hold the same basic philosophy, AR has often focused on a specific issue as a means to improve teacher practice. PAR (historically) was the term researchers used when the study focused on an issue that directly affected a community. People in the community would work together collaboratively to conduct the research and the necessary actions to correct the situation. As mentioned in the Introduction, the communal nature of education and the need educators have to work in groups outside the small company of colleagues in their school buildings led this book to embrace PAR as a means of both focusing on an issue to improve education and expanding the collegial base of the study to larger groups of educators, preferably working with community members, as well.

Three attributes that contribute to the efficacy of PAR for educators are as follows:

1. The participatory elements of PAR aid in building a community of practice in schools (Wenger, McDermott, & Snyder, 2002).
2. PAR is a means of professional development that involves a wide variety of stakeholders in the improvement of educational practice.
3. The above-mentioned qualities significantly improve the involvement, expertise, and sense of professionalism in PAR practitioners (Greenwood & Levin, 1998; James, 2006a, 2006b, 2006c; Zuber-Skerritt, 1992).

A **community of practice** is defined as "a group of people who share a concern, set of problems or passion and who deepen their knowledge and expertise through regular interaction" (Wenger, 2004, p. 4). The process is democratizing and engages participants to seek solutions for problems they face. Greenwood and Levin (1998) complement the work of Paulo Freire (1986) and his pedagogy of adult literacy as a means for oppressed people to engage actively and to find a democratic voice within their environments. One measurable outcome for this research framework relates to the increase in participants' professional capacity and control over their own situations (Zuber-Skerritt, 1992).

A community of practice developed in the Vancouver (British Columbia) School District as the school district worked to implement "substantial changes in pedagogy, school organization, and professional development" in order to address language issues brought to the fore by changing community demographics (Early, 2001, p. 174). Early reported on a single-school case study for the second phase of the language issue project. The school chosen for her report had a school population where 70% of the students spoke at home 1 of 20 different languages other than English. The collaborative or participatory work for the project included the school's ESL and content teachers working together. This mutual process proved so successful that it continued after the project was over. Because of the nature of AR, the specific ESL processes implemented were specific to the teams of teachers developing them. Early concludes that the process was successful in drawing the attention of teachers to the role of language as a medium of learning in education for all students, and to intentionally plan for greater support between language development and educational development (2001, p. 175).

PAR is a relevant form of professional development for educators and community members because it considers both the context and the content of the issues being studied. While other forms of research set up controlled studies to focus their studies, PAR projects focus on phenomena within the community and school context in which they occur.

Reports produced from PAR studies are intended for a specific constituency, often within the educators' local context, school, or school district. This does not preclude the applicability of PAR findings to state and national educational issues, which are described in Chapters 10 and 11. The reports allow other administrators and teachers to compare and contrast contextual elements and draw their own conclusions about the validity, credibility, and application of the process/outcomes to their own schools and classrooms. PAR outcomes, when used as professional development for educators, are outlined in Table 1.1.

Finally, it is the purpose of professional development to leave practitioners motivated and energized to create needed change by involving them in the study and improvement of their practice. Most educators will agree that trainings frequently do not meet that intended aim. The following two quotes, one from a principal and the other from a teacher, point to the differences in viewpoint about this outcome.

Table 1.1 PAR Outcomes for Educators

PAR Methodological Outcomes
PAR practitioners can expect to develop their professional capacity through critical reflection.
PAR promotes a level of focus on the issue being studied that results in long-term engagement with the issues. This bodes well for any school reform effort.
PAR studies develop local expertise
PAR studies leave the practitioners more motivated and energized about their work than when they began the project

As an administrator, if I was frustrated that teachers weren't doing what I wanted them to do, then I would consider PAR because it gets people involved in "doing." Also it will help the school to be more effective. You can tailor it to the situation. You can get the data to support the issues, or find assumptions your staff are struggling to overcome. For us, I know we haven't done a good enough job of assessing data, but going and telling teachers that won't make that happen. I will need to guide my staff to find out for themselves where we're missing the target. Then they'll own the process, be excited about it, and make some changes. PAR helps me do that.

When I began my participatory action research, my goal was to help my highly mobile students find enjoyment in school and feel more comfortable in the school culture. I really had no goals for my own growth as an educator, yet the lessons that I learned because of doing my research were profound. . . . One of the biggest things I learned through the course of my project was that no matter how busy teachers get, we could do that little bit extra to make a difference in our students' lives. There were times when I was absolutely exhausted by the end of the day and the last thing I wanted to do was stay after school for an extra hour to meet with my group. I found that once we got started and I saw their enthusiasm and appreciation, I reenergized (Reynolds, 2005).

REFLECTIVE QUESTIONS

- What types of research have you done in the past?
- What was your experience of the process?
- How much time do you have to conduct research now?
- With whom will you be working, and what skills do they bring to the process?

SECTION 2: RESEARCH AND ACTION IN THE PAR PROCESS

As previously mentioned, there are many similarities and differences between PAR methodology and forms of traditional, nonparticipatory research. A great deal of this difference is the result of PAR's equal emphasis on knowledge (obtained through research) and action. These two elements influence each other throughout the process. Research methodology influences how constituents of a project discuss and judge its findings and conclusions. Similarly, actions taken during these efforts equate to the larger context of school reform and influence the process in the next round of research. The methodology determines the day-to-day process of the research team, and the resulting strategies in school reform efforts establish the actions taken by school staff. Within PAR, strategic inquiry process and research methodology are so close that they seemingly merge. Within the wider context of educational research, PAR contains both a continuum of methods and a focus on the cyclical process of research and action.

A journal reflection from an elementary school teacher illustrates his broader understanding of this participatory, nontraditional type of research.

My personal background is in the sciences, and I have always thought of research in a traditional scientific sense, with the researcher as an observer, collecting "hard" data that is easily measurable. . . . Action research was extremely difficult for me to wrap my head around. . . . I did not understand how journal entries and personal reflections counted as data sources. . . . PAR is not about finding a definitive answer to a research question using hard data and controls; it is about making a difference through action. I was not a researcher first, I was a teacher, and my responsibilities were to my students. I was dealing with ten- and eleven-year-old human subjects with varied life experiences, feelings, and needs, both educational and emotional. When I put all of that into perspective, I realized that action was the most important aspect of action research (Reynolds, 2005).

Research methods are defined as a series of steps taken to complete a certain task, such as learning the answer to a question or to reach a certain objective, such as finding solutions to a problem or analyzing the effectiveness of a solution in place. Research methods are generally divided into two camps: quantitative (numeric and statistical evidence) such as surveys and assessments, and qualitative (words, often coded for frequency) such as interviews and focus groups. **Focus groups** are interviews conducted with a small group of people, all at one time, to explore ideas on a particular topic. The goal of a focus group is to uncover additional information through participants' exchange of ideas.

Quantitative analysis may appear safer, as it is designed to eliminate the ability of researchers to manipulate analysis to serve their own ends. The safety factor is not fail-safe, as quantitative researchers can display bias with the design of the research questions and also through statistical analysis procedures. Conversely, **qualitative research** is seen by some as suspect, as it may be harder to separate evidence from subjective analysis. Qualitative research is a field of social research that is carried out in naturalistic settings and generates data largely through observations and interviews. Compared to quantitative research, which is principally concerned with making inferences from randomly selected **samples** to a larger population, qualitative research is primarily focused on describing small samples in nonstatistical ways.

Participatory teams use both qualitative and quantitative measurement to their advantage. Since life experiences often defy quantitative measurement, researchers employ qualitative methods (which are discussed at length in Chapter 4). Similarly, since quantitative measurement adds a sense of the concrete to the responses of people in interviews or focus groups, PAR practitioners frequently employ mixed methods design. Working with both together allows educators to make the most of time constraints while studying and improving educational practices in their schools.

The function of PAR practitioners differs from that of other types of researchers. While the daily process is almost identical to the more common "scientific" methodologies (and therefore these are the focus of the first four chapters of this book), ultimately it is the actions that result from this research that create the difference. For a PAR project to be credible, the actions taken must lead to positive results for the populations affected. PAR practitioners make pragmatic use of relevant and available data, collecting evidence to better understand the situation of study. Then they move forward to take action, resulting in changes that affect later measurement.

Another difference between PAR and other research methods lies in the role of reflection as data. During the process of research and action, PAR teams reflect and make subjective decisions based on their personal experiences. These reflective notes are also treated as data *and* are incorporated into the theoretical **research design** to which they adhere. Research design is defined as the plan to be followed to answer the research objectives, the structure or framework to solve a specific problem. PAR researchers work with others and rely on group synergy in building their research designs to aid them in validating the final analysis of the situations they study. Participatory groups add the element of diverse backgrounds and insights, which PAR research employs as an additional form of data through which to build evidence.

The process of research in PAR becomes cyclical as it moves between research (diagnosis), action, research (measurement), and reflection. PAR practitioners engage in multiple cycles using the process described in Table 1.2.

Table 1.2 PAR Steps

PAR Steps
Diagnose: Learning communities or teams of educators serve as participatory groups to evaluate what is currently known about the topic to be studied. They surface their assumptions about the topic and research and evaluate factors that contribute to the status quo. In addition, team members research theory and literature to understand what others have done in similar situations.
Act: Based upon this research, they work individually and with their group to plan possible courses of action and ways to measure it. In all cases, their plans are conceived with the intent of moving status quo to an increased level of effectiveness.
Measure: Implementation is followed by measurement as participants work to achieve student-level outcomes. They use multiple forms of measurement with which to study how their actions affected the populations they are studying.
Reflect: Individual participants reflect on their process, their actions, and their outcomes both singly and as a group. During this reflection, they also brainstorm alternative situations and additional steps. PAR research includes reflection as a source of qualitative data through which they guide their process.

During each iterative cycle, PAR researchers start these same series of steps again. This creates a cyclical motion of increasing knowledge and understanding and then implementing change based on data findings. Because educational issues are complex, the cycles will not be as uniform as the ones in Figure 1.1. PAR researchers may find that before attending to the issue of academic achievement (for instance), they may need to address other issues (i.e., regular attendance, adequate nutrition, sufficient school supplies) within the context of their communities.

Nevertheless, a simplistic but informative drawing of the cycles of PAR is shown in Figure 1.1.

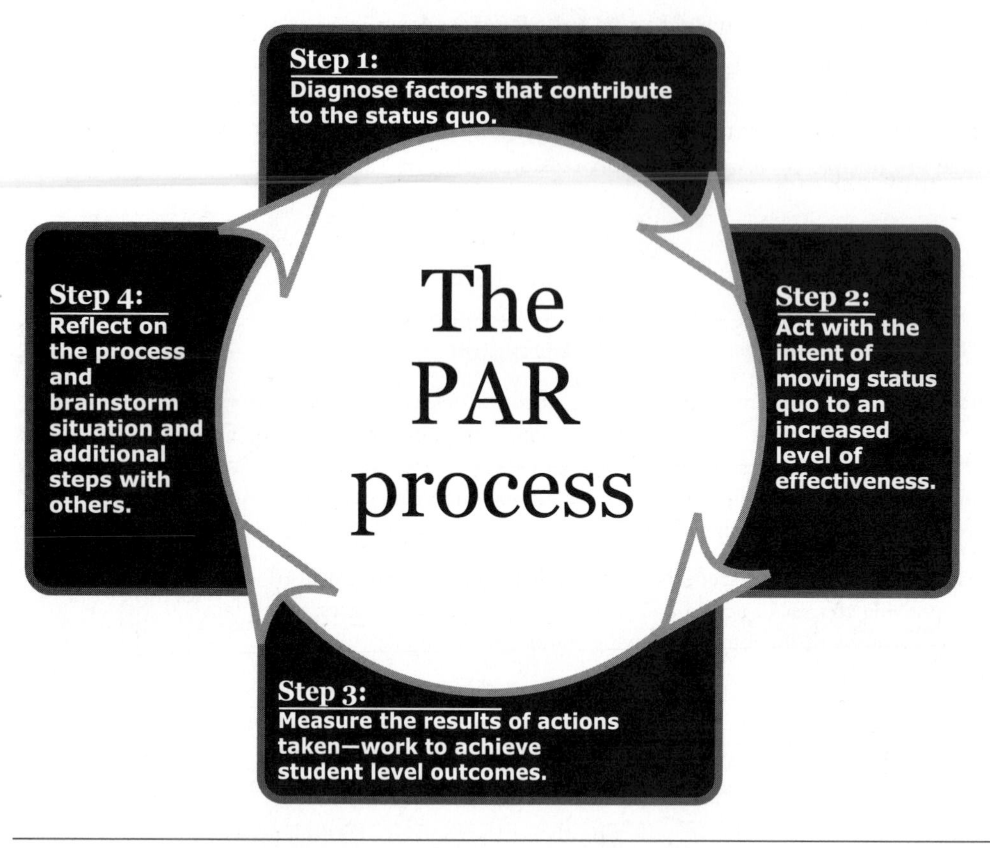

Figure 1.1 The PAR Process

SOURCE: Alan Bucknam/Notchcode Creative, 2005.

REFLECTIVE QUESTIONS

- Think of a time when you worked with a group of people to accomplish a task. What were the challenges related to group work?
- When does working with a group become more efficient than working on your own?
- What guidelines would you set with a new team to ensure success?

SECTION 3: PARTICIPATORY RESEARCH AS A TOOL TO ADDRESS ADAPTIVE CHANGE

As mentioned in the first section of the chapter, this book is written as an aid to educational leadership. PAR as a process allows educational leaders to engage and involve their school communities in tackling some of the hardest questions in education. Issues such as the discrepancies in socioeconomic standing or ethnicity within schools are called **adaptive problems,** where the distance between the real and the ideal is great enough to cause distress for those who try to unravel a problem. If the distance to solving the problems seems insurmountable, such as with complex issues internal to poverty, then educators become discouraged and shut down. These adaptive issues require perseverance from educators trying to close the very real gaps between populations within their schools. PAR has demonstrated its efficacy in helping leadership address adaptive issues by creating a **holding environment,** defined as a situation set up by a leader to diminish discouragement of team members as they address the problem and face a difficult and complex set of issues. This critical concept is discussed at greater length in Chapter 11 (Heifetz, 2000). The PAR process provides such a holding environment for participants when they encounter difficult challenges (James, 2005b, 2006a, 2006b, 2006c).

Think of the holding environment as a pressure cooker. The cook regulates the pressure by turning the heat up or down, while the relief valve lets off steam to keep the pressure within a safe limit. If the pressure goes beyond the carrying capacity of the vessel, the pressure cooker can blow up. On the other hand, with no heat, nothing cooks (Heifetz, Kania, & Kramer, 2005, p. 12).

This discussion raises the question of whether and to what extent research can be used by leadership to solve problems. Enter AR, in general, and PAR, specifically, as an answer. Typically, the gathering and reporting of data on particular topics is useful to decision makers, and therefore some evaluation or research is employed. PAR studies deliberately engage the people who do the work to create the change. These same individuals inform the decisions that influence their school environments. Similar to professional learning communities, PAR researchers can examine procedures, for instance, of classroom behavior management plans, while concurrently addressing the plans during the action cycles of their studies. Nonparticipatory formats for research may study these issues but solicit external consultation and do not involve the people performing the work to measure or design the changes that are indicated.

Steps that would be taken during a nonparticipatory pattern for research (taken into an educational realm) would include the following:

- A topic of interest generally defined by a stakeholder such as national, state, or school district administration or some other authority with access to funds, privately or through government support. Stakeholders finance the research and drive the topic to be studied.
- A proposal or contact written by researchers to the funding agency. These outline how they would accomplish the outcomes desired. Decision makers select and contract with the research agency. The funding entity may or may not understand the research process well.
- **Informed consent** from the subjects (people) to allow a specific aspect of their lives to be used as data. Defined as the agreement between concerned parties about the data-gathering process and/or the disclosure, reporting, and/or use of data, information, and/or results from a research experiment in an educational setting, informed consent in education holds fewer restrictions than other fields, such as medicine. As is discussed in Chapter 2, educators have some latitude through legal means to utilize educational data, such as scores from tests and demographics, for school improvement efforts. This type of data may be drawn upon without the active consent of the subjects.

In this example, nonparticipatory researchers (a) collect data from the subjects or large educational databases, (b) draw conclusions based on gathered data, and (c) report findings to funders. Stakeholders have the primary concern for long-term improvements related to the issue. Seldom do they consult the researchers or subjects for agreement with policies derived from the research findings. For these reasons, the above model describes a hierarchical stance. The funding stakeholders possess the most power related to the research results. The subjects participating in the research hold the least power, while the researchers' position would be placed somewhere in the middle.

The holding environment created through the PAR process flattens the traditional hierarchy mentioned at the beginning of this section. Research practitioners have input in all aspects of the project: research design, data collection, analysis, and conclusions. The participatory team is encouraged with a sense of their own expertise (Freire, 1993; James, 2005a). To the extent that all voices are included in the process, from students, teachers, and community members to school district administration, a PAR team creates a democratic means of establishing policy.

Let's imagine that a traditional nonparticipatory research team was commissioned to investigate a drop in attendance in a school. They begin their data collection using quantitative measures and report the percentages plotted over the school year. They hold interviews with teachers and/or focus groups with parents or students for additional evidence to add context to their quantitative data for the report. Because the research team is outside the school and working on multiple projects simultaneously, their ability to gain access to data and schedule appointments adds time constraints to their process. Upon completion of the study, they take a semester to file their report with the school principal, who reads the report, when convenient, and proceeds to implement the policy changes recommended.

In contrast, if a PAR group were established to study the same issue in the same school, the team would include, at minimum, a teacher, an administrator, the attendance clerk, and concerned parents. The PAR process would force them out of their comfort zone and, because of that force, would act as the holding environment. They would query the same sources, probably dividing the work among them. They would face the hard task of home visits, personal interviews, and focus groups with students and families who were low attenders. Convening regularly to share results, they would discuss the situation from each of the unique vantage points they represented. Ideas would surface for which they might decide to implement a new approach on a temporary basis. The results of any new actions would be measured and would add to their data. At the end of the same period of time as the previous study, their school would have the advantage of key stakeholders informed and invested in the process. The participatory team would have implemented a few ideas to test impact on the issues faced. Most likely, ideas would be flexible according to the school's particular situation, which this school-based research group would understand in depth.

This model is equally useful for larger organizational structures such as school districts, state educational agencies, and national initiatives focused on specific educational issues.

An Example of PAR Use in the Classroom

Tobey was a fifth-grade teacher in Columbine Elementary School in Longmont, Colorado, when she participated in a statewide educational leadership group convened to improve educational practice for students experiencing H&HM

due to financial instability. Her PAR group consisted of school administrators and teachers paired in teams and representing rural, small town, suburban, and urban educational settings whose academic standing was impacted by student transience.

Tobey's story is useful, for it provides a glimpse into how cycles of research aid educators to understand the complex issues they experience. She began her study pointing out the following:

As a third-year teacher at Columbine, I saw a need for greater attention to be placed on students from our H&HM population. Many of the students in my class would leave for several weeks or months and return numerous times throughout the year, their academic progress often suffering (Bassoff, 2004).

Tobey's PAR group met every other month throughout the school year. These sessions were a time to exchange ideas, to discuss the work they were doing, and to challenge each others' assumptions.

When I presented my goal of helping H&HM students become more academically competent to my colleagues in the PAR group, they found it to be too broad. They helped me narrow my focus, challenging my assumptions about my students. I didn't actually know whether or to what extent my H&HM students were lagging academically (Bassoff, 2004).

As the project started, and due to discussions within her participatory group, Tobey became aware of how students' lack of food, shelter, clothing, and school supplies could impact their performance in her classroom. A concern related to students' basic needs became her first cycle of research. Tobey sought to better understand why a few students arrived late to class and whether or not they had jackets or had eaten breakfast.

My most startling discovery was that one of my students rode a bus to school even though our school had officially eliminated the need for bus service. It turned out that he wasn't eating breakfast in the morning because the bus dropped him off at school just before the bell rang. Due to his conscientious effort to make it to school on time, he elected to miss breakfast. However, he would perform poorly in class as a result (Bassoff, 2004).

Tobey's work continued to transform through four cycles of AR. In the second cycle, she went on to ask, "Since students can't learn if their basic needs are not being met, how can I ensure that my students' basic needs are being met?" In the action portion of this cycle, Tobey gathered school supplies, backpacks, and so on to have on hand for H&HM students and proceeded to measure whether and to what extent this support affected their adjustment to her classroom. In her third cycle, influenced by the PAR team's discussions on welcoming school culture, her topic question evolved: "I was led to unexpected paths. This time I questioned whether or not the classroom felt welcoming." In the action portion of this cycle, Tobey set up table tents, folders, and other supplies and left a few empty desks in her classroom. With these steps she could easily welcome a new student and could efficiently have a desk and supplies ready when the youth joined the class.

The learning cycle that Tobey experienced through this professional development project culminated in her fourth cycle, when she directly confronted her need to change educational practice to enhance the reading performance for these students. Tobey's increased understanding of her students lives, gained through Cycles 1 through 3, caused her to change the poetry section of a nationally developed curriculum to include poems about homelessness. Quickly her results showed an increase in motivation with some students who were initially hesitant to memorize poems but now were ultimately eager to share.

As I reflected on the interests of the class and went back through my journal, it dawned on me that what my students needed was an opportunity to express what they had learned from their own experiences. Operating under my currently successful guided reading model of instruction, I began to look at ways in which I could make the model flexible. I wanted to tap into my students' strengths as tellers of their own stories (Bassoff, 2004).

Tobey used computerized reading materials to measure her progress in boosting academic achievement. Her story is also noteworthy because her students encountered above-average test results.

Even though my school year is only three quarters complete, student achievement on the computerized reading assessment program in my class increased an average of 200 lexiles for my stable student population and over 300 lexiles for my homeless and highly mobile student population. The average student is expected to grow 75–100 lexiles in one school year (Bassoff, 2004).

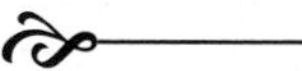

Task 1.1: Beginning a Reflective Journal

In Tobey's example, the reflective journal was key to her recollection of points of decision making as she progressed through the cycles of PAR. The purpose of the task outlined below is to get your PAR project off to a solid start by starting a reflective journal. While the topic of "reflection as data" for PAR projects is covered in Chapter 3, Section 3, the reflective questions that precede each section in every chapter offer many potential reflective prompts as you engage in the PAR process. Reflections provide not only data for your study but also a starting point for discussion with your participatory team as your research develops.

Procedure

Step 1: Decide upon a place and method of recording reflective data that has a high likelihood of becoming part of your daily or weekly routine. This may be starting a file on a computer and placing a regular reminder in your calendar or diary. You may also choose to start a notebook where you can jot quick Post-it Notes and organize them periodically. Other PAR practitioners found that keeping a journal in more than one location (at home and at school, for instance) allowed them to re-sort the notes by date when it was time to share reflections for team analysis.

Step 2: Begin all reflective journal notes with the date.

Step 3: Decide what other issues you may want to regularly reflect upon:

- What have you recently learned?
- Are you satisfied with your progress?
- What challenges are you facing, and how have you overcome them?
- What do you want to do next?
- What inhibits the outcome for which you search? The outcome you are trying to achieve?
- Who might help overcome challenges?
- How is the dynamic of the participatory team working?
- What new assumptions have you uncovered?
- How will these assumptions be tested?

Step 4: Review your recent progress and write a closing sentence that sums up this stage of your PAR project.

Step 5: Record as well your conversations with your participatory team, your classmates, or your professor as you have the opportunity to discuss your progress with them.

CONCLUSION

People working together to solve local problems is the essence of PAR work. This process involves concerned individuals and aids them to overcome the challenges experienced when conducting research. To the extent that participants work collectively to include proven research methodologies and rigorous designs, PAR blends the best of community involvement, research, and action. The PAR process

- Is situated in research methodology, most often as a mixed methods approach.
- Uses a team approach, which addresses the complexities of a situation.
- Puts equal emphasis on inquiry or research and action.
- Is a cyclical process that repeats the four steps of (1) diagnose, (2) act, (3) measure, and (4) reflect.

While situated within a mixed methodological approach, PAR has both similarities and differences when compared to other types of research. PAR is similar to scientific research in that a project typically makes pragmatic use of mixed research methodology, incorporating both qualitative and quantitative evidence. PAR is different from scientific studies in that research and action are given equal emphasis and the researcher is encouraged to influence the ultimate project outcomes. Also, because the researcher is seen as a valuable voice in the team process, each team member's regular reflections are used as data. PAR's emphasis on practical results creates a process of iterative steps that continue until the PAR practitioners are satisfied with the results. The four steps—(1) diagnose, (2) act, (3) measure, and (4) reflect—are rarely clear-cut or obvious, yet they incorporate standard methodological procedures and drive the process through to a positive conclusion for educational practices and communities.

PAR is an exceptional tool for educational leaders because it builds on the professional learning community environment found in schools. One of the most intriguing aspects of the process is its ability to provide a holding environment that diminishes the natural tensions created by school reform. PAR allows administrators and teachers to focus on the difficult adaptive work to reduce the distance between the ideal of high standards of achievement and the sometimes discouraging reality of standardized test scores. Whenever educational leaders wish to build sustainable results, communication is key—among participants, within their communities, and with all stakeholders. The PAR process ensures the integrity of the resulting actions to solve demanding, multifaceted school problems due to the active engagement of multiple factions of the school community.

New PAR practitioners are urged to remember that they will have several cycles during which they can approach an issue from different vantage points. Use of reflective journals, started at the beginning of the research project, will prove to be of assistance with the analysis of the individual and collective learning of team members throughout the study.

CHAPTER 2

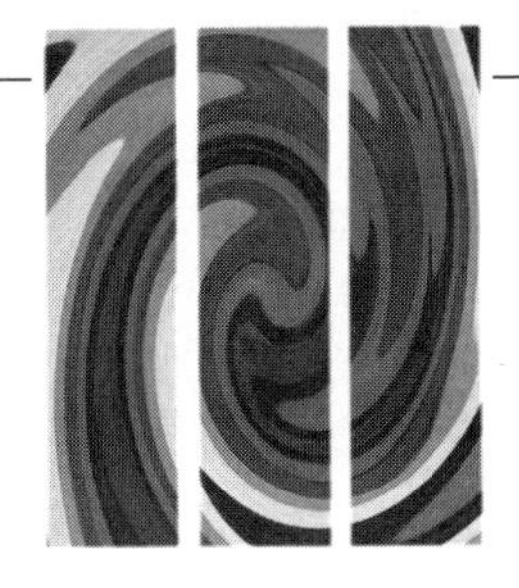

The Tenets of PAR: Ethics, Purpose, and Logic

As shown in Figure 2.1, we believe ethics, purpose, and logic to be ideas that overarch all of research and are worthy of discussion before PAR begins. The research process is similar to curricular design in three ways, described here as the **tenets**, or basic beliefs upon which each discipline is built. While, like values, tenets are defined and subscribed to on an individual basis, they are confirmed through increasing development of capacity. First, both demand that practitioners behave at all times in a way that is respectful to the people toward whom their actions are directed. The ways to ensure this respect is discussed in Section 1 on ethics. Second, both judge their outcomes against firmly established goals or purposes. The power of **purpose statements** in PAR studies is discussed in Section 2. Purpose statements are one or two sentences that convey the motivation behind the PAR project, to help researchers keep focused close to their goals. Third and finally, both branches of learning require that new strategies and knowledge build on previous knowledge. The use of a logic model that incorporates previous studies found in the literature is covered in Section 3. These tenets result in educational practices aimed at improving learning and building improved practices and curriculum while treating students with the utmost respect.

REFLECTIVE QUESTIONS

- What do you believe to be the most important ethical standards for educators when working with students and families?
- What steps do educators take to ensure student confidentiality?

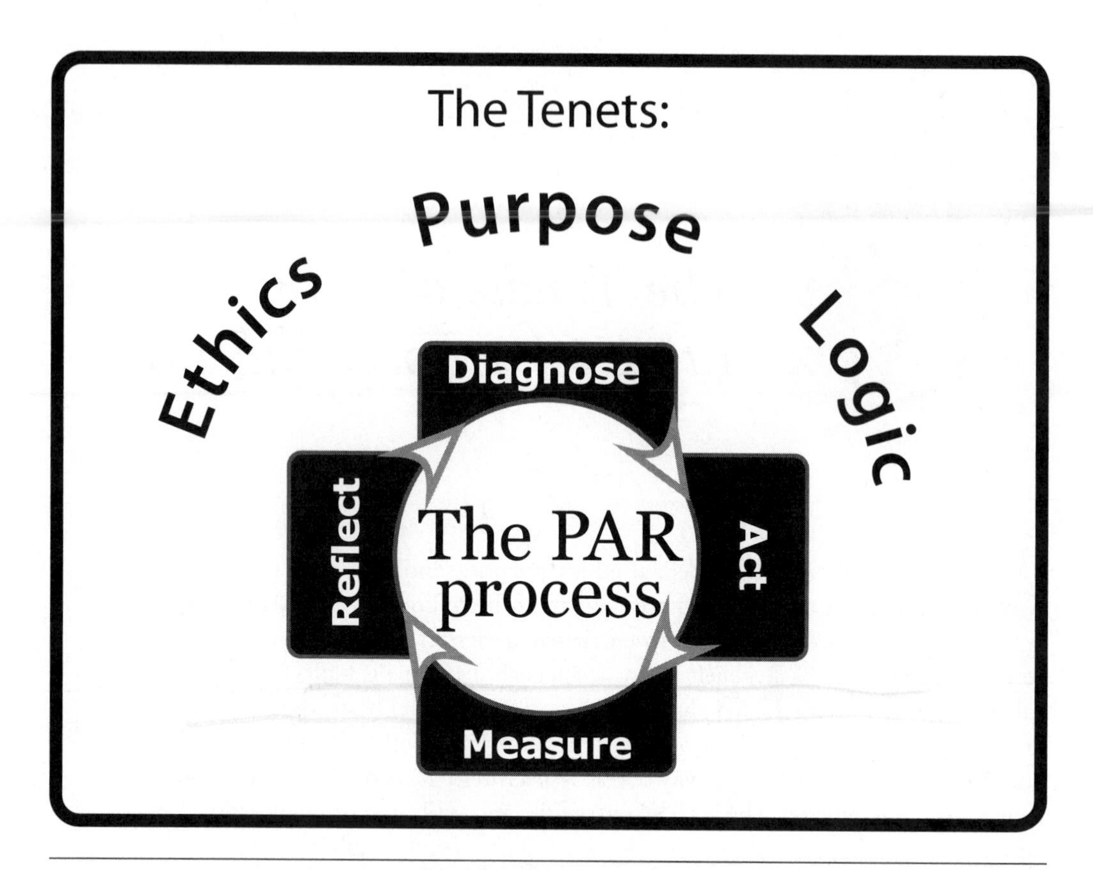

Figure 2.1 Prior to the PAR Steps

SOURCE: Alan Bucknam/Notchcode Creative, 2005.

SECTION 1: ETHICS

The ethics of education work to prevent students from harm. Nevertheless, insecurities, embarrassment, or ridicule still take place in schools. **Do no harm** means do not cause injury or damage to individuals in research through the misuse of research subjects, often related to "informed consent" protocols in educational studies. This is the first ethical principle in medicine, education, and all fields of research (Goree, Pyle, Baker, & Hopkins, 2004; Sommers & Sommers, 2004). Using balls to represent types of qualitative methods and cubes to represent quantitative research methods, the relationship of these three foundational elements is displayed in Figure 2.2.

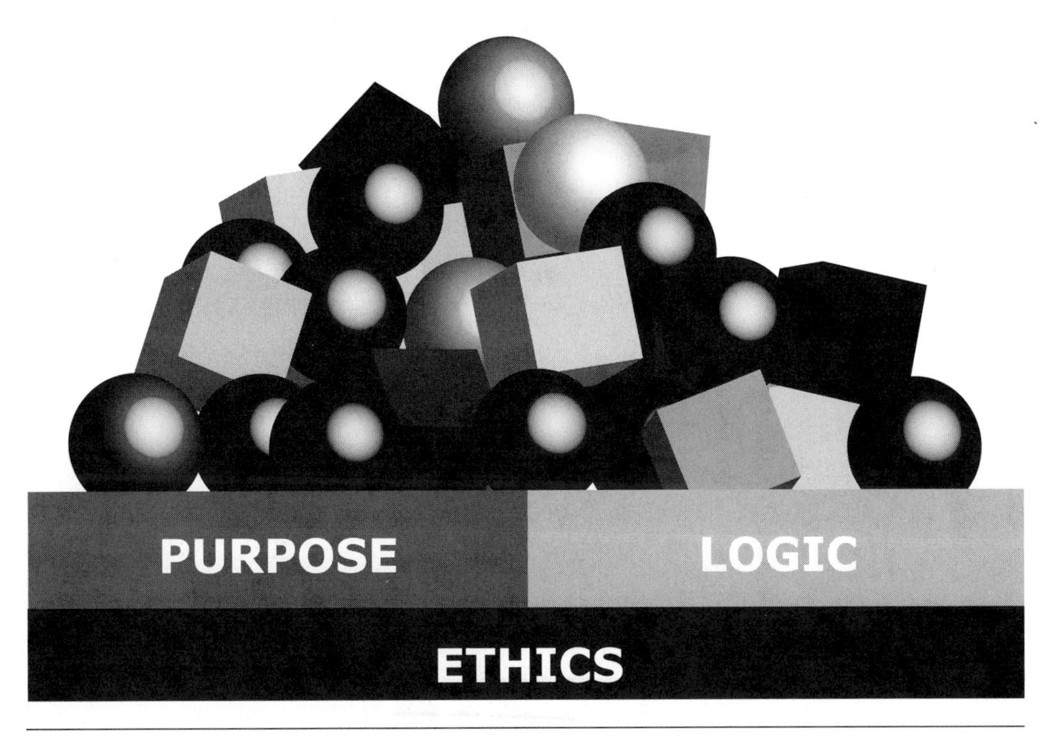

Figure 2.2 Foundations of PAR

SOURCE: Alan Bucknam/Notchcode Creative, 2005.

Purpose statements and logic models are basic foundational methods with which PAR practitioners bind their projects and ensure success and are discussed in the following two sections. Ethics, as illustrated in Figure 2.2, is the tenet without which the others do not stand. Research has not always adhered to these standards, with the most highly reported cases of unethical behavior occurring in the biomedical arena; perhaps the most horrific cases are those of physicians and scientists who had conducted biomedical experiments on concentration camp prisoners (National Institutes of Health, 1979). Unfortunately, research atrocities have occurred in the United States as well. One of the most publicized cases is the Tuskegee Syphilis Study from 1932 to 1972 in which 400 poor, mostly illiterate, African American migrant workers were enrolled in the research. Subjects were not told they had syphilis, and even though penicillin was commonly acknowledged as a successful treatment by 1948, the drug was withheld from many of the subjects to boost the scientific evidence of how the disease spreads and kills (Reverby, 2000). The Belmont Report of 1974 established ethical principles for all research of a biomedical or behavioral nature (National Institutes of Health, 1979). All research for publication or federally funded studies must undergo a rigorous institutional review board (IRB) and receive approval before data may be collected. Readers of this text who consider a PAR project as part of their practical experience at a university should discuss the potential of review with their professors.

PAR teams may be required to complete a formal application outlining the research design. Applications are reviewed against standards that deem some educational research exempt as follows.

EXEMPTION 1 (45 CFR 46.101(b)(1))

Research conducted in established or commonly accepted educational settings, involving normal educational practices, such as (i) research on regular and special education instructional strategies, or (ii) research on the effectiveness of or the comparison among instructional techniques, curricula, or classroom management methods (U.S. Department of Health and Human Services, 2005).

An awareness of local school district policy on data collection from students and families is a first step for educators initiating a PAR project. Even though many studies are exempt from federal review, the local school district may have implemented controls, which will have bearing on the amount of confidentiality and type of consent needed before data are collected.

Ethical Elements

PAR research practice is ethical when educational researchers

- Obtain informed consent by requesting permission from students and their parents after completely outlining their data collection strategies, disclosing the intent of the research, its benefits and risks, and the parties who will have access to the information gathered.
- Work to ensure that no subtle or overt harm is done to the subjects who allow personal information to be included in the research.
- Hold the knowledge of personal experience in a strictly confidential manner.
- Add to the body of knowledge about the subject under study.

- Employ research techniques that are as valid and rigorous as possible.
- Take action to overcome the issues they study.
- Care about their subjects, the education they receive, their ongoing success in life, and the democratic ideals implicit in education.
- Are completely honest during and following the research study, disclosing both pros and cons about the research. These lessons include what was beneficial and components that would be done differently if the project were to be repeated (Creswell, 2002, 2003; Goree et al., 2004; Noddings, 2003).

The basis of informed consent is a complete disclosure of the reasons, benefits, risks, and potential outcomes of the research. As mentioned in Chapter 1, informed consent is defined as the agreement between concerned parties about the data-gathering process and/or the disclosure, reporting, and/or use of data, information, and/or results from a research experiment. Children under 18 are protected subjects, requiring consent from both parent(s) or guardian(s) as well as their own. When requesting consent, educators reveal the tie between their research efforts and the improvement of academic practices. How these data are gathered, from whom, the type of analysis, and the expected benefit should all be transparent to the fullest extent possible, given the age of the student to be studied. For instance, parents would need to understand that research would include reviewing school records, conducting interviews, holding focus groups, and so on and that results would not name their child directly but would be a report of aggregate data. Students and their family members need to understand that they can refuse to participate in the research without any risk of consequence.

One specific risk in **quantitative research** (which uses primarily some variation on the survey to gather evidence that it reports numerically) or qualitative research (which uses some variation of the interview to gather evidence reported in words) that requires researcher awareness and diligence is risk of embarrassment. Should participants in the study experience embarrassment or discomfort at any time during or after the research, informed consent regulations require researchers to explain clearly participants' rights to withdraw without consequences (U.S. Department of Health and Human Services, 2005).

PAR practitioners need to consider another aspect of the ethic of beneficence—or do no harm. Researchers may do harm when they enter into their studies with a strong presupposed **bias** as to what they will find. Bias is created by influences that distort the results of a research study. While the issue holds greatest concern in medical and psychological fields where researchers have the option to prescribe medication or studies involve the investigation of emotional conditions, it is also relevant to the field of education. Whether conducted in a subtle manner or not, to encourage or to project a predetermined outcome on participants devalues their responses and voice. Bias creates harm to the subject, to the constituency, and to the field of study when researchers release a report of flawed research.

School culture is often built with an attitude of a team of professionals working together to support students. Because school staff often work with the same students, they occasionally share information freely about particular children. Some professionals perceive this action to be to the benefit of the students, holding the belief that once school personnel understand the issues individual students face, the staff will treat each student with concern. In the PAR process, ethical considerations of research override well-meaning—but inappropriate—communication, and practitioners must put aside well-intentioned reasons for sharing personal information about students.

Research data collected for a specific project must be held in strict confidence within the PAR practitioner team. Quotations should only be cited without names or significant identifiers. Student stories should be reported with clarifying phrases such as, "this student will be called Jose" or "the name has been changed to Sally." Another phrase that PAR practitioners may find of assistance is "data will be reported in aggregate form." Translate this to students and families as "I won't report anything you say as your thoughts but will pool all the interviews together when I tell others what I have learned."

PAR adds to the body of knowledge about lessons learned by educational leadership in diverse local communities. PAR reports have been used to influence state and local educational policy and the actions of school boards. Because of this ladder of influence, it is important that every participatory group or team act as **critical friends** for each other. In a 1993 article, Arthur Costa and Bena Kallick defined *critical friend* as "a trusted person who asks provocative questions, provides data to be examined through another lens, and offers critique of a person's work as a friend. A critical friend takes the time to fully understand the context of the work presented and the outcomes that the person or group is working toward. The friend is the advocate for the success of that work" (p. 50). While the topics of validity, credibility, and reliability are readdressed in Chapter 5, it is important to note that PAR seeks to construct a "holistic understanding of the dynamic and complex societal world" (Stringer, 2004, p. 55). PAR projects, ethically, demand as much rigor as is possible to show that the conclusions are formed from a valid mixture of data, not merely one or two individuals' private agendas.

It is vital to remember that the middle word, and the second step, in a PAR cycle is *action*. Frequently during the first round of research, especially when the topic is relatively complex or obscure, the action amounts to the collection of more data than was available when the project began. From the second cycle on, however, it is ethically important that well-planned actions begin to improve the situation under study. It is also critical to have a clearly defined target outlined by the purpose statement.

Task 2.1: The Formation of an Ethical Plan for PAR Projects

This task encourages both administrators and teachers, working individually or as part of a PAR team, to investigate the ethical considerations inherent in their projects and to plot informed consent.

Procedure

Step 1: Investigate the school district policies that may influence or constrict your research. Request guidance from the school administration regarding requirements for informed consent. Remember, general guidelines indicate that program coordinators have a right to investigate their program outcomes and school personnel have a right to investigate their student outcomes without causing concern.

Step 2: Read through the ethical considerations and determine which, if any, may be (a) covered under school district or organization guidelines of which you should be aware and (b) difficult to ensure, given your individual PAR project.

Step 3: Craft ethical guidelines addressing the considerations outlined in Section 3. Each may be a statement of your intent to address this topic to the best of your ability, or, as in informed consent, which follows, the issue may need more elaboration.

Step 4: Develop preliminary guidelines for gathering informed consent from students and their families or use the procedures provided by your local school district. Discuss these guidelines with your PAR team. Act as critical friends for each other. Discuss worst-case scenarios to ensure that all team members agree that all potential ethical issues have been covered.

Step 5: Report your final ethical strategies to your project stakeholders, which may include school administration, community members, or university classmates and professors.

REFLECTIVE QUESTIONS

- In your role, what concerns do you have related to education?
- What are a few specific topics that you would like to investigate to improve educational practice?
- For each idea, what would be the goal or desired outcome of your inquiry?

SECTION 2: THE POWER OF PURPOSE

School reform efforts aim to improve education. The core motivation in education is for all students to learn and through learning to become successful. When educators lose the ability to measure success in terms of increased student achievement, school reform goes astray. Good research is similarly built upon an understanding of the specific purpose that drives the study (Creswell, 2002). PAR practitioners address two types of purpose: what they want to learn (research) and what they want to improve because of that learning (action).

In its simplest form, a purpose statement is one or two sentences that convey this twofold motivation behind the PAR project. As an example, administrators who want to look into school attendance issues might phrase their purpose statement as follows: "Our purpose is to understand the mitigating factors that lead to poor attendance and to establish new support systems to help students attend more regularly." A teacher also might write, "My purpose is to understand what causes some students to come to school less frequently in order to establish flexible instructional strategies that improve their academic success." Participatory groups similarly need to work with the ideas and motivations that bring them together until a clear purpose for increased understanding and resulting action is established.

It is surprisingly easy for researchers to set off on a research journey, take a few interesting side trips, and end up miles away from the desired destination, just weeks before the end date of the project. Purpose statements help researchers keep focused on their goals. This is not to say that research must move rigidly in a straight progression toward the established goal. The wonder and joy in PAR methodology is its support of side trips that potentially add valuable data and new dimensions to the original study. The interesting side trips taken by Tobey in the Chapter 1 case study allowed greater understanding of the issues faced by her students than previously imagined, which she then applied to improve academic outcomes. Purpose statements guide side trips back toward the destination.

Format for Purpose Statements

To some extent, the way in which researchers fashion their purpose statements will determine the methodology they use to complete their research. John Creswell (2003) writes about a variety of forms of purpose statements, pointing out stylistic differences for diverse research methodologies. We assume (a) that most PAR projects contain at least some qualitative evidence and (b) that busy educators grab whatever data they can as they proceed with their study. This second characteristic makes PAR practitioners pragmatic (practical and down-to-earth) in their use of mixed methodology, resulting in the following list of elements to include in purpose statements for PAR projects.

In the first sentence,

- Begin with "The purpose of this study is to . . ."
- Include action verbs, such as *investigate, transform, explore.*
- Include both general and specific descriptions of the educational issue under study.
- Include both research and action outcomes.

In the second sentence,

- Indicate the methodology; this may be "participatory action research using a mixed methodological design for data collection and analysis."
- Inform the reader as to the **population** and context of the study. Give an example or further explanation for this step.

The population is a group of persons that one wants to describe or about which one wants to generalize. To generalize about a population, one often studies a sample that is meant to be representative of the population. Context is situated information and/or environment that have specific characteristics that may not be transferable.

Task 2.2: Multiple Journal Entries Define Purpose

The purpose of this task is to guide you through a repetitive journaling process that ultimately leads to creating a solid and motivating purpose statement. This individual exercise will need to be adjusted for use with a participatory team.

Procedure

Step 1: Spend 1–2 minutes journaling the answers to the following sentence stems: "The concerns I have with my teaching or educational practice are . . ." "What I want to accomplish with this project is . . ." Write everything that comes to mind; do not worry if it is false, repetitive, or exaggerated. Do not allow your mind to think "but that is impossible"—just write everything that comes to mind. When done, put the notes aside for a few days.

Step 2: Repeat Step 1 with the sentence stem "What I need to understand before I can accomplish my goal is . . ."

Step 3: After resting from these thoughts for a period, read what you first wrote and determine which of the purposes you would rank as one and two. Consider which are the more interesting, provocative, and exciting to you and why that might be true. If the purpose(s) you selected appear completely impossible to accomplish within the time allotted for this project, break it (them) down into smaller subsections that would lead toward the larger aspirations.

Step 4: Spend another few minutes reflecting on the reasons you wish to accomplish both of these purposes, and for each think about these questions: What is motivating about the idea of learning about this topic or accomplishing this purpose? How will it improve the lives of students, teachers, or staff? Would this purpose be interesting to others? Will it improve school achievement? And so on.

Step 4: In the final session, craft three or four ways in which you could state one or two favorite purpose statements using the format discussed.

Step 5: Choose the statement that you like the best and discuss it with your team, participatory group, classmates, or professor.

Step 6: Examine your purpose statement and those of others and look for passion, excitement, reasonableness, and attainability. Share your thoughts with others.

REFLECTIVE QUESTIONS

- Think about your favorite lesson or curriculum. What other knowledge contributes added richness to the content?
- What are logical steps of this lesson or curriculum?
- In what ways can the learners experiment and draw their own conclusions?

Logic models provide "lesson plans" for the PAR practitioner. Developed in the 1980s for use in program evaluation, logic models are employed in PAR to help practitioners focus on their purpose and find the literature they need to solidify their diagnosis of the problem as they work through each cycle (James, 2006c).

SECTION 3: LOGIC MODELS

Every process has a logical progression of steps to help ensure success for the individuals who implement the processes. In research, the basic process includes defining the problem to be researched, checking previous literature to establish a theoretical and practical understanding of the issues, proceeding with data collection and analysis, and finally reporting results. This rational progression of steps is known as the logic model and was developed during the 1990s from the momentum for logical program evaluation. We have modified this tool to serve as an aid for PAR practitioners.

The following five questions guide the logical flow of analysis from purpose to research design:

1. What is the purpose behind your study, and what questions emerge from that purpose that need to be addressed?
2. Who has previously studied these topics?
3. What elements/variables were shown to be important in their studies?
4. How would I measure those same elements/variables, given my situation?
5. What form of analysis would I need to implement?

It is normal for the purpose of a PAR project and the resulting **research questions**, or focus for the study, to evolve over time. Once a research question is defined, the logic model, an iterative tool, will be edited and will change throughout the study. Consequently, practitioners who may experience hesitancy when asked about the study's purpose may gradually gain confidence by working through the process in vague or loose terms. Specific questions will emerge over time. To support this evolving PAR process, it may be helpful to journal through a series of questions such as "What do I really care about? What interests me? What would I like to accomplish with my study?"

As an example, a PAR study in the group we facilitate on issues regarding homeless students might have a general question such as "How many of our students could fit under the definition of homeless and/or highly mobile?"

When they started reading the literature, they found that, while the total number of students in this population would be learned through their school records, many authors had written about the general effects of homelessness on students. The PAR team then revised the question to cover the specific issues that seemed to affect their school. The final study question became "How many of our students have (a) difficult health issues, (b) self-identity issues, and (c) gaps in their academic understanding, due to periods of homelessness?"

Table 2.1 illustrates a typical first cycle of research for a PAR study that builds upon one group's answers for these same questions. In this example, teachers (one of whom is a graduate student) work in a middle school and teach the same core subject. The purpose of their project is to understand the elements that affect their students' comprehension and to improve their teaching strategies in this area. They started by asking what others have done to improve reading comprehension. They found two studies that were of interest and then listed the most provocative strategies and ideas. Finally, after reading Chapters 4, 5, and 6, they filled in the last two columns, listing how they would measure and analyze what they were currently doing in order to improve.

As previously mentioned, PAR practitioners work four steps into each cycle of research, as shown in Figure 2.3.

The logic model helps practitioners diagnose the situation by forcing them to look at the research and pull from it the elements they wish to study in their own research design. These elements, or *variables,* are then measured,

Table 2.1 First Cycle of PAR

Questions to be addressed	*Previous studies*	*Variables elements to be measured*	*Local measurements*	*Form of analysis*
What have others done when wanting to improve reading comprehension?	(Harvey & Goudvis, 2000) (Keene & Zimmermann, 1997)	Strategic thinking Strategic reading Bridges Synthesis Visualization/ sensory images Inference	Teacher observation Student writing Tapes of lessons Artwork with students explaining	Qualitative coding

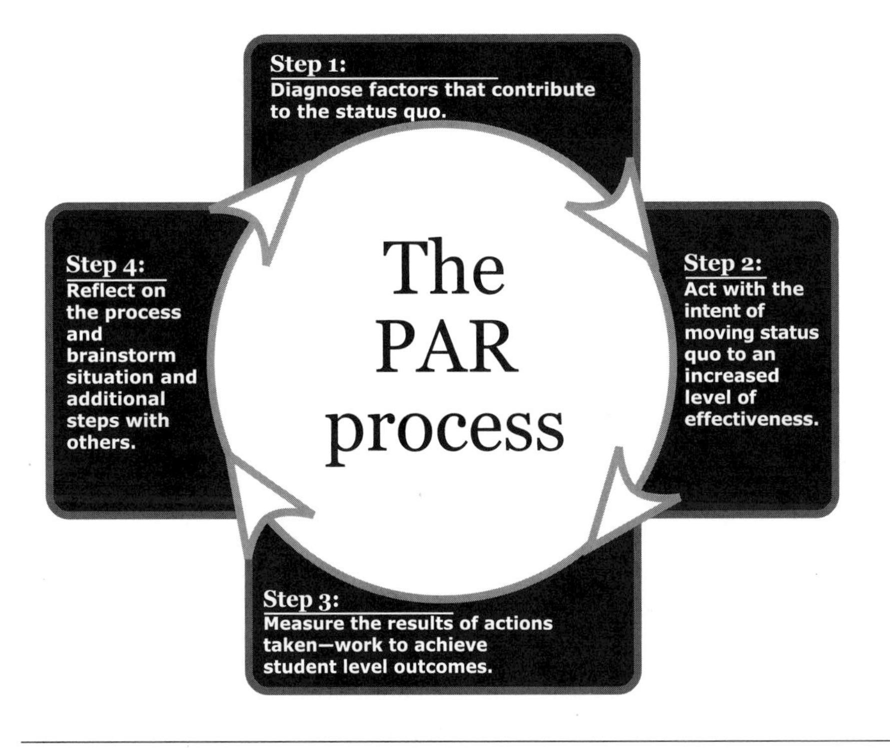

Figure 2.3 The PAR Process

SOURCE: Alan Bucknam/Notchcode Creative, 2005.

implemented, and measured again during the action/measurement cycles. A **variable** is defined as an attribute or characteristic of a person or an object that varies within the population under investigation (e.g., age, weight, IQ, test scores, attendance). Finally, the analysis of data and the reflection on what has been learned take place as PAR practitioners move from measurement to research.

Logic models support flexibility and openness during the study's evolution by maintaining the standard of basing all subsequent cycles on literature. After the teachers in the example followed the strategies laid out in their literature sources, they realized that their background and upbringing were very different from that of their students. The difference hampered their ability to help students work with sensory images as suggested in the reading. For their second cycle of research, the team decided to learn more about their students' lives to accommodate student learning. Part of their **review of literature** included the work of Ruby Payne (Payne &

Evans, 1995), who had analyzed the language differences between lower, middle, and upper economic classes of families in the United States. Payne's work provided suggestions about explicitly teaching the formal register of language.

The second round of research, as shown in Table 2.2, while different in its focus, builds on the first.

During the group's second cycle of research, the teacher who was earning her master's degree learned from a college professor that Strauss and Corbin (1998) present a clear theory about utilizing multiple types of qualitative evidence and gleaning the most from them. Sharing the information with her fellow PAR researchers, the team decided to include grounded theory in the second column of the logic model chart. **Grounded theory** is a systematic methodology used to uncover meaning from the methodical analysis of, and generation of, a theoretical understanding from qualitative data.

Table 2.2 Second Cycle of PAR

Questions to be addressed	*Previous studies*	*Variables elements to be measured*	*Local measurements*	*Form of analysis*
What have others done when wanting to improve reading comprehension?	(Harvey & Goudvis, 2000) (Keene & Zimmermann, 1997)	Strategic thinking Strategic reading Bridges Synthesis Visualization/ sensory images Inference	Teacher observation Student writing Tapes of lessons Artwork with students explaining	Qualitative coding
How is reading comprehension affected by the community and lifestyle of the students and their families?	(Payne & Evans, 1995) (Strauss & Corbin, 1998)	Use of casual or formal register to language Storytelling Hidden rules	Home visits Student journals about their neighborhoods	Observations and journals are coded using (Strauss & Corbin, 1998) grounded theory

At the end of their second cycle of research, this PAR team had an improved understanding of the culture of their students. They understood similarities and differences between their own children and their students, relative to free time interests and central aspects of home life. The team still did not fulfill their purpose to discover what accommodations were necessary to help their students improve reading comprehension. As they accumulated ideas and researched multiple strategies other professionals implemented, the group moved into the third and final cycle of research.

The third cycle of research led this PAR team to investigate methods to incorporate the expertise of their students about their culture, their interest in sports, and key elements of their daily lives with selected reading materials. Using the research of other professionals, the team linked their understanding of the students' culture to the adapted curriculum. The teachers continued to measure results, this time using quantitative evidence derived from reading comprehension tests (see Table 2.3).

At the end of the three cycles, what do the PAR practitioners gain through the consistent referral to their logical plan? In addition to help in guiding their cycles of study, the logic model provided insights about their process. As they complete their final reports, they could easily

- Extrapolate their plan of action from the literature.
- Demonstrate the theoretical links between their research and the actions that resulted.
- Track the sources of data and methods of analysis.
- Illustrate the relationship between the various cycles of research and the student outcomes they achieved.

As practitioners move through the steps of the PAR process, it is easy to become so focused in the learning that they forget to effectively manage the research methodology. This is perhaps the most difficult part of PAR: merging a cyclic learning process with linear research methodology. We have found the logic model aids beginning PAR practitioners in being attentive to both the learning process and the methodology. The diagrams we use throughout the remainder of the book will merge these two components. As shown in Figure 2.4, the various uses of the logic model advance the research portion of the PAR process.

After PAR practitioners have diagnosed the selected issue, written a purpose statement, and drafted initial research questions, they employ the logic model and initiate a review of the literature to determine how to measure the group's study topic. A review of the literature is a survey of the research on a

Table 2.3 Third Cycle of PAR

Questions to be addressed	*Previous studies*	*Variables elements to be measured*	*Local measurements*	*Form of analysis*
What have others done when wanting to improve reading comprehension?	(Harvey & Goudvis, 2000) (Keene & Zimmermann, 1997)	Strategic thinking Strategic reading Bridges Synthesis Visualization/ sensory images Inference	Teacher observation Student writing Tapes of lessons Artwork with students explaining	Qualitative coding
How is reading comprehension affected by the community and lifestyle of the students and their families?	(Payne & Evans, 1995) (Strauss & Corbin, 1998)	Use of casual or formal register to language Storytelling Hidden rules	Home visits Student journals about their neighborhoods	Observations and journals are coded using (Strauss & Corbin, 1998) grounded theory
What accommodations will improve reading comprehension?	(Bransford et al., 2000)	Personal expertise Expression Feelings in communication	Computer program test results Writing journals	Frequency testing Coding of qualitative evidence

topic and is generally presented at the beginning of a research paper to explain how research questions are developed. Use of the literature review findings helps clarify necessary action steps. Once these actions or new practices have been implemented, the team reinitiates the logic model to determine how to measure the success of the actions. When finished measuring the effects of the changes, referring back to the logic model will provide other points of view

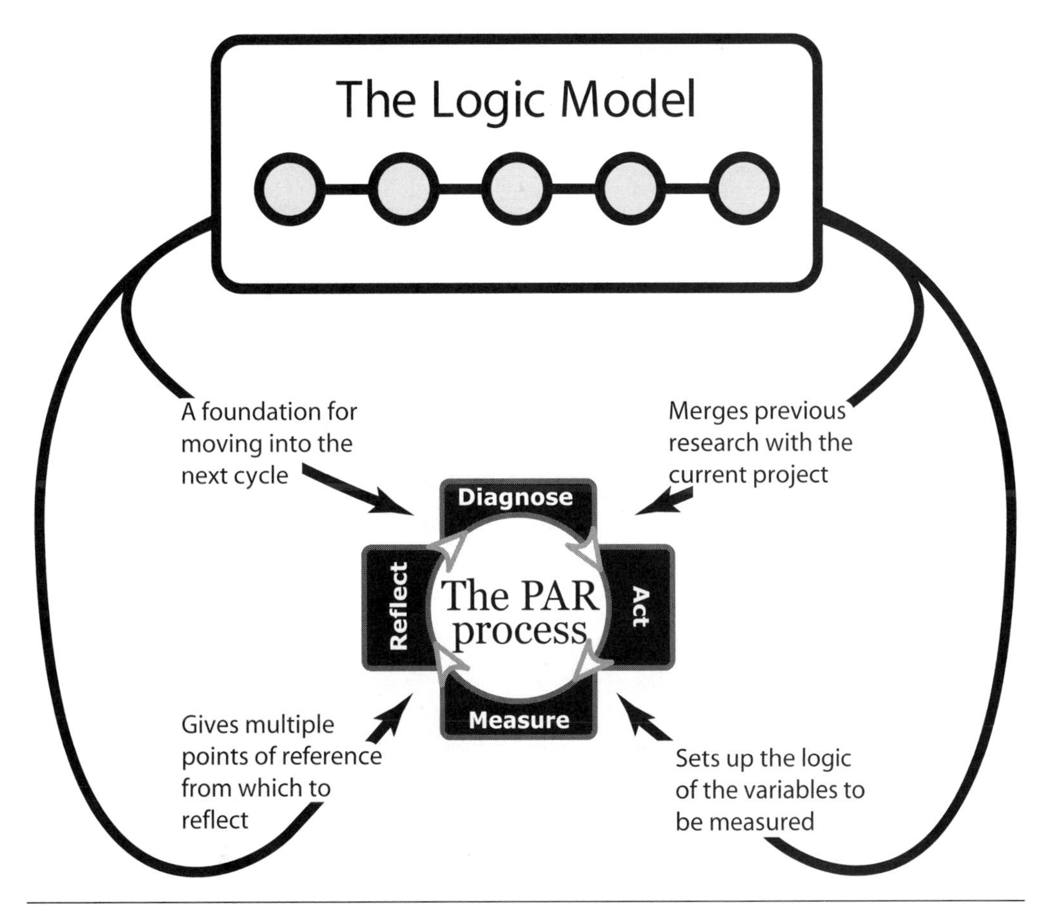

Figure 2.4 How Logic Is Used With PAR Steps

SOURCE: Alan Bucknam/Notchcode Creative, 2006.

on the same topics. Finally, after reflection, PAR researchers refine their individual studies in subsequent cycles, each of which begins a new line on their logic models.

Because of the interrelationship between the PAR steps and the logic model, we present them side by side throughout the rest of the book. Variations of Figure 2.5 introduce appropriate sections in the following chapters to clarify the components of the PAR process being currently presented.

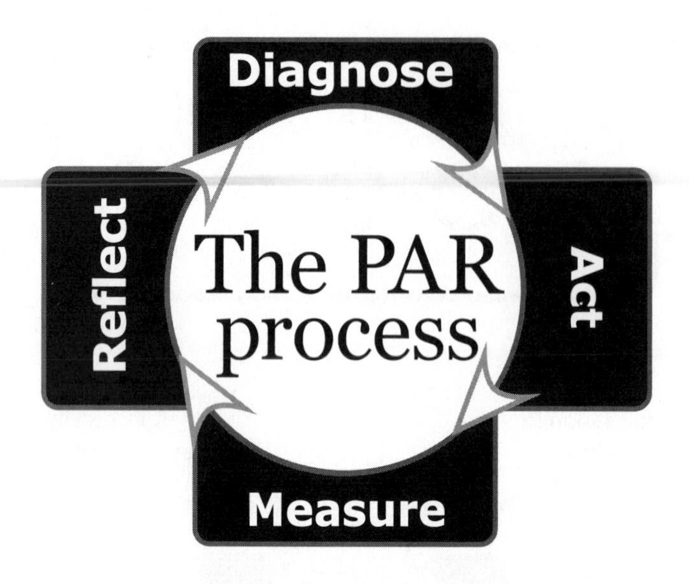

Questions to be addressed	Previous studies	Variables elements to be measured	Local measure-ments	Form of analysis
What have others done when wanting to improve reading com-prehension?	(Harvey & Goudvis, 2000) (Keene & Zimmer-mann, 1997)	Strategic thinking Strategic reading Bridges Synthesis Visualization /Sensory Images Inference	Teacher observation Student writing Tapes of lessons Art work with students explaining	Qualitative coding

Figure 2.5 Chapter 2's Stage of the PAR Process

Task 2.3: Planning Your First Draft of Your Logic Model

The aim of this task is to guide you through the original creation of a logic model and map of logistical issues for the PAR project.

Note: during this phase of PAR design, your ideas about the projects will most likely develop and evolve with each new exercise. A few words of caution when completing this task: (a) stay unattached to any single approach, as new requirements and evidence will change the understanding on which you base these ideas, and (b) do not be discouraged if, at first, you cannot fill in all areas of the logic model. The last two columns are addressed in Chapters 4 and 5.

Procedure

Step 1: Build a five-column, three-row table and copy the headings from the logic model example in Section 2 of this chapter. Fill in as many columns as are possible. Future chapters help you fill in the rest.

Step 2: Add two research questions that closely align to your favorite example of a purpose statement in the first column of each of the two blank rows. (Chapter 3 expands upon the topic of research questions.)

Step 3: Insert as many types of research methods or data collection methods that make sense as you consider how to measure experiences to help answer the selected research question. Place the list of data collection techniques in the fourth column after the research questions. Do not worry if this is your first time working with these methods. As your project progresses, you will most likely revise the listed methods.

Step 4: At some point, you may choose to add two more columns for consideration as a means to tighten your design and potential for success: (1) Time Line and (2) Person Responsible. By adding these columns and discussing them with your PAR team, you can establish due dates for individual team member accountability of the divided work tasks.

Step 5: Share the first draft of your logic model with other participants, colleagues, or classmates and, if appropriate, your professor. Discuss similarities, differences, or questions you may have.

CONCLUSION

Purpose statements form a foundational cornerstone for PAR methodology. A well-crafted purpose statement reminds practitioners of the preliminary concern and enthusiasm that initiated the research project. These statements stand as directional signposts for study and engender continued motivation within a research team. When other circumstances and ideas invite the practitioners to travel off course, the purpose statement guides them back toward the original outcome.

Logic models developed throughout PAR projects aid researchers in building a strong and convincing case pertaining to project outcome that supports changes in curriculum, teaching strategies, or school policies. The logic model presented here aids administrators, teachers, or educational students to

- Make the most of available sources of data.
- Develop projects grounded in literature and theory.
- Move into measurable actions.
- Connect iterative cycles of research and action.

Seven ethical considerations form the foundation on which PAR practitioners design each cycle of research and action: (1) obtain informed consent; (2) do no harm; (3) respect confidentiality; (4) develop knowledge; (5) hold to validity, credibility, and reliability as standards; (6) act to the benefit of others; and (7) report results honestly. Researchers are responsible to themselves, students, parents, and the rest of their stakeholders that no harm will come to study participants because of their work. The PAR process will only be as strong as the foundation upon which it is built.

CHAPTER 3

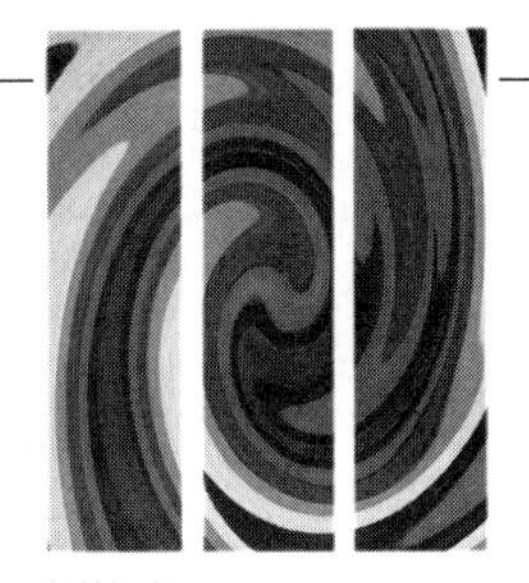

Starting to Research

Research may seem like a complex process to PAR novices. However, when groups persevere together, the seemingly complex mental gymnastics become much easier. Chapters 3–6 cover these mechanics, ultimately helping the potential of all PAR projects to be meaningful within the world of educational practice. Asking good questions that are free from assumptions, reviewing literature as background, and assessing methods of study are the components covered in this chapter.

REFLECTIVE QUESTIONS

- What concerns do you have about your educational practice?
- What would you like to improve?
- How can you word these concerns or improvements as an appropriately neutral question for research?

SECTION 1: ASKING GOOD RESEARCH QUESTIONS

Consider the analogy of driving a car to a destination. In research, the purpose statement (discussed in Chapter 2) provides the destination. The research question, discussed here, establishes the route. Variables (introduced in Chapter 2, again in Section 3, and discussed further in Chapters 4, 5, and 6) serve as signposts along the way. These elements must synchronize, or researchers may end up with data that do not answer their questions or lead them to their intended destination. A lot of mental work is done during the diagnosis stage of a PAR project when the logic of the research is set up. This section focuses on the first column of the logic model as shown in Figure 3.1.

It is usual for several research questions to emerge from a single purpose. For instance, administrators trying to improve the culture of their school may ask, "Do visitors and new students feel welcome when they enter the building? Are staff courteous? Do we have the procedures in place to ensure that new students can find their way around the school?" and so on.

What makes for good research questions? They should be provocative and act as natural motivation to the individuals asking the questions. They serve to challenge practitioners to change their practices as they uncover the answers. The answer to a significant question is not yes or no. Two problems PAR practitioners experience with research questions are (1) asking sweeping general questions, which become impossible to study, and (2) using phrases that reflect predetermined beliefs or bias. A manageable question is neither too complex nor too simplistic and facilitates naturally evolving actions. When the initial question is too broad or complex, practitioners will not be able to collect enough data to confirm an answer or to unpack the situation sufficiently to convince their constituency of needed action. When a research question is too simplistic, the answer will not compel the wider constituency or provoke action. When researchers do not address their underlying bias, the data collection tends to confirm the bias, rather than supplying new information in a neutral manner.

An advantage that PAR methodology holds over other research methods lies in the cycles of research. A small question may grow more complex and provocative over time, while a complex question may narrow in further cycles. It is not likely

Table 3.1 Traits of Good Research Questions

Good research questions are
1. Significant, interesting enough to practitioners to carry their interest throughout the project
2. Manageable, within the scope of practitioners' influence and abilities
3. Clearly stated and unambiguous
4. Self-reflective, involving the researcher in the practice
5. Neutral, allowing for data that support or refute the possibilities presented

SOURCES: Caro-Bruce (2000); Creswell (2003).

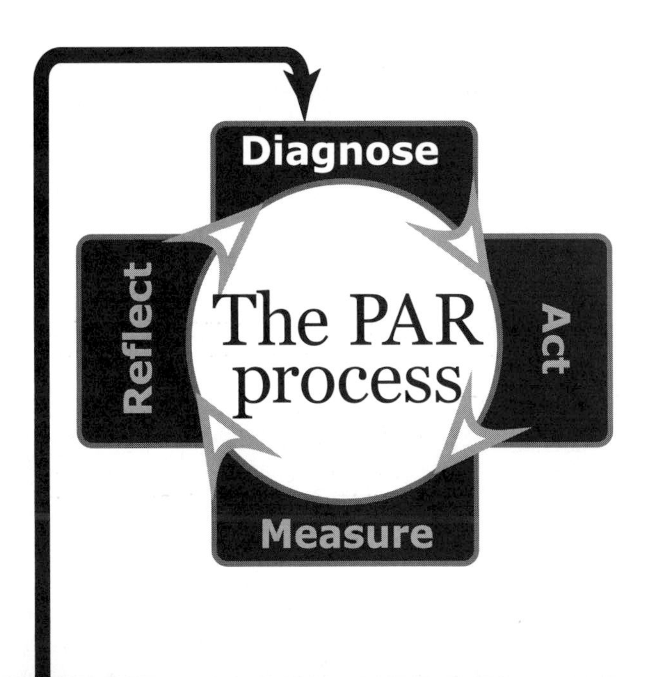

Questions to be addressed	Previous studies	Variables elements to be measured	Local measure-ments	Form of analysis
What have others done when wanting to improve reading com-prehension?	(Harvey & Goudvis, 2000) (Keene & Zimmer-mann, 1997)	Strategic thinking Strategic reading Bridges Synthesis Visualization /Sensory Images Inference	Teacher observation Student writing Tapes of lessons Art work with students explaining	Qualitative coding

Figure 3.1 Chapter 3 Sections 1 and 2's Stage of the Process

that the initial research question will be the sole question addressed through a PAR project. The research team has the option of dividing a cycle to investigate multiple questions, and the data gathered can round out each others' understanding of the challenges they face in the study.

A clearly stated question accurately reflects a range of possible answers rather than directing a specific response. For instance, the question "Is X a circumstance related to Y?" might be better rephrased as "Whether and to what extent is X related to Y?" A good research question also contains both the focus and scope of the research. Therefore, an improved **iteration** (the act of doing something again) of the previous question would be "Whether and to what extent is X related to Y in our school and community under these circumstances?" When the research question is clearly stated, the practitioners immediately have ideas about how to gather the data necessary for the study.

Research questions can also be self-reflective, such as "How can I become a better teacher?" (McNiff, 1993). PAR methodology can be self-indulgent, allowing practitioners the luxury of focusing on their daily lives. Reflective process then becomes one source of data to use in later cycles for guiding decisions and actions. For that reason it is perfectly appropriate to narrow the scope of the research question to personal practices and concerns.

Finally, clearly stated research questions do not box in the PAR research team. Questions are neutral and do not aim to guide actions but rather offer a base of understanding on which to guide actions. For instance, rather than asking, "How can we . . . ?" you could ask, "What is known about the situation that contributes to . . . ?" To test a theory of action ask, "What happens if . . . ?" rather than "Does . . . work?" as the latter could be answered by yes or no.

The following scenarios depict two school/community teams as they develop and begin PAR studies. Their research questions evolve as group members raise issues. PAR researchers have the benefit of multiple cycles within diverse groups of collaborators, allowing teams the freedom to address an issue from many angles.

Scenario A: The principal in a middle school wants to increase parental involvement in his school as part of his agenda to raise test scores. The PTA president agrees because membership has dwindled to six or seven parents. They ask a few teachers and parents to join them in using PAR as a process to foster this change. Their first research question is "How can we improve parental involvement and increase student success?" Their discussion entails the fact that

- The inquiry is two questions, not one.
- They have a clear bias that parental involvement *will* increase academic success but do not currently have data to confirm this belief.
- They do not know much about parents who are not involved.

- They wonder if parents are engaged with their teenagers' lives in general but not involved with their children's school.

They realize that they have two things they need to sort out quickly. First, they need to test whether and to what extent parental involvement is a factor in their students' success. The principal and teachers in the group decide to adopt this research question. The parents and PTA president, on the other hand, decide to go out in the community and investigate what types of parental involvement are common in their community. Chapter 4 discusses their data collection.

Scenario B: The neighborhood surrounding the elementary school has recently started to change. The school population includes new students coming from a variety of cultures, many of whom do not speak English as their first language. The school is host to a community school project, and the project director wants to help the school transition into a welcoming environment for all parents and students. She assembles a group of teachers and parents to initiate a PAR process. The question she throws out for discussion is "How can schools develop more welcoming cultures?" As the group discussion begins, some parents share stories or anecdotal evidence that illustrate their belief that the community either does or does not perceive the school as welcoming. Their initial questions display a bias that the school is not welcoming. Various cultures may have different expectations of the school. The group realizes that they need to know more about their local context. Subsequently, the group rephrases their question as whether and to what extent Midvale Elementary is perceived as welcoming by the populations it serves.

Task 3.1: PAR Practitioners Reflect On and Share Their Initial Ideas for Research Questions

The purpose of Task 3.1 is to begin reflective journaling to define research questions. Each member of a PAR team can do the exercise individually and compare results, or the exercise can be carried out as a group. If administrators and teachers using the PAR process have not already done so, this task officially begins the reflective journal required for sound PAR studies. As mentioned in Chapter 2, reflective journals provide a source of data for final PAR reports. At this point ideas are archival evidence, and notes will be condensed later to describe the process.

Procedure

Step 1: Write for 5 minutes in a stream of consciousness fashion. Note (spontaneously without judgment) the issues within the field of education that you think of as potential subjects for your research.

Step 2: Discuss these ideas with your participatory team and the stakeholders for your project, who may include classmates or your professor. In your reflective journal, record their responses or critiques. Be aware of whether the wording of your question points to an assumption or bias about the issue under investigation. In other words, do you already suspect certain things to be true?

Step 3: List potential research questions in sequence of preference. Review each against the list of ideal qualities and reword as necessary.

Step 4: Using your participatory partners as critical friends, list the pros and cons of each question. Include any limitations in your ability to gather data (e.g., challenges with time). Also include elements that might make one question easier to study than other questions.

Step 5: Ask yourself, and your team, whether there are smaller questions within those selected questions that might be a good focus for a first cycle of research.

Step 6: Choose the top three choices for your initial research question.

Surfacing Assumptions

Most educators can remember a time when they made an assumption about why a student was behind in class, only to discover mitigating circumstances that explained the behavior. Rather than start a PAR project only to find that the premise for the research questions were presumptuous and disputed by evidence, PAR practitioners will benefit from surfacing assumptions about their topics in the beginning of the study. Building research questions and uncovering the assumptions on which the questions are based requires continuous attention until solid research questions have emerged.

A dictionary cites three interesting and relevant definitions of *assumption*:

1. The act of taking for granted: *assumption of a false theory.*
2. Something taken for granted or accepted as true without proof; a supposition: *a valid assumption.*
3. Presumption; arrogance (Lexico Publishing, 2006).

It is a natural human foible to assume we know and understand any context or circumstance in which we find ourselves, whether we base that assumption on verifiable data or not (presumption, arrogance). Indeed, if people could not assume that their understanding was correct, they would spend all their time verifying evidence and never move forward on projects. On the other hand, to base a research project on an assumption is to base its reasoning on unsure ground from the very beginning. For this reason, it is necessary to become conscious of what is an assumption and what is not. Finally, as with cultural proficiency issues, assuming we know something about the lives of other individuals without checking those assumptions before we make decisions creates a presumption and may be perceived as arrogant—the third definition above.

Task 3.2: Surfacing Assumptions

To better understand which ideas are based on data and which ideas are assumptions is a critical skill to learn when conducting a research project. PAR practitioners and participatory teams may help each other by acting as critical friends and asking questions that point to assumptions that other practitioners may be making.

Procedure

Step 1: Open a word processing document and begin a table that has four cells such as the one shown in Table 3.2. You may wish to use a landscape orientation for your page (11" wide and 8.5" tall) in order to give yourself enough room to write. Insert the column headings as shown.

Table 3.2 Questions on Assumptions Template

What you know or think you know about your topic	Qualitative data available to verify this knowledge	Quantitative data available to verify this knowledge	Rate on a scale of 1–10, where 10 constitutes a convincing argument and 1 is a pure assumption

Step 2: In the first column, list thoughts and beliefs you have about the issue or topic you plan to study. You may wish to draw upon conversations you have had with your participatory teams or fellow students. Use this column to list your current beliefs about your topic. As an example, an elementary principal

wants to study referrals to the office for behavior problems. This administrator assumes that some classes of students have more behavioral problems than others. He or she enters that assumption in the first column.

Step 3: In the second column, list qualitative evidence that supports the statement in the first column. Qualitative evidence includes information other people told you or observations or reflections that you have previously recorded. Our administrator has heard that the current fifth grade has "always been trouble." That type of hearsay data is noted.

Step 4: In the third column, list quantitative evidence that supports the statement in the first column. For the purposes of this example, the quantitative evidence would be a tally of referral slips sorted by teacher per month. The principal in our example may run simple statistical tests to show that there is a significant difference in the number of students referred to the office by fifth-grade teachers compared to those in other grades.

Step 5: Consider the strength of all evidence and, in the fourth column, rate all information on a scale of 1–10 to ascertain if the documentation builds a convincing case for the truth or validity of the statements. If it is clear that you have strong evidence for your statement (an 8–10), this is an unlikely choice for further research. If there is no evidence (0–4), then it is an assumption and you will need to conduct a basic search of the literature before you can adequately decide if you want to pursue this statement further. Five to seven points may suggest that this issue is an adequate choice for a first round of inquiry, as you would be basing your research on some knowledge but obviously need additional proof for verification.

In this example, the principal rates the strength of the evidence as a 5 since, while there were more referrals from Grade 5, the majority involved only two students. Our administrator wonders whether the evidence may be traced to discipline problems in the classrooms of first-year teachers. As the PAR project moves into its second round, the principal will conduct periodic, unscheduled observations in all the classrooms.

REFLECTIVE QUESTIONS

- Have you recently investigated a topic by searching the Internet for new resources?
- What is exciting and what is frustrating about investigating resources?
- What standards do you apply to determine the credibility of your resources?

SECTION 2: INFORMAL AND FORMAL REVIEWS OF LITERATURE

As shown in Figure 3.2, Section 2 continues the discussion of work done during the diagnosis step and, as represented in Column 2, includes a review of literature. This section discusses the investigation of other research studies on the selected or similar topics.

Examination of published research studies and journal articles builds more in-depth understanding of topics relevant to PAR studies. As research affecting the field of education is published continuously, it is essential for PAR teams to peruse university databases and the Internet on a regular basis to ensure they employ current ideas about the topic in their projects.

A review of the literature may be informal or formal. In an informal manner, it is useful for PAR teams to divide their topics, fill out their logic models, go to the Internet, and discover what other professionals write about the subjects. An informal review of literature is useful for PAR teams as they discuss their research questions. Using a common search engine such as Google or Google Scholar (www.scholar.google.com), researchers will find Web sites that contain all levels of evidence and opinion about their topics, some more valid than others. However, PAR practitioners need to be aware of whether and to what extent sites have been peer reviewed and are academically accurate.

It is important to note that not all research is equally valid, credible, or reliable. While these three concepts are covered in depth throughout the discussion of methods and analysis, the point here is that peer-reviewed journals, such as those found in university libraries, subject all articles to rigorous examination prior to publication. While no process is foolproof, peer-reviewed journals contain studies of exemplary quality. The credibility of the evidence and conclusions of these articles is heightened through the scrutiny of others in the relative field. A parallel can be seen with PAR projects concerning the work of critical friends, who examine and critique every step of the studies to improve the quality of research.

PAR teams search the literature they gather to find the types of variables that other researchers have used when studying similar topics. Variables are the elements that researchers use to measure the issues they intend to study, defined in Chapter 2 as an attribute or characteristic of a person or an object that varies within the population under investigation (e.g., age, weight, IQ, test scores, attendance). As an example, attendance may be used as a variable in studies focused on improving school bonding or attachment. Other variables common in PAR projects may include age, gender, academic levels, comprehension, or time on task. Perusal of the literature helps PAR practitioners discover what variables other researchers have measured in order to find guidance for their own studies.

Students tend to write formal reviews of literature, reporting the perspectives of each author or set of authors in turn. Their work becomes Author A said

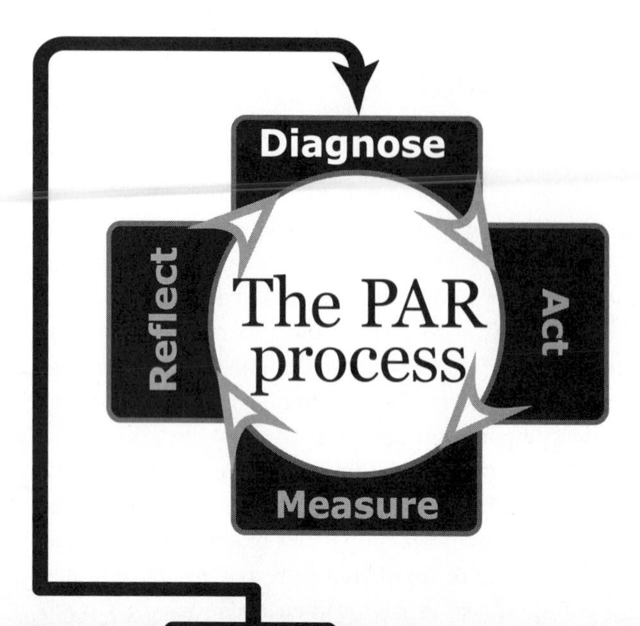

Questions to be addressed	Previous studies	Variables elements to be measured	Local measure-ments	Form of analysis
What have others done when wanting to improve reading com-prehension?	(Harvey & Goudvis, 2000) (Keene & Zimmer-mann, 1997)	Strategic thinking Strategic reading Bridges Synthesis Visualization /Sensory Images Inference	Teacher observation Student writing Tapes of lessons Art work with students explaining	Qualitative coding

Figure 3.2 Chapter 3 Section 2's Stage of the PAR Process

1, 2, and 3. Then the next paragraph says, Author B said 1, 4, and 5. Finally, the third paragraph might discuss how Author C pointed out a different interpretation of 1, refuted 4, and agreed with 3. Formal reviews of literature are more interesting to readers when organized to cover discussions from multiple authors about a particular topic, rather than the thoughts of a sole author (Hart, 1998). The following task will help researchers sort ideas they have discovered. For those whose constituency requires a formal review of the literature, this task will also help to organize the writing.

Task 3.3: The Mini "Lit Review"

This task aids individuals or PAR teams in developing a chart of explorations of the literature surrounding their topics of interest. When conducting a formal review of the literature, it is beneficial to cross-reference the research collected in the mini lit review. Whether your constituency requires that degree of formality or not, it is valuable to construct a chart to organize your understanding of research findings that correlate with your study.

The procedure below outlines the progression of the lit review. Your individual topics will determine the final structure of your chart. Nevertheless, this idea will begin the process of organizing literature.

Procedure

Step 1: Go to the library or an online university database to search for peer-reviewed research pertaining to your PAR topic. Note ideas that improve or relate to your research, regardless of agreement with your view of the topic.

Step 2: Create a list of the main ideas from each author and number them in sequence. In addition to key ideas, or as an alternative method of sorting, you can make a numbered list of the variables discussed in these articles. As you continue to read, make note when new authors explore, confirm, contradict, or deny the ideas of other writers or make use of similar variables.

Step 3: Track the reference information for each source on separate pieces of paper or in a database. Include authors, year published, title of book or article, title of journal, publisher, place published, journal issue, month or time of year published, page numbers for key ideas and for the article as a whole. Use the reference list at the end of this book to determine what information you need.

Step 4: Build a table. The columns will be headed (in order from left to right) Author and then the top 5–7 key ideas you gathered from your reading, and Notes. The lists created as part of Step 2 provide and number the key ideas. Leave a wide column on the far right for notes. Use one row for each referenced source of information. As an example, a perusal of educational leadership materials provided five key ideas, numbered as follows: (1) collaborative leadership, (2) 360-degree planning, (3) value-driven leadership, (4) strategic change, and (5) adaptive work. Table 3.3 was developed.

Table 3.3 Key Ideas

Author (year)	1 collaborative leadership	2 360-degree planning	3 value-driven leadership	4 strategic change	5 adaptive work	Notes

Step 4: Fill out each subsequent row, noting the correct citation for the book (author, year) and placing Xs in each box that refers to an idea referenced in the list created for Step 1. An example of what this might look like is shown in Table 3.4.

Table 3.4 Key Ideas Continuation

Author (year)	*1*	*2*	*3*	*4*	*5*	*Notes*
Sergiovanni (1994)	X		X	X	X	Strong on value-driven work
Fullan (2001a)	X		X	X		Believes in distributed leadership
Schèon (1983)		X	X		X	Watch for defensive organizations
Fullan (2001b)			X	X		Need for community involvement in the equation

SOURCES: Fullan, 2001a, 2001b; Schön, 1983; Sergiovanni, 1994.

Step 5: Use Table 3.4 as a guide for your writing if you are completing a formal literature review. Using the example above, the item in the third column, "value-driven leadership," is the one most often discussed by other authors on your topic. Therefore, you would choose to discuss it first, as it has the most agreement. For each idea, you note the authors who have made points on this topic, present their ideas, and compare and contrast their points of view. Point 4 will be the next discussion about your topic, because it has the second highest number of authors who discuss it.

Step 6: Discuss the following questions with your PAR team:

- What did the literature say about the issue?
- What main topics emerge in several authors' work?
- To what extent do they pertain to our local situation?
- What variables should we derive from these studies for our own research?

REFLECTIVE QUESTIONS

- To what extent do you feel comfortable with quantitative and qualitative data collection?
- As an educator, how do you use both types of data in your work?
- Do you prefer learning from numbers (statistics) or learning from people? Why do you think this is so?

SECTION 3: A BRIEF OVERVIEW OF THE BASIC RESEARCH METHODS

Everyday problem solving and research maintain strong resemblances. When a problem needs to be solved, groups of concerned people might

- Discuss the issue from multiple angles.
- Look into how others have solved similar problems in other locations.
- Divide the investigation so that different group members return with a variety of inputs and possible solutions.
- Discuss the solutions proposed by individual team members.
- Break those solutions into steps.
- Proceed with a solution while measuring the results.
- Meet again to determine whether the outcomes were sufficient.

Research methods follow a similar process except that PAR practitioners employ basic research methods throughout their investigations. The utilization of both qualitative and quantitative methodology includes a set of practices for data collection and analysis that have been proven over time. The adoption of these methods aids the PAR team in producing valid, credible, and reliable results.

Qualitative Methods

At a theoretical level, qualitative research methods can be seen as analogous to teachers' relationships with their students. When teachers need to understand why students behave certain ways, they delve into the students' lives searching for mitigating circumstances. While time consuming in the broader sense of gaining knowledge about only a few students, the strategy provides insights into the motivation behind students' actions and insights into their lives.

The processes of using qualitative methods aid researchers in extracting the depth and richness of the human experience from their subjects. Qualitative methods add body and life to the data. Data collection methods can include interviews, focus groups, observations, and each researcher's personal reflections. Studying issues qualitatively involves the collection of thoughts through words or pictures.

Time is a major logistical constraint when using qualitative methods as compared to quantitative methods. Asking questions directly of people (as compared to giving them a survey) results in data that generally take less time to collect, less time from which to gain a glimpse of meaning, but more time to fully analyze. Time needs to be factored in by considering the number of people from whom data should be gathered in order to give the project an appropriately broad view of the issue being studied. For example, in an interview with a single adult, asking four or five questions and probing responses for depth of understanding might take an hour, with relatively little preinterview preparation being required. On the other hand, it takes hours to prepare the questions and test them prior to implementing a survey, but then data are collected from potentially large numbers of people (Anderson, Herr, & Nihlen, 1994; Creswell, 2002; Ritchie, 2003). Surveys are a whole exercise of measuring people's opinions on a topic. Don't confuse a survey with a questionnaire. Some people say, "The interviewer did 50 surveys," when they mean 50 interviews for one survey. Finally, with an interview, researchers may discover that the answers do not get to the issues they are trying to study, and so the interviewers can continue to probe in order to gain more knowledge. With surveys, when the data are inconclusive, an entirely new survey needs to be developed (Hoyle, Harris, & Judd, 2002; Lewis, 2003; Snape & Spencer, 2003; Thomas, 2003).

More should be said about why qualitative evidence may be lengthy to analyze. While a surface understanding is apparent at the time of an interview, a body of evidence requires contemplative review. First, peoples' words need to be transcribed and re-sorted, then examined for similarities and differences in meaning and tone. This step provides rigor, ensuring that personal biases or selective hearing did not flaw analysis. The use of software can aid a researcher in extracting meaning from qualitative evidence, although many techniques can accomplish similar analysis by hand.

Quantitative Methods

The quantitative methods used in PAR include tests, standardized tests, questionnaires, and surveys. Measures may be collected using multiple choice responses or **scales**. Scales are a group of related measures of a variable that can be sorted along a continuum according to some weight or opinion. For example, a **Likert scale** can be employed to judge whether an issue is "not applicable" to "very applicable" on a scale of 1–5. A Likert scale is a scale on which survey respondents can indicate their level of agreement or disagreement with a series of statements. The responses are often scaled and summed to give a composite measure of attitudes about a topic. Theoretically, administration of such tests is easy with spreadsheet software such as Microsoft Excel that is used for record keeping and analysis.

These methods are used to extract information from a large number of people and to run simple or complex statistical analysis on their information, highlighting the frequencies and relationships in which different variations occur (Creswell, 2002, 2003; Gorard, 2003; Nelson, 2002). Researchers may extract the data using various types of *sample populations* and, with proper time and resources, to conduct **random control trials**. The knowledge from this type of investigation can be extrapolated to much larger populations (Leedy & Ormrod, 2005). Sample populations are a representative selection of a population that is examined to gain statistical information about the whole; for example, a group of subjects selected from a larger group in the hope that studying this smaller group (the sample) will reveal important things about the larger group. Random control trials are basically understood as the comparison between two identical or near identical groups of subjects. In the typical random control trial, one group receives an intervention while the other does not, and the results are compared.

Logistically, quantitative methods require planning and diligence to ensure that the instruments are in place when the researcher intends to gather evidence. Prior to use in the study, PAR participants need to conduct a pretest using the survey questions. What appear to be well-developed questions can hold many meanings in the multiple-choice answers. If questions or answer choices are misunderstood by the respondents, the resulting data are useless. A well-crafted, reliable survey ensures that respondents do not feel coerced to provide the answers they believe the questioner wants to hear. The logistical considerations between quantitative and qualitative evidence also include whether, and to what extent, data are needed from large numbers of people. For instance, it is difficult to understand the why and how of a situation through a questionnaire. Finally, quantitative methods take minimal time, relatively speaking, to administer. Analysis is also less time consuming than qualitative evidence but may require software equipped to crunch the numbers through a variety of tests.

Table 3.5 illustrates the comparison between the two general types of qualitative and quantitative instruments in the researcher's toolbox.

Table 3.5 Logistical Considerations for Qualitative and Quantitative Instruments

Qualitative tools provide rich evidence about personal circumstances, feelings, and thoughts of a relatively small number of people	**Quantitative tools** provide researchers with demographic data and snapshots of skills, beliefs, and attitudes of a potentially large population.
Require thought before implementation, but can be refined during use if necessary.	Require preparation, research, and pretesting before an instrument can be used to gather data. Instruments cannot easily be refined during use.
Take time to implement as each focus group or person interviewed requires the same attention.	In general, are faster to implement once planning and development work is done, as quantitative instruments require only a small amount of time to administer to large populations.
While qualitative software will be necessary for large studies, a person with notes, a highlighter pen, and a place to cut and paste significant ideas will be able to build a convincing argument.	May require software for analysis, but takes relatively little time.
Should the first analysis not work out, data can be reexamined to draw out a more convincing argument.	In the final analysis, the data either present a convincing story or they do not.

The best research, in the opinion of many in the social sciences, uses both qualitative and quantitative measures, known as *mixed methods* or *mixed methodology*. Most PAR studies in schools will be some form of primarily qualitative mixed methods. Discussed at greater length in Chapter 5, the back-and-forth comparison of data from different sources, known as **triangulation,** is defined as using a variety of research methods to compare diverse sources of data pertaining to a specific research problem or question. This process helps to enhance the validity of results, since they do not overly rely on any particular method of study.

Reflective Practice

In our experience, most educators believe themselves to be reflective practitioners. Sagor (2000) defines **reflective practice** as looking at one's work so that "reflections on the findings from each day's work inform" strategies and outputs for the next day (p. 7). Educators often hold the belief that they are reflective when they think about their work and occasionally discuss it with other teachers, but not because they regularly engage in a formal reflective practice. As mentioned in Chapter 1, educators who use PAR to study some aspect of their practices need data to back up their research process and frequently draw on their reflective journals for part of that data (McNiff, 1993; Noffke & Stevenson, 1995; Sumara & Carson, 1997). Building the habit of a regular reflective practice is a mainstay of PAR practice. While included as a critical step in its own right after measuring the outcomes of action, reflective practice best serves the practitioner if done on an ongoing basis.

Reflective practice has four parts: (1) debriefing sessions, (2) discussion of feelings and thoughts, (3) discussion of next steps, and (4) new possibilities or ideas. First are the ongoing debriefings of recent events, for individual team members and the group as a whole. What happened and why does the PAR team think it occurred this way? What have members of the PAR team done, and what have been the outcomes? The second step questions what the group thinks and feels about those circumstances. Are they satisfied? If not, why not? Was there something different they wanted to happen? When groups or individuals engaging in PAR have small triumphs, the process of reflective practice encourages them to celebrate and to record the accomplishments in their journals as well. Third, reflective practice asks the question "What next?" This query invites the PAR team to analyze next steps, to review timetables, and to address the issue of partner support, a critical component for the PAR team to be successful. Finally, PAR groups need to be open to new possibilities and ideas and should always ask, "What are we missing?" While some of the emerging ideas cannot be addressed currently, the new thoughts can be held in abeyance for another cycle. PAR participants may use a separate section of their journals, or write in a different color, to include interesting questions and musings that can be picked up in a later cycle (Caro-Bruce, 2000; McKay, 1992; Sagor, 2000).

The following quotations from administrators and teachers involved in PAR projects state the importance of reflective practice in their final analysis and results:

One principal in a small town wrote,

> *I asked questions about how to improve and clarify data, questions, and technical issues in my reflective journal. I found reflection helped narrow the focus. It also helped me recognize that this process works.*

A fifth-grade teacher noted,

> *I used my reflective practice to search for incorrect assumptions. I was interested in thinking about the nature of action research compared to traditional research. My journal helped me "get my arms around" PAR methodology.*

A principal in an urban elementary school who was studying mobility in his school wrote,

> *I used reflection to aid my identification of the magnitude of the issue. I realized we have a need to coordinate school services.*

Finally, an elementary Title Math teacher wrote,

> *Surprisingly, I found reflecting and observing helpful instead of burdensome. The PAR project kept me focused with a great deal to learn and little time to learn it compared to a classroom teacher, I had fewer variables competing for my attention.*

These educators found that they gained important knowledge throughout their PAR cycles by looking back on what they had written in their reflective journals. Later chapters detail the use of reflective data as part of a qualitative data collection strategy and its use in the final analysis and conclusion component of PAR projects.

Task 3.4: Reflective Journal Practice

If you have not already done so, beginning a regular reflective journal practice may be the single biggest boost you give to your PAR project as an individual.

CONCLUSION

Research projects start by sorting potential ideas, deciding on a research question, and plotting how to begin the investigation. Research questions need to be small enough to be manageable yet still lead to greater understanding of the educational issues under investigation. Good research questions

- Help practitioners design next steps and guide them to the answers they seek.
- Are significant, manageable, and clearly stated, including the scope and context of the situation to be studied.
- Are neutral, allowing data to be gathered that may agree with or dispute the researchers' ideas about their subjects.
- Engage and motivate the participatory team toward action.

Ideas that the PAR group do not test, but take for granted as "true," may negatively impact the PAR project at a later stage. For this reason, time is required to surface assumptions. Because assumptions are a natural part of life, practitioners need to be alert to the presence of the team's suppositions.

There are three ways in which informal and formal reviews of literature are important to PAR participants. First, they engender new ideas about the topic being researched and keep PAR practitioners current about their topic. Second, they provide material for discussion within participatory teams. Third, they are instrumental as a tool to categorize the readings about the topic into ideas for application in the study. These ideas are then translated into variables used for measurement during the data collection phase of a specific cycle of research.

PAR research methodology centers on quantitative and qualitative methods and reflective practice. Qualitative methods probe the richness of human experience. Quantitative methods gather snapshots of the experiences of large numbers of people. Reflective practice, which is a qualitative method worthy of its own category, keeps PAR practitioners personally involved and aware throughout. Both types are necessary when creating a holistic picture on which to build successful and sustainable action. PAR researchers need to consider the logistical time constraints inherent in a particular method as they begin to format research questions to address in the first cycle of research.

Reflection in PAR projects holds a more central role than it might in other types of educational practice because it also serves as data. Strong reflective practices not only ask the what, when, where, why, and how of the situation but also uncover practitioners' feelings and thoughts about the situations they experience and what evidence they might be missing.

CHAPTER 4

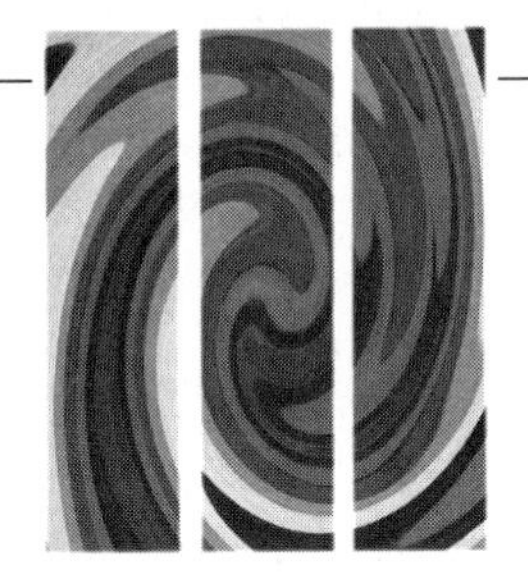

Qualitative Data Collection

Educators live in a world where everyone has an array of thoughts about education. This multitude of ideas, opinions, and beliefs, generated throughout people's lives, makes the world of qualitative evidence both rich and confusing. The purpose of this chapter is to help the novice PAR researcher sort through and implement qualitative data collection. Conversations, notes, e-mails, voice mails, interviews, and focus groups all have potential to become qualitative data. PAR research holds itself to the standard of being responsive to the community in which the researchers are based. Therefore, qualitative data collection will be some part, most often the greatest component, of the data on which a PAR team draw their conclusions.

People experience the same set of circumstances differently. This concept is vividly illustrated in Akira Kurosawa's film *Rashomon* (Kurosawa, 1950), in which a crime witnessed by four individuals is described in four mutually contradictory ways. The theme of the movie relates to the difficulty, if not impossibility, of gaining an accurate view of a situation or story from witnesses whose stories conflict. The story, based on the accounts of five different characters—the Woodcutter, the Priest, the Bandit, the Samurai, and the Samurai's wife—is summarized as follows:

> In 12th-century Japan, a samurai and his wife are attacked by the notorious bandit Tajomaru, and the samurai ends up dead. Tajomaru is captured shortly afterward and is put on trial, but his story and the wife's are so completely different that a psychic is brought in to allow the murdered man to give his own testimony. He tells yet another completely different story. Finally, a woodcutter who found the body reveals that he saw the whole thing, and his version is again completely different from the others. (Lohner, 2006)

Seldom will qualitative data in schools provide such dramatic examples of how everyday experiences provide multiple perspectives. Nevertheless, PAR practitioners must stay vigilant to capturing enough evidence that the range of possibilities emerge.

Qualitative data collect information as written or visual images and report findings as words. Yet qualitative data collection is more than just conversations, records, or observations. Rigorous collection and analysis of the words and pictures, gathered as evidence about a topic, enhance the position of educators to build a convincing body of knowledge on which to improve educational practices. Once PAR teams have decided upon their first research questions and searched through previous research for ideas, resulting in a clear and logical reason for gathering data, they are ready to begin. Qualitative evidence, collected during the PAR diagnosis and measurement steps, is shown in Figure 4.1 along with the portions of the logic model where PAR practitioners record their local measurements.

HOW IS QUALITATIVE EVIDENCE USEFUL?

Qualitative evidence, when rigorously analyzed, makes it possible for PAR teams to uncover, expose, and consider the complexities within their community. While no scientist would endeavor to measure a situation with an infinite number of variables, this is precisely what school leaders do when investigating educational issues. Qualitative evidence extracts depth and adds body to the conclusions drawn by PAR teams. Data collection and analysis tools are employed when practitioners need to delve deeply into circumstances and understand the human motivations involved. These data are particularly informative to answer questions of

- *Meaning:* The significance of situations (held in peoples' minds as meanings) are subjective and vary, depending upon personal experiences. More than other types of queries, a question about meaning will surface the biases of both the individuals who ask the questions and the individuals who respond.
- *Context:* Influences understanding. This is true whether it is a personal context (e.g., age, gender, or cultural background) or the community context (e.g., wealthy or poor; rural, suburban, or urban; stable or changing demographics; economically stable or unstable).

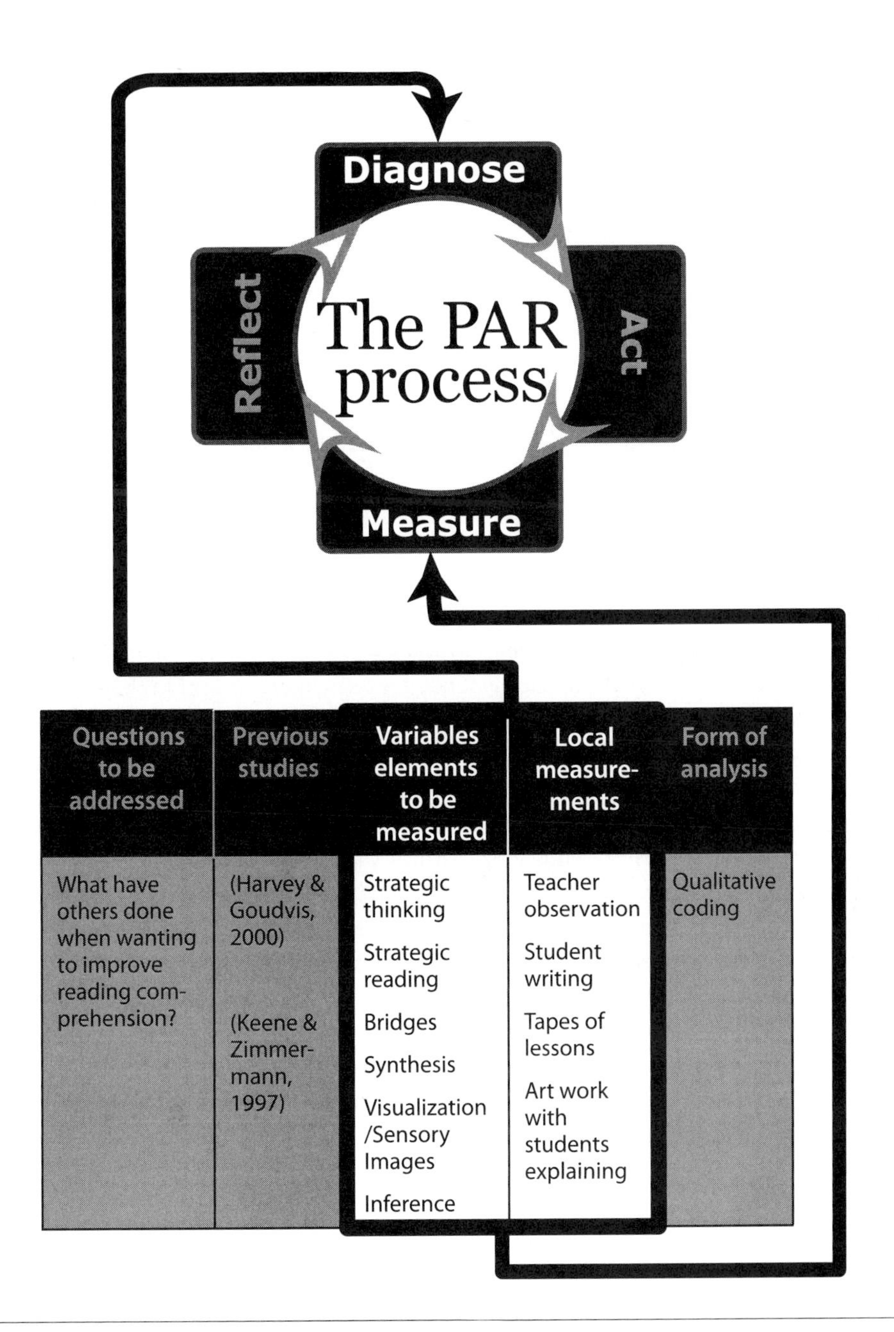

Figure 4.1 Chapter 4's Stage of the PAR Process

- *Understanding of process:* In order for the PAR conclusions to be transferable to other contexts, the background that led to the situation and the actions that resulted need to be understood and reported. In addition, the reporting on either the success or failure of programs in schools calls for understanding both the planning and implementation phases of program development.
- *Causal relationships:* Understanding the complex situations that cause people to take action is key to understanding the cultural and societal mechanisms that make up the fabric of life within a community or school. The study of causal relationships requires a strong chain of logic, with a wide range of diverse opinions collected and analyzed at each link in the chain (Maxwell, 1996).

WHAT MAKES QUALITATIVE EVIDENCE DIFFICULT?

Qualitative evidence collection is subject to the biases of the people involved, both in collecting the evidence and in providing it. Researchers may have a preconceived notion about the evidence they are likely to find in their investigation. Unconsciously they may ask questions phrased in such a way as to heighten the chance the respondent will answer as expected. Likewise, the respondent may have biases about either the researchers or their topic and may not be willing to disclose personal ideas or feelings. This is likely to occur when issues connected to power, sensitive feelings, or cultural values enter the topic under study. PAR teams, acting as critical friends, help each other through diligence to search out and overcome biases.

As mentioned before, qualitative data collection extends beyond a sole conversation, record, or observation. Likewise, the understanding to be gained from gathered evidence exceeds simple reflection. Covered in the next chapter, qualitative data analysis requires breaking down the data (words or pictures) in such a way that each bit can be analyzed and resorted. Subsequently, with a sufficient accumulation of "bits," new understanding develops.

REFLECTIVE QUESTIONS

- What are all the ways you receive information from other people?
- What concerns do you have as you begin to ask people questions?
- How can your PAR team help to address your concerns?

SECTION 1: QUALITATIVE DATA COLLECTION METHODS

As mentioned earlier, qualitative data are particularly appropriate for PAR projects because they can help us understand people's reactions, beliefs, and behavior more clearly. This section outlines the ways to collect qualitative data and discusses practical considerations that researchers need to take into account as they implement these strategies. Though distinct categories are listed, in reality these categories may seem much more ambiguous to researchers gathering data in the field. Nonetheless, it is useful to divide them here for the purpose of discussion (Byrne-Armstrong, Higgs, & Horsfall, 2001; Maxwell, 1996; Patton & Patton, 2002; Snape & Spencer, 2003; Strauss & Corbin, 1998).

Table 4.1 divides the three general categories of data collection methods discussed in this chapter into separate strategies. As mentioned above, these groupings and definitions are pliable.

Table 4.1 Categories of Data Collection Methods

Data collection strategy	*Attributes*	*Challenges*
Data collected directly in words from people		
Interviews: one-on-one question-and-answer sessions where the researcher may use a variety of techniques. Interviews average 30–45 minutes per person.	Reveal information about the worldview of a single individual. This is a flexible strategy that (with care) can be massaged during data collection as needed to heighten results	Interviews are a time-consuming form of data collection. To gather data from one person requires preparation, the time of the interview, and the time of transcription.
Focus groups: group interviews, using the same variety of techniques and taking approximately the same length of time as interviews.	More time effective than interviews but with slightly less flexibility. The group process may encourage results from shy or hesitant people when the group brings up topics with which they agree.	The group dynamics may interfere with complete or accurate data.

(Continued)

Table 4.1 (Continued)

Data collection strategy	*Attributes*	*Challenges*
Data collected once or throughout a process of change		
Reflective journals: handwritten or verbal account of an event, or group of events, over time. These often unveil how writers subscribe meaning to their topics	Subjective account of the event from the point of view of the writer, who may be the researcher or a subject of the research. Can be collected once or throughout a process of change	Similar to interviews, reflective journals display the worldview of single individuals. They also frequently require transcription.
Field notes: written explanations or data taken, often by multiple observers at a single event, capturing interactions of interest to the larger topic under study.	May follow a prescribed format or be open-ended. Generally gathered by the PAR team and therefore likely to target the topic of study.	Somewhat more objective than reflective data although still subject to the biases of the writer.
Data collected during the event(s) being studied		
Anecdotal evidence and logs: data taken from people often outside the research team that report the facts of the interactions as understood by the writer.	May follow a prescribed format or be open-ended. May be more objective about the topic of study, since not constrained by the biases of the PAR team's discussions of the topic under study	Somewhat more objective than reflective data although still subject to the biases of the writer. Generally not gathered by the PAR team and therefore may not center on the topic of study.
Observations: stylized note taking about predetermined portions of an event or group of events under study, generally taken by more than one observer. Observations often tally the number of times an event takes place.	Are often collected over a period of time. Can be collected by a variety of people, thereby increasing the possibility of reliable results. Accuracy may be helped by voice or video recording prior, with multiple people taking part in analysis.	Accuracy may be constrained by the point of view of the person recording the data.
Student work:	Can also be collected over time and with the intention of showing growth.	May be hard to interpret accurately.

One PAR study will serve as an example throughout this chapter. The research team in a medium-sized elementary school took on the challenge of improving parent and community involvement.[1] While involved in a broader study focused on other issues, their principal read an article by Gerardo Lopez titled *On Whose Terms?* (Lopez & Mapp, 2002). In the article, Lopez investigated parent involvement from the perspective of migrant farm workers and concluded that these parents felt very involved with their children's education yet saw no reason to interact with schools. The elementary school principal in our example decided to ask a team of teachers and parents to join him in investigating whether and to what extent these results might be true for the families in their school. He knew from his test scores that many students were reading below grade level. Were these parents involved in supporting their children's education, and how could the school improve the success of those efforts?

Data Collected Directly in Words From People: Interviews and Focus Groups

The PAR team in our example decided that they first needed to interview a few parents who were involved with the school in traditional ways, such as class sponsor or parent/teacher organization (PTO) member, and a few who were not currently involved. These conversations helped the team understand the topic's parameters and the need to rewrite and reorganize questions from a parent's point of view. Next, they organized pizza parties for parents in the different grades and conducted focus groups. During each party they asked the same short series of questions that had evolved from the initial interviews. The team paired off for the pizza parties. While one person asked the questions, the other recorded the answers.

Interviews and focus groups are similar methods, as both allow researchers to question subjects and probe responses with further questions. In both settings, researchers

- Develop their questions through an iterative initial process, testing the way in which they ask the questions to help ensure that their questions are understood by their subjects.
- Work to set up an environment that enhances the potential for full disclosure, being both comfortable and safe from a research subject's point of view.
- Keep a short list (four to five questions) of the topics from which they are gathering evidence, with the backup of a longer list of potential probing questions they may use.

- Commit to starting and ending between 45 and 60 minutes to avoid participant fatigue.
- Utilize multiple means of collecting data. In the ideal, there is someone taking notes on a computer, the tape recorder is running to help capture exact words, and the facilitator is working with a flip chart to provide feedback to the subject's responses and from which to ask clarifying questions.

Take time to ensure that the surrounding area is quiet and that electronic equipment is in working order. It is best to not depend exclusively on the use of electronics and to be prepared in case of equipment failure or difficulties. This can be accomplished by having at least one person taking notes. Then if the recorders fail, all data will not be lost.

Both interviews and focus groups are flexible methods for gathering qualitative evidence, offering PAR practitioners insight into the human dynamics in the situations they are studying. To achieve the greatest benefit, researchers must balance the time taken for data collection with considerations about analysis (Byrne-Armstrong et al., 2001; Maxwell, 1996; Patton & Patton, 2002; Snape & Spencer, 2003; Strauss & Corbin, 1998). For example, if PAR practitioners decide to record interviews rather than intrude on the conversation with note taking, time allotment for tapes transcription will be needed prior to data analysis. On the other hand, should transcription services be available, full transcriptions offer researchers the richest data. Tapes may take, on average, 4 hours to transcribe 1 hour of conversation.

These two methods of collecting data are dissimilar in other ways. An interview allows in-depth personal probing of a response until researchers feel they understand the answer and its implications to their topic. However, in a focus group, the facilitator needs to progress with questioning and balance his or her curiosity related to specific responses with the need to maintain momentum in the group process. Besides time, other factors may influence the decision to question people as individuals or in groups.

Traditionally, these data-gathering techniques have been segregated into three categories: structured, unstructured, or semistructured (Maxwell, 1996; Strauss & Corbin, 1998). The divisions relate to the relationship of ideas and concepts to the manner in which data are gathered. For instance, a structured interview is one in which all subjects are asked exactly the same questions—the questions are based rigorously on prior evidence. These questions may take the form of "Please relate your understanding of the relationship between X and Y." The researchers have structured the questions to focus the subjects' responses in a particular way. **Unstructured interviews** start with general ideas or areas of concern, and the specific questions asked are likely to change, depending on the subjects' responses and interests. Unstructured questions may be open-ended, such as "Tell us about your experience of this topic."

In our experience, the semistructured middle ground is effective for PAR practitioners (James, 2004; Reynolds, 2005). **Semistructured interviews** are developed when researchers know what the literature says about their topic and map out pertinent questions with possible probing subquestions. Semistructured interviews allow the opportunity to digress from the primary question and probe a response to understand more clearly what is seen as a provocative remark on the part of the interviewee. Such remarks may come in two categories: (1) the researcher has not heard that position stated before or (2) what has been said seems to be in contradiction to comments others have made previously. In situations when the research subject is particularly articulate, with pertinent responses useful for direct quotations, an interviewer may take extra time and effort to capture not only the subject's meaning but the exact words of the response.

Structured interviews also have value in PAR studies. In this more formal technique, researchers decide upon a series of questions and read the questions exactly to individuals to establish an understanding of their ideas on a topic. For example, in a PAR study on homelessness, the research team asked respondents a series of questions about attitudes toward families and children who lived without homes in their community. An interview was solicited from every fourth person who came out of a mall on a given Saturday (James, 2005b).

McKernan (1996) and others (Legard, Keegan, & Ward, 2003; Stringer, 2004) present the following list of question stems as appropriate for interviews and focus groups: "Why," "Should," or "How important is . . . ?" In addition, a researcher may want to query affect by asking about feelings and emotional responses. It is appropriate to form a leading question by asking, "What do you think about . . . ?" or "Do you remember your experience of . . . ?"

Data Collected Through a Process of Change: Reflective Data/Field Notes/Anecdotal Accounts

The PAR team in the above example based their investigation on Epstein's (2001) book on parent involvement. The group decided they needed data from a variety of sources to capture the relative effectiveness of their current support strategies for parents helping their children with homework. To start, they focused on parent/teacher conferences that were held multiple times during the year. Team members kept reflective journals noting their activities before, during, and after the conferences. They each reflected on what they thought went well and ideas for improvement. Prior to the conferences, the PAR team discussed what types of evidence might display both positive and negative communication between teachers and parents during the conferences. They then circulated at the event, taking **field notes** pertaining to observations. Field notes are written explanations or data taken, often by multiple observers at a single event, capturing interactions of interest to the larger topic under study. Finally, the team asked teachers and parents to write anecdotal accounts of the same conferences. These included details about attendance and topics discussed.

Some individuals are not comfortable with the concept of reflective work or keeping journals and may wish to substitute *field notes* or *anecdotal evidence* for reflective writing. All three methods have much in common:

- All three allow people to capture details and ideas about events.
- PAR team discussions prompt the topics identified or addressed in the notes.
- Individuals delivering the data supply as many details as possible.
- Data make note of both the date of the incident and the reporting date of the incident. Each is recorded as close to the event as possible.
- Data may include attachments of other types of evidence as well.
- Systems that help the people capture the data in digital formats aid PAR practitioners in analyzing one data set as compared to another.
- All three methods allow researchers to note the politics, the power issues, and other subtle interactions that ultimately influence the success of any educational implementation.

Student participation logs and student journals are viable sources of qualitative data and come under the loose headings of reflective journals or field notes. The degree of insight that they offer is directly tied to frequency and quantity of the writing. For instance, a single entry in a student journal may not be as indicative of an overall theme as entries where one or several students mention the theme regularly. Sagor (2005) reminds us that, especially for older students, the ethics of informed consent applies to the use of student journals as research data. It should be clear to the students whose work is being used whether and to what extent these journals are to be used as data, whether or not results will be reported in aggregate form, and whether further permission will be obtained prior to the use of direct quotes. Student names should not be used in documents without both student and parent permission.

Anecdotal evidence is accounts written directly after an incident and include explanation, setting, and contextual information as well as reporting the facts of who did what and so on. Potential interpretations may also be included, but the writer must take responsibility by indicating when these descriptions may be an interpretation of the incident and not simply facts reported ("The expression on her face implied to me that . . ."). Examples of anecdotal evidence frequently found in schools include student behavior summaries, field trip activity forms, or injury incident reports. All include the date and time of the occurrence as well as the date and time of writing. Specific details help provide accuracy with important situational facts that may become lost or become vague at a future time.

These three types of data differ in (a) their relative amount of subjectivity and (b) how closely they follow the PAR team's prescribed format for data collection. A more objective format, which clearly delineates topics or questions to be addressed, is more likely to produce data that are useful to the study yet less likely to reveal unexpected insights or ideas. Subjective data may present fascinating new ideas, although taking longer to read, and may contain elements that are unconnected to the topic under study.

Data Collected During the Event(s) Being Studied: Observations/Student Work/Logs

As their study progressed, the team members in our PAR example decided to focus on parent involvement with homework. To study what types of homework help occurred and to help parents learn new strategies, the team offered a series of clinics after school. They collected two types of qualitative evidence during these sessions. First, a series of examples of student homework was collected prior to the clinic, during the clinic, directly after the clinic, and work turned in a month later. The PAR team also collected observational data about the ways in which students interacted with their parents and the methods parents used to help their children before and after coaching.

Observations (a research technique in which no direct questions are asked, but individuals in a public place [e.g., shoppers and drivers] are watched and their behavior recorded) are often collected over a period of time to measure the variance in a particular set of behaviors (e.g., actions on the playground, interactions during peer tutoring). The basic process to capture observational data over time is to observe first, create a checklist next, then observe again using the checklist. Repeat the process until the list functions as an accurate and easy way to capture the behaviors under study. Observations, examples of student work, and logs are similar in the following ways:

- All develop a type of trend analysis by measuring the same phenomena over time.
- All include the weakness of the human element, for the recorder's focus may shift and skew these data.

- For each type, the more structured the approach, the tighter the observations will fit researcher objectives.
- All are similar to journals and field notes in that a high degree of structure also means that observers will be less likely to capture new or unexpected events.

Sagor (2000) gives an example of shadowing, where one aspect of a school reform effort includes teachers following students throughout their school day to observe and to better understand the school context from students' perspectives. This technique could make use of parent observers as well. One group found that the technique of shadowing varied from elementary to middle and high school. One significant difference was the participation of the student being shadowed. Younger students could be shadowed anonymously. Older students should give their consent for the shadowing and for permission to use the observations as verifiable data (Sagor, 2000).

Reviewing class disruption reports led one alternative high school PAR practitioner teacher to uncover trends related to interruptions of instruction:

> After discussing different possibilities, we decided to track attendance, tardies, verbal disruptions, and technology disruptions (phones, CD players, etc.) that interrupted instruction. I created a tally sheet and made certain taking a tally didn't also interrupt instruction. I split verbal disruptions into minor (those that interrupted instruction briefly) and defined major interruptions as those that stopped instruction for thirty seconds or more. Absences are quite high and tardies are significant early in the day. Phones and music machines show fewer interruptions than I anticipated. As I examined the data displayed for this report, the attendance/grades balancing act was starkly presented by the high number of absences. (Ecord, 2006, n.p.)

This teacher continues to track student work and measure their relative success against the number of disruptions in class. He will present these data to his students so that they will be able to make informed decisions and potentially change their patterns of behavior. AR cycles will measure whether and to what extent they take responsibility for their disruptive behavior after confronting these data.

Observations may also include photographs and videos. An advantage in employing digital recording techniques lies in the ability to record information in a constant and passive way that is easily ignored by the person being observed and therefore is likely to capture unrehearsed moments. Another advantage is that as a data collection strategy, such evidence can be viewed repeatedly. A challenge of digital recording relates to its transcription into written accounts; therefore, it is difficult to compare with other types of data for purposes of triangulation. Photography has the added disadvantage of the interpretation of events being open to very subjective levels of interpretation by others.

Observations and student work are dissimilar in the locus of control of data to interpretation. For instance, the students are completely in control of their work, with only the data interpretation subject to the ideas of the researcher. On the other hand, observations of what is recorded and its interpretation are subject to the interpretation of the researcher, who may or may not experience events as students do. One very positive way to eliminate such disparities is to include students in the participatory teams of the project who directly interpret events in their lives or their schoolwork.

Task 4.1: Collecting a Variety of Qualitative Data

The purpose of this exercise is to gather data about an event employing multiple sources of qualitative data collection. This may be completed after the event as an exercise, keeping in mind that the greater the distance from the actual event, the less likely the data are accurate.

Procedure

Think of an upcoming event that relates to the topic you are studying. As an example, the PAR group from the chapter example described a back-to-school night.

Brainstorm a list of questions or topics and categorize them under the four types of qualitative evidence: meaning, context, process, or causal relationships. Add other questions as appropriate to cover each type of evidence

Go through the chart and descriptions of the three categories of qualitative evidence: those collected directly from people, throughout a process of change, or during an event. Choose a variety of data collection strategies and brainstorm what questions could be answered.

Rate the relative difficulty of proceeding with that data collection strategy on a scale of 1–10.

Proceed with planning and implementing those qualitative techniques that appear to be the most efficacious to advancing your research.

You may wish to use the following graphic organizer as you analyze use of these techniques. The first line of the following table illustrates the ideas in the example above.

Table 4.2 Graphic Organizer for Qualitative Data

Questions	*Meaning, context, process, or causality?*	*Who has the information/When does it occur?*	*How might we gather data?*	*Relative expense of time and resource/Value*
Do parents know how to help with their children's homework?	Understanding a process	Parents and children/ nonclass time	Interviews or focus groups with students and parents. Observations during homework clinics.	Time consuming/ Valuable Less time consuming/ Group chose to do them both.

REFLECTIVE QUESTIONS

- Looking back on the description you wrote for Task 4.1, to what extent did you investigate the event from others' viewpoints?
- What other questions might you have asked that would have made your description more complete?
- What other data collection techniques might you have decided to use?
- To what extent might quantitative evidence, such as what you could gather from a larger population with a survey, help strengthen the evidence from these data?

SECTION 2: MAXIMUM SUCCESS AND RIGOR

We agree with Maxwell (1996) that qualitative evidence cannot nor should not be collected and analyzed in a linear fashion. Our experience has been that data collection and analysis are an inherently complex interplay of choice-making elements. Figure 4.2 demonstrates PAR practitioners' best approach to qualitative evidence by (a) discussing what they know or understand; (b) gathering data to confirm, deny, or enhance that understanding; and then (c) analyzing their data shortly after the data are collected. The actual process may move in a loop between any two steps before proceeding. New results help to fine-tune the practitioners' next phase of data collection.

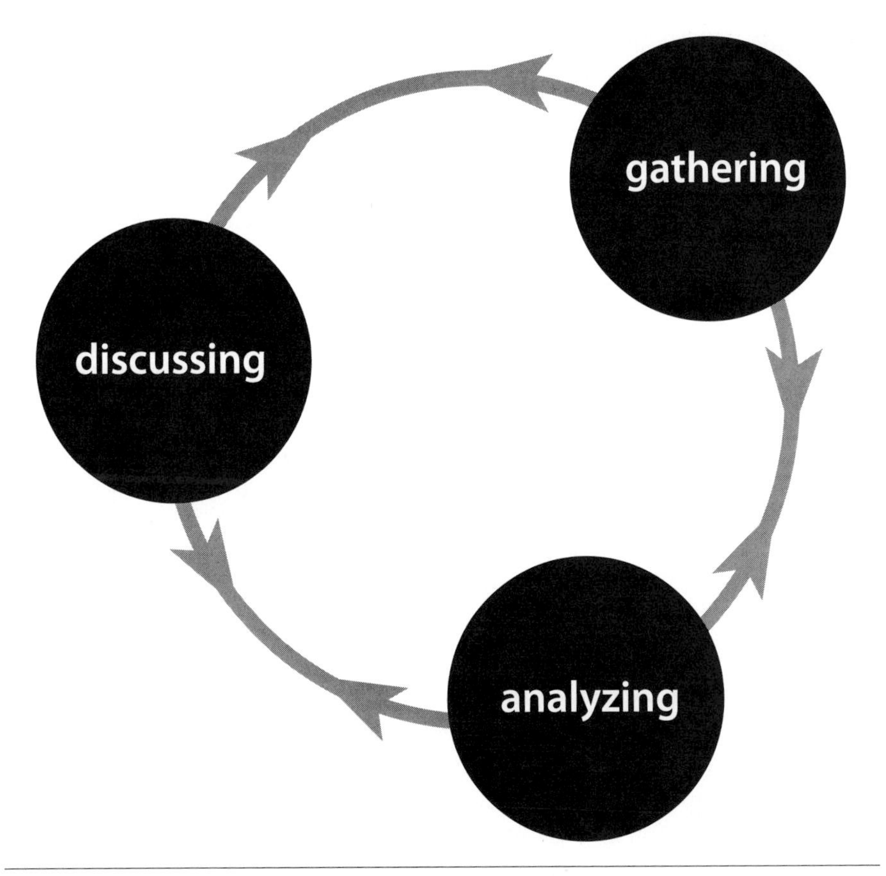

Figure 4.2 Process of Qualitative Data Collection

SOURCE: Alan Bucknam/Notchcode Creative, 2006.

This interplay allows PAR practitioners to build projects with valid and reliable results. While discussed in more detail later, practitioners demonstrate validity by gathering data from multiple sources in order to confirm their conclusions. Reliable conclusions are demonstrated through the ability to improve educational practice in a local context and the transferability of these findings to other settings.

Managing Time and Resources

Journals, scrapbooks, case notes, portfolios, field notes, observations, and so on all have one factor in common: the conscious collection of thought as data.

This is a daunting task, since people have more thoughts in a day than they can count, in fact more than they are aware of. Educators frequently feel caught in a system that requires them to work long weeks during the school year. Many tasks require their attention, some of which add to their educational settings but do not directly affect students. The secret to successful completion of a PAR project, without undue stress, is to wrap the project creatively into as many ongoing tasks as possible. The following six strategies will help the new PAR practitioners with time efficiency:

- Aim for the collection of digital data, capturing the exact words of the subject. To the extent that all data hit this target, analysis time will be shortened.
- Know when the data gathered are "enough." Enough qualitative data can be convincingly quantified. For example, we found that when we questioned 20 parents (out of a class of 30) about their involvement in their children's education, we found that the majority attended parent-teacher conferences (80%). A research team may judge data as adequate when it becomes clear that they have captured the major themes, usually when subjects repeat what others have already stated. At this point, researchers may consider confirming their results using new techniques or from new sources. When two techniques produce similar responses from a variety of subjects, these techniques hold sufficient evidence for the researchers to consider moving into action.
- Make it easy for subjects to participate in the collection of data. Will an e-mailed self-report questionnaire work? If so, then do not make appointments for interviews.
- Make data gathering part of normal work activities. Observations are a good example of data collection wrapped into the educator's day.
- Students can be assigned a time to reflect on their participation during the day, allowing the educator time to write as well.
- Incentives may influence whether subjects will make themselves available for focus groups. Many educators using PAR have used food as an incentive.

How to Make It More Rigorous

PAR practitioners who increase the rigor with which they approach both data collection and analysis do much to enhance the efficacy of reports to their constituencies. To add rigor, we recommend the following strategies that require little time.

- Maintain a strict time line for data collection and analysis (Glanz, 2003). PAR groups hold each other accountable to time lines and plans, acting as critical friends to ensure that everyone stays on task.
- Capture the number of respondents and percentages of agreement as qualitative data are collected. Qualitative evidence is more descriptive and convincing when reported side by side with numbers and percentages.
- Divide the note-taking sheet into two columns. On the left, take notes as usual. On the right, write down comments that come to mind. The right-hand column becomes a qualitative record of your critical thinking about the ongoing procedure.
- Use any existing whole-faculty study groups or professional learning communities that already exist to further data collection efforts. For instance, when the example PAR group shared their ideas with the faculty study groups in their school, others offered to gather information from the parents working on special projects in other areas.

Introduction to Mixed Methodology

Pragmatic use of mixed methodology means that PAR practitioners make use of all available data (both qualitative and quantitative) in order to build a rigorous, cohesive set of conclusions about their topic. They do this through the triangulation of multiple sources of data. Triangulation is defined as using a variety of research methods to compare diverse sources of data pertaining to a specific research problem or question. This process helps to enhance the validity of results, since they do not overly rely on any particular method of study.

This chapter has clarified the use of several types of qualitative data. Comparison of data collected at different times, which uses different methods or populations, builds a strong analysis of the issues. The comparison also ensures that resulting actions take into account meanings, context, processes, and causality. Some types of qualitative data ask similar questions, and when compared, these data types verify the consistency of human experience across any given issue.

However, there are times when qualitative data alone will not be sufficient to alleviate doubt about the outcomes achieved through PAR projects. As an example, in a hypothetical research project, 100% of the parents in a focus group, all with children from the same classroom, thought that the school did not offer worthwhile volunteer possibilities. Would that necessarily make it true? What if the researcher instead recorded that the five parents who attended the focus group had their children in the same class of 30 students and that a subsequent questionnaire distributed to the whole class showed that 65% of the parents reported the need for a greater range of volunteering possibilities? Both of the statements were true, and both quantified their results, but the reactions to the two reports, with two size samplings, might be very different.

Reporting situations for large groups will likely be more valid, credible, and reliable by verifying results with quantitative forms of measurement. In the example case, the PAR team studying parent involvement designed a questionnaire to validate information originally acquired through a focus group. PAR researchers need to evaluate their data and ask, "If an experience that exists for a few students or parents also exists for many students or parents, does it exist for the population as a whole?" Larger populations are more easily studied using quantitative techniques that are covered in Chapter 6.

Task 4.2: Data-Planning Matrix

The following exercise is adapted from Maxwell (1996, p. 83). Researchers can employ the exercise to plot individual and group needs for data in PAR projects. This planning matrix can be used for both qualitative and quantitative data, and we suggest that, like the logic model, PAR groups employ the task throughout multiple cycles of the PAR process.

Procedure

Any of these may be tracked using a graphic organizer as follows:

- Establish a table with six columns and multiple rows in a landscape format.
- Label each column from left to right as follows:

  What do I need to know?

  Why do I need to know this?

  What kind of data will answer the questions?

  Where can I find the data?

  Whom do I contact for access?

  Time line for acquisition

This example has been filled out by the team whose work was discussed throughout this chapter. Note that the three main sources of qualitative data overlap. Table 4.3 shows that the team is realistic about the substantive amount of work needed to collect evidence within the period of a few months.

Table 4.3 Planning Matrix Graphic Organizer

What need to know	*Why need to know It*	*Data*	*Who/where data*	*Time line needed*
Whether and to what extent parents are involved in their student's education	What can be done so that their involvement aids academic standing	Interviews with involved and noninvolved parents Reflections and field notes Student work and homework clinic observations	Parents and students/library pizza party and PTO meeting Parent/teacher conferences Homework clinic	One month: can be done by next meeting Design field notes and test during conference with counselor and use at parent/teacher conferences in 3 weeks. Plan and advertise homework clinic, then gather homework and observe

As an individual or group, fill in the table until all questions have potential sources of data listed.

Discuss access to data issues and assign group members to each. When implementing an individual PAR project, review the table with a critical friend to ensure a high level of sensitivity related to data collection issues.

CONCLUSION

Qualitative evidence can be words or pictures. Whether collected from individuals, throughout a process of change, or during an event, PAR teams rely on strategies that balance time and resource constraints while collecting enough evidence to rise above the subjective nature of understanding. Overall, the strongest strategy is to collect data from multiple sources and then compare results.

Discussed in this chapter were (a) collecting individual data from interviews and focus groups, (b) collecting data throughout a process of change from reflective journals, field notes, and anecdotal evidence or logs, and (c) collecting data at the event through observations or student work. Each has positive attributes that help these data add to the richness and variety of understanding on which the PAR team will base their conclusions. These strategies are constrained by either issues of time, subjective understanding, or the biases of either the researcher or subject.

The people collecting qualitative data can take steps to ensure that their work is accurate and precise. PAR teams further the quality of these data when they work as critical friends to establish usable tools, double-check for bias, and adhere to a regular timetable for date collection. Finally, data emerging from various qualitative and quantitative strategies should be compared. Mixed methodology aids PAR teams to build a rigorous, cohesive set of conclusions about their topics.

NOTE

1. Several PAR studies, which took place during the 2003–2004 and 2005–2006 school years, are blended in this example (James, 2006a, 2006b, 2006c).

CHAPTER 5

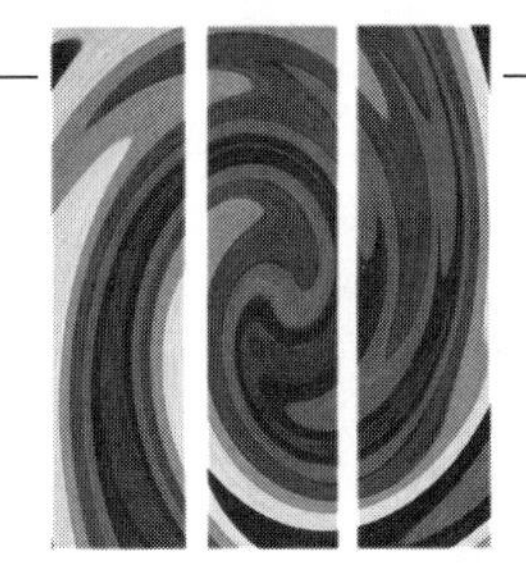

Qualitative Analysis

As mentioned in Chapter 4, data collection and analysis are iterative processes that play off each other throughout the use of qualitative methods in a PAR project. This chapter covers early qualitative analysis for PAR practitioners who have collected some qualitative data but are not yet ready to reach their final conclusions for their projects. We will return to the final analysis in Chapter 9, which discusses issues related to documentation, results, and final conclusions. The analysis of data takes place twice in the PAR steps, either directly after diagnosis or after measurement. As shown in Figure 5.1, analysis refers to the last column in the logic model.

An analogy appropriate to open this discussion compares qualitative researchers to archaeologists who sort through bits of pottery, ash, and bones at an ancient site. By the time the public view the site, it is uncovered and reassembled into recognizable shapes such as walls, skeletons, outdoor cooking areas, and dwellings. This is not the same "stuff" that the archaeologist initially sees when the pieces are discovered while digging. It is a similar story with the qualitative researcher. Data from research subjects originally come bundled with other bits and pieces. It is only through the sorting and re-sorting of these data that the key concepts across topics are tied together at the end of the study. While an archaeologist may find the missing piece to finish the pot at a distance from the rest of its remains, so may the missing concepts in an important idea be delivered to the PAR project from an unexpected source or situation. An archaeologist may have participated in previous digs and initially may be looking for familiar shapes; yet when settling into the site, the focus remains on the found bits and pieces. A PAR practitioner learns to erase what one thinks one "knows" and to sort and re-sort ideas, gleaning new perspectives.

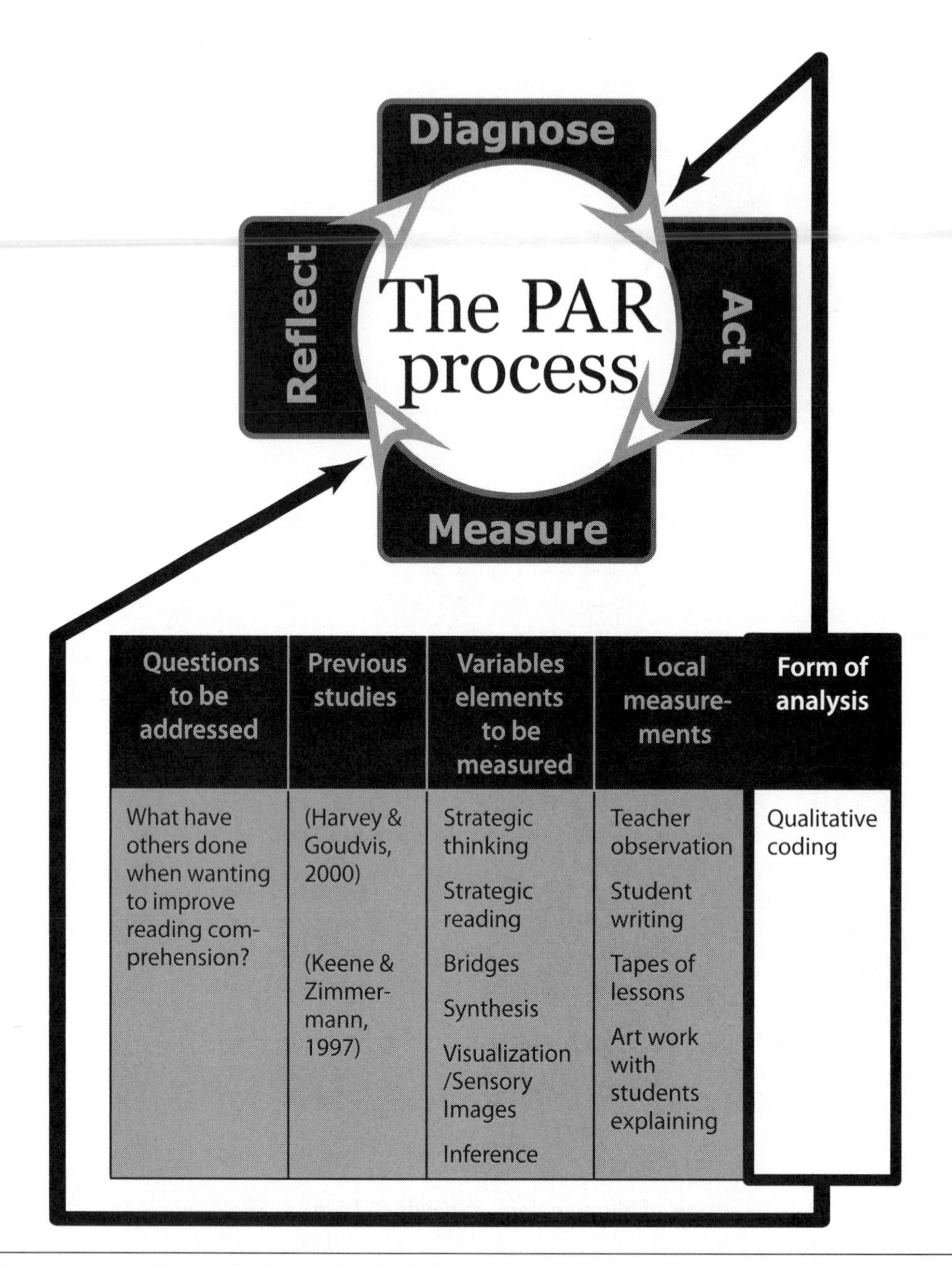

Questions to be addressed	Previous studies	Variables elements to be measured	Local measurements	Form of analysis
What have others done when wanting to improve reading comprehension?	(Harvey & Goudvis, 2000) (Keene & Zimmermann, 1997)	Strategic thinking Strategic reading Bridges Synthesis Visualization /Sensory Images Inference	Teacher observation Student writing Tapes of lessons Art work with students explaining	Qualitative coding

Figure 5.1 Chapter 5's Stage of the PAR Process

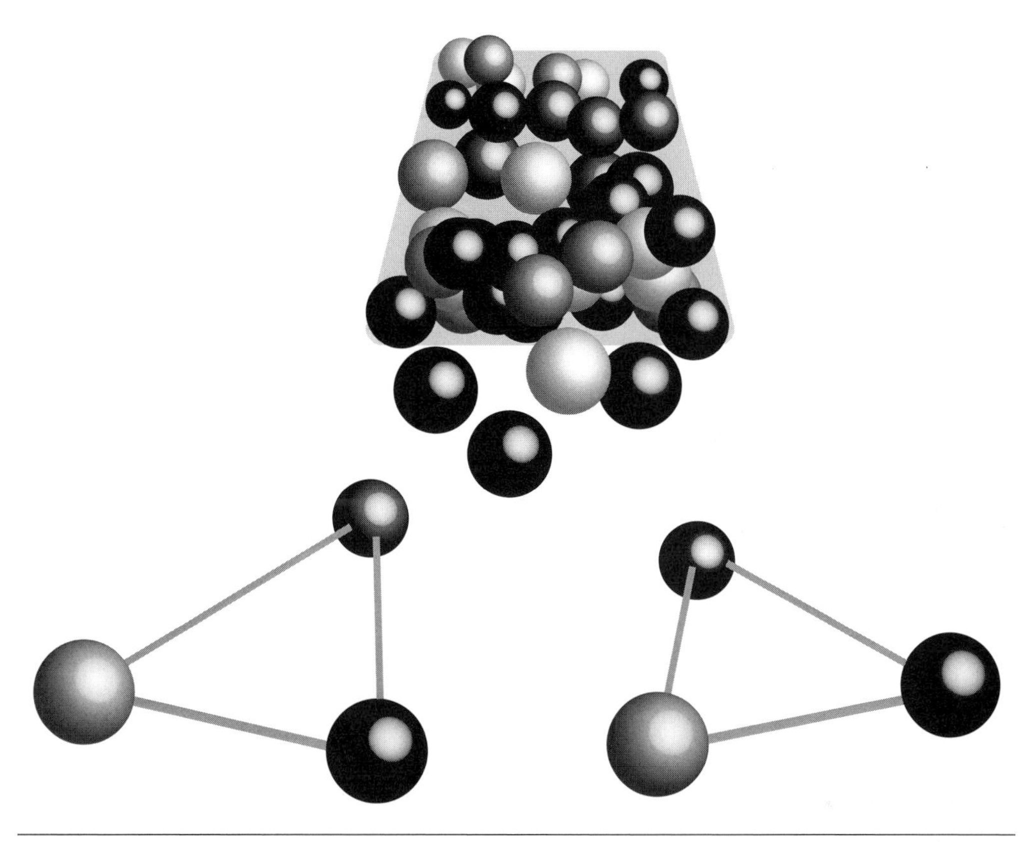

Figure 5.2 Making Sense of Qualitative Data

SOURCE: Alan Bucknam/Notchcode Creative, 2005.

Figure 5.2 shows the first processes where qualitative data (shown here as balls) are sorted until they hold together as new meaning.

The qualitative collection and analysis process is not complete at this point, however. The PAR researchers' task is to continue gathering and sorting until these beginning data reconfigure and their underlying insights emerge. The stages of analysis that build figures such as the one depicted above are covered in Chapter 9.

Directly after collecting qualitative data, it needs to be transcribed or made ready for analysis. Digital formats allow for maximum flexibility later during the analysis process. For instance, upon completion of interviews, interviewees' responses and PAR practitioners' notes should be word processed into documents. Answers that contain exact quotations from research subjects need to be recorded as quotations.

REFLECTIVE QUESTIONS

- How might you analyze the data from a series of reports on the same topic?
- What preparation would you make before you started?
- What strategies would help consistency?

SECTION 1: STAGES IN ANALYZING QUALITATIVE EVIDENCE

Qualitative analysis requires sorting and re-sorting data until the overarching conclusions or theoretical understandings emerge. Strategies generally fall into two categories: those used for sorting (graphic organizers, memos, codes, and families) and those used for comparison (triangulation and rubrics).

PAR teams begin by reading or reviewing the evidence they have collected. This starts when there is sufficient data to compare and contrast the ways in which subjects understand the topic being studied. Teams do not want to wait until they have so much data that just to read through it seems ominous.

Graphic Organizers

Graphic organizers are any method that PAR teams use to classify and organize newly gained knowledge. Tables aid discussion and display evidence where others can reflect on the information. When people first read the evidence, they can employ a simple graphic organizer as a means of sorting data. The easiest way to begin is to use a table with a column for each main idea. Rows signify the different instances where other evidence confirmed or disagreed with the column heading. Groups can employ a similar technique with a white board. Individuals may opt to write on adhesive notes that can be rearranged and may disclose new ideas in a further discussion.

Codes

Codes can be defined as labels put on data that summarize the data's content or highlight a primary idea. Depending on the research question, one piece of text can be coded in various different ways. Codes serve to separate and sort text into different categories, allowing researchers to look at it with fresh eyes and in new ways (Creswell, 2003; Maxwell, 1996; Patton & Patton, 2002; Strauss & Corbin, 1998).

Prepared by carefully documenting their work as described above, PAR researchers begin to read and analyze their data. They do this in one of two ways. In the first, they read their data with no preconceived idea as to what is important and start to open code ideas that come to mind, pointing to similarities and differences within data as they become apparent (Strauss & Corbin, 1998). **Open codes** are much like reading through student work. Single words or short phrases that capture the patterns of ideas begin to emerge as researchers read through qualitative data. Later, data are reread grouped in sections with like or similar codes, and larger theories or understandings emerge. Researchers try to review the data without preconceived notions of what they will find.

The second general method of coding is **selective coding.** The researcher starts coding with specific themes or ideas in mind and then sorts the data according to these preselected categories. Teams can selectively code statements or ideas that they know they will cover in multiple data sets because they pertain to the general topic, or they code topics introduced through the literature and/or researched through multiple data collection strategies (Patton & Patton, 2002; Strauss & Corbin, 1998).

If PAR practitioners have access to qualitative data software such as Atlas/ti or NVIVO, the software can mark codes and tally locations of every coded passage, which eases the data analysis process. For practitioners without the help of software but whose data are word processed, each code can be highlighted with a different color or copied and pasted into new groups on separate documents. The example PAR team did not have their data in a digital format. Nevertheless, they started reading their data with three codes in mind: red for what parents looked for in involvement opportunities, yellow for data about barriers to involvement, and pink for data that aided understanding of community context. They used highlighter pens to mark passages and then reviewed just those three color-coded sections.

Memos

Memos are used to catch ideas as they become obvious during analysis. For instance, the PAR practitioners studying parent involvement noticed that all data coded yellow (for barriers) discussed the time constraints of working parents. The memos included questions about such diverse ideas as what short-term volunteer activities would be useful and whether the school should be open in the summer to accommodate youth who needed child care. Memos are a flexible technique that allow teams to capture a breadth of ideas when brainstorming (Maxwell, 1996) by tagging each individual's ideas a different color. The above PAR team passed their data around the circle, with each group member using a different color of Post-it Note on which they wrote their ideas. Their memos were later sorted into ideas for action steps and topics needing further investigation (McKernan, 1996).

Families

As data are sorted into codes, they are separated from the root document. As the PAR researchers read through their data again, they focus on one code at a time. This step encourages practitioners to see new overarching themes congregated under the ideas captured in codes and memos. These themes are called **families.** For instance, the PAR team noticed how their codes for barriers to involvement clustered with data describing the attitudes of the previous school administration, which was not adept at building a welcoming culture in the school. Parents who were new to the school did not perceive that barrier, but parents who had been volunteers prior to the change in administration were hesitant to be involved again. By tying data together in families or groupings, specific linkages of cause and effect appear, such as the one related to the former principal's relationship with the community. This information allowed the PAR team to understand the underlying barrier to involvement for some parents.

PAR group members, acting as critical friends (McNiff, Lomax, & Whitehead, 1996), may support each other by reading coded data and memos with a fresh eye. Once separated from its root questions and re-sorted into codes, an objective viewer may understand the data linkages in new ways, creating avenues for future study. The PAR team found that the parents' thoughts about involvement clustered around issues of time, travel, and amount of direct contact with students. This led the PAR group to propose that involvement would increase when opportunities were developed across those continuums. As a result, new parent involvement opportunities did develop, some with a small time commitment, some connected to field trips, and others that involved monitoring student behavior rather than working directly with them on projects.

Triangulation

After families of ideas begin to form, researchers quickly draw conclusions about these data and begin to employ methods to test their ideas, often starting with the test of triangulation. As discussed in Chapter 4, triangulation is the comparison of one data set to another, often derived from very different methods of collection or from different populations (Creswell, 2003; Maxwell, 1996; Patton & Patton, 2002). For instance, suppose the PAR team from our example wanted to test whether offering a wider range of volunteer activities might increase parent involvement. To do so, they could (a) distribute questionnaires in the neighborhood asking these questions, (b) make a site visit to a school with many volunteers and interview those individuals, or (c) conduct interviews with parents who are currently involved. Any or all of these three ideas could yield additional data to triangulate with the PAR team's original analysis.

The challenge with triangulation is that for firm conclusions to be drawn, data on all sides need to be analyzed in a consistent manner. For instance, if open coding of interviews from the school that implemented a wide range of volunteer activities develops entirely different data categories from another source of data, then their evidence will be difficult to compare. Again, PAR teams can help each other by acting as critical friends (McNiff et al., 1996) and challenging new data collection methods until everyone believes the likelihood of comparability is high.

Rubrics and Multiple Observers

Many PAR projects in education focus on increased student achievement. In these studies, multiple analyses of student work in portfolios may be important. **Rubrics** are written guidelines by which student work is assessed, articulating the standards for how student work is judged and allowing for the cross-tabulation and inclusion of multiple viewpoints in the analysis. The differences in observational records and measurement of student work varies from day to day due to a number of factors such as the mood of the person making the records and the context under which they were made. Students' analysis of their own work through grading rubrics will also add new and unexpected insights. No matter who is employing a rubric for analysis purposes, every attempt should be made to capture exact quotations, which are a rich source of data.

The potential differences inherent in rubrics can be viewed as a weakness during a **trend analysis**, where differences over time are measured as a way of demonstrating change. Two tactics for alleviating these challenges are (1) establishing grading rubrics, outlining clear expectations for poor, medium, or superior work across all variables that affect project outcomes and/or (2) training multiple observers who work together repeatedly until their observational notes and rubric grading patterns are consistent with each other. To maintain overall consistency, it is important that neither the grading rubric nor the observers change throughout the complete trend analysis.

Similarities and Differences

Codes, memos, families, and triangulation are similar in how their use varies along the continuum from unstructured to structured. As with data collection methods, these separations merely serve to admonish PAR practitioners to look at their data from multiple angles and to uncover as much meaning as possible. Unstructured coding and resorting stems from grounded theory made famous by Strauss and Corbin (1998). It is based upon the belief that truth emerges from patterns that become apparent as the data are analyzed repeatedly. Unstructured techniques break the data down into small bits and then re-sort the data until new ideas or organizational patterns emerge.

The strength of this approach lies in the potential for uncovering completely new understandings of the relationships in the world (Strauss & Corbin, 1998). The biggest disadvantage for PAR projects is that it requires a high degree of objectivity and the greatest amount of time. Open coding is perhaps the most successful when outside researchers, not involved in the situation, gather data and return to their universities to study it rather than when community groups study situations in which they are involved.

Structured data sorting flows out of an understanding of the literature on their topic, the practitioners' own logical processes, and the research subjects' conceptual understanding of the world (Noffke & Stevenson, 1995). Having definite ideas of what they will be looking for, their codes, memos, and families grow naturally out of these initial understandings. A structured method of sorting and grouping data also aids in forming comparisons and allows for greater ease in triangulation between data sets (Creswell, 2003; Maxwell, 1996; Patton & Patton, 2002). As an example, the PAR team read Joyce Epstein's (2001) work on family involvement in schools and, as a result, coded their data according to her six types of communication. The strength of this approach was that it gave them a fairly exact idea of which of the six strategies were working. The weakness of this method was that it did not allow the team to uncover as many nuances of how the Latino culture differed from the Caucasian families they served.

Semistructured analysis allows for the strengths of both unstructured and structured analysis and is most often recommended for PAR projects. PAR groups read the existing literature and base both their questions and the initial coding of their material on the findings of the literature review. Then they reread the material, noting all passages that do not fit within the neatly arranged structures. These "misfit" passages become the resources for further discussion, open coding, and the focus for the development of new families or types of information. An alternative approach is to ask neutral parties to read their data before the data are coded and to offer suggestions as to how they sort across data collection techniques.

REFLECTIVE QUESTIONS

- To what standard do you measure the credibility of statements made by others?
- What evidence would show you that an educational practice could reliably transfer to your school setting?

SECTION 2: VALIDITY, CREDIBILITY, AND RELIABILITY IN THE ANALYSIS OF QUALITATIVE DATA

Our discussion now turns to the three concepts of validity, credibility, and reliability. Throughout analysis, PAR practitioners need to ask whether and to what extent their conclusions will be perceived by others as

- **Valid:** the degree to which data and results are accurate reflections of reality. Validity refers to the concepts that are investigated, the people or objects that are studied, the methods by which data are collected, and the findings that are produced.
- **Credible:** the degree to which the person reading the report thinks the conclusions make sense. This is a subjective judgment and requires that PAR researchers be cognizant of their audience and context.
- **Reliable:** the consistency and dependability of the research findings in general but, also specifically, as to whether and to what degree the findings would transfer to another context.

PAR groups help each other achieve these levels of validity, credibility, and reliability by serving as critical friends. The two main types of help they offer are (1) discussions on whether and to what extent conclusions match the evidence and (2) challenging whether and to what extent evidence that might refute these claims is adequately covered.

Spencer, Ritchie, and Lewis (2003) stress the importance of researchers engaging with each other in difficult but productive conversations. PAR teams help each other when they are willing to double- or triple-check their work in order to verify that analysis remains grounded in data. Qualitative research, like education, is often dismissed as "soft." By writing and rewriting until the connection to these data is evident, researchers overcome many of the barriers inherent in these processes. As new data are gathered, all parts of the analysis process need to be revisited repeatedly, including the overall organization, emerging themes, agreement and disagreement, or associations within data and between groups of data. When the same variables or elements can be observed or measured from three to four vantage points, PAR practitioners will be able to convince their constituencies that their conclusions are valid (Anderson et al., 1994; Higgs, 2001; Maxwell, 1996; McKernan, 1996).

Occasionally, PAR projects take detours as practitioners follow ideas that seem promising. These side trips may prove to be gems or they may lead to dead ends. PAR team members can be vigilant for the traps and warn each other to ignore data that do not seem to advance the project toward its overall purpose; by doing so, they increase credibility.

Task 5.1: Practice Analysis of Data

The following task provides PAR practitioners the experience of analyzing qualitative data. These data may be derived from any of the data collection methods described in Chapter 4. If possible, you will need a team of at least three people for this exercise.

Procedure

If the PAR team has already collected qualitative data, use it for this exercise. If you are doing this exercise by yourself and using prewritten reflective data, make sure that at least 24 hours elapse between reflection and analysis. This will give you sufficient time away from these data for increased objectivity.

- Each person in the group reads through the data and makes a preliminary set of potential codes.
- Discuss the potential codes with each other. Choose a color with which to highlight each.
- Read the data a second time and code and highlight passages in the colors you have chosen. Remember that data that conflict with each other but pertain to the same topic receive the same code. For instance, a person agreeing with or disagreeing with a school policy will still be coded as an opinion about that policy. If one passage may be coded multiple ways, copy and paste it next to itself so that it can be highlighted accordingly.
- If any new ideas about the project as a whole come to mind, capture them as a memo and set them off to the side.
- Read through the data again, one highlighted color at a time, reflecting on themes, or families of ideas, that emerge. You may want to copy and

paste each highlight color into its own document. Make note of your reflections.

- Read the data again—looking for whether material contained in the uncoded areas adds to or delineates any themes.
- Compare your codes, memos, and families with the others in your group. List similarities and differences.
- As a group, if you were to have a conversation with an outsider about your project *using only the codes you have identified*, what would you say? Write a paragraph adding as many measurements as possible to make your description concrete. For example: "Seventy-five percent of the parents agreed that . . ." or "The majority (5) pointed to this, while a small minority (2) pointed to that."
- In your own words, document the process that you just used. In two or three sentences, include whether and to what extent open codes add to the selective coding of the data and how themes emerged.

CONCLUSION

Chapter 5 presents an overview of qualitative data analysis. As data are collected, they are analyzed, and the results provide feedback to advance new collection strategies. Qualitative analysis involves the fragmentation and regrouping of data derived from conversations or written accounts. These data are coded, and families of evidence are grouped together throughout the data collection process. Data are also tagged with memos relating to further investigations through multiple analyses. Initial results are confirmed by triangulating data with other data derived either from different sources (both qualitative and quantitative) or through multiple analyses against a rubric. Each result is considered relative to validity, credibility, and reliability.

In the end, PAR practitioners need the ability to justify the validity, credibility, and reliability of their conclusions. Results will be valid to the extent that they accurately portray the issue under study from the subjects' various points of view. Credibility is judged against the standards of the researchers, the people involved in the study, and the constituency to which they report. Finally, reliability indicates that the actions that result from these studies will improve education in their communities and may be of interest across a wider arena.

CHAPTER 6

Quantitative Evidence

Because of the standards movement, educators in the United States have become well-informed consumers of quantitative data, the strength of which is to demonstrate a small amount of precise information as it pertains to a large population (usually of students). Many public school districts throughout the United States provide some level of data about their schools on district Web sites to help parents and other members of the public become adept at reading student and school-based data as well. A review of the Web site from a large metro school district showed quantitative school data segregated into five subgroups: Overview, Academics, Teachers, Students, and Ethnicity. This site broke down district-level statistical information by school name and categorized the data as follows:

- Overview included State Accountability Rating, Parent Satisfaction, Attendance, and Suspensions.
- Academics included Improvement Rating, Percentage of Students Passing State-Administered Standardized Reading and Math tests.
- Teachers included Percentage With Advanced Degrees, Percentage With More Than 11 Years of Experience, Absence Rate, and Percentage Not Fully Licensed.
- Students included Attendance Rate, Percentage Free and Reduced Lunch, Stability Percentage, and Dropout Rate. Stability was determined by 3 years' attendance in the same school.
- Ethnicity was broken down into African American, American Indian, Asian, Hispanic, and White.

DATA FOUND IN SCHOOLS

PAR methodology easily aligns with several current trends in education. While we also review this topic in Chapter 11, here we discuss quantitative data in the context of data collection and assessment work in connection with the continuous school improvement movement. This nationally implemented initiative has been instrumental in giving educators the necessary methods for data-driven decision making. This model includes the following process steps: planning, implementation, evaluation, and improvement (Bernhardt, 2004), which correlate to the PAR steps of diagnose, act, measure, and reflect.

Bernhardt (2004) points to four types of measures that administrators and teachers can use to understand their schools. These include measures of demographics, perceptions, student learning, and school processes. These data are a mix of information currently available in schools and regularly utilized in school improvement efforts. Demographic information is usually found in registration data. The collection of data on perceptions about the school employs a mix of qualitative techniques such as interviews and focus groups, which can be confirmed through quantitative surveys. Data about student learning builds on a base of information in regular school records in the form of test data, cumulative records, and so on. Adding student portfolios, observations, and other forms of authentic assessment enriches standard quantitative records. Bernhardt's fourth measure, school processes, can be outlined through student handbooks, curriculum lists, and minutes from meetings and can be enhanced with survey data.

Standardized Tests

Standardized tests are generally a yardstick against which educators measure the progress of their students (Bagin & Rudner, 1994). There are two general categories of standardized tests used in education: those that measure achievement and those that measure aptitude. Both are rigorously designed and validated to deliver comparable results across large populations (Zenisky, Keller, & Sireci, 2004).

The general use in education of standardized test scores is to report on progress, diagnose strengths and weaknesses, and/or evaluate progress (Bagin & Rudner, 1994). There are two caveats for their use. First, one standardized test score cannot be compared easily to a score derived from another test, as standardized tests are created on different scales of reference. The test developers design this purposefully, so that comparisons become invalid. For instance, one student's ACT scores cannot be compared to another student's SAT scores.

Scores are never 100% reliable, as most published tests provide a "standard error of measurement" that establishes what they consider the margin for error when implementing their test.

As mentioned above, while one of the most publicized forms of information available about public schools in the United States, standardized tests are one of many types of information. Though not to be used in exclusion, standardized tests become powerful methods when presented in combination with other achievement data. In addition, standardized tests should not be used for placement, as the results of these tests alone will not demonstrate a holistic interpretation of student achievement or aptitude.

REFLECTIVE QUESTIONS

- What quantitative data at your school do you have available for your review?
- How are these data discussed, and what influence do these data have on school strategies?
- What types of questions arise from your review of data, and how might those questions be measured?

SECTION 1: QUESTIONS ANSWERED BY QUANTITATIVE AND MIXED METHODS EVIDENCE

In general terms, quantitative data answer questions about how things are. These questions come up at two points during PAR steps, either during or directly after the diagnose and measurements steps, as shown in Figure 6.1.

These data collection and analysis techniques include methods that classify (demographics) and address questions such as "Who are our students?" Or they show change (pre-/posttests, observations, and time studies) and answer questions such as "How are third graders progressing in comprehension skills?" They may compare groups (correlation analysis), asking, "Does reading for pleasure influence student achievement?" Finally, they may report opinions or levels of satisfaction/agreement (surveys, Likert scales), asking, "Do parents feel welcome in the school?" or depict outcomes (standardized assessments) by answering the question, "How many fourth graders scored proficient in writing skills on the state assessment?" As introduced in Chapter 3, when combined with previously gathered and analyzed qualitative evidence, these data give educators

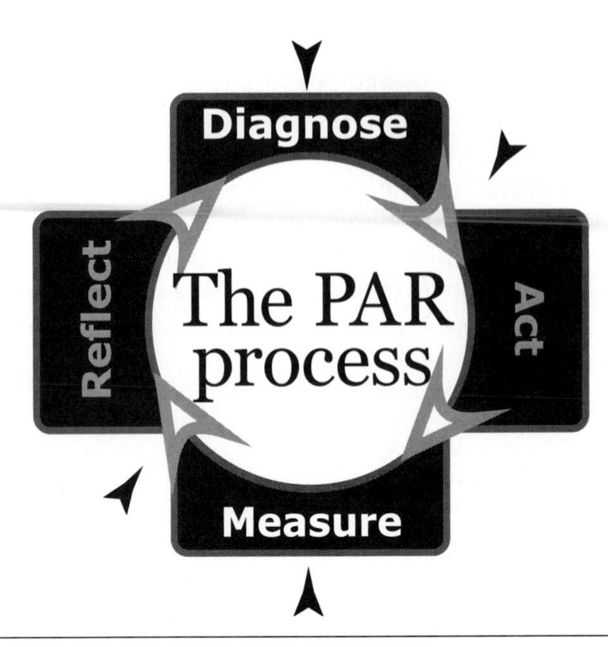

Figure 6.1 Chapter 6's Stage of the Process

a sound basis on which to make decisions and to build educational programs. Next we present brief descriptions of three types of quantitative studies and the resulting types of analysis with the questions targeted by each methodology.

Observations and Time Studies

Observations in quantitative studies frequently examine a particular behavior as it is monitored in a group over time. These studies generally address the efficacy of particular interventions or answer questions about how widespread a behavior is within a school. When PAR practitioners are concerned with change over time, it is prudent to collect data in the beginning, during regular intervals, and at the end of any situation under study. While inconclusive by themselves, observational data augment other forms of data to develop a holistic and convincing view of a situation.

Surveys or Questionnaires

At a practical level, PAR teams are most likely to implement questionnaires or surveys to collect additional or confirmational evidence for their PAR studies. When surveys are well written and tested prior to implementation, they reliably test the opinions and perceptions of larger populations than can be reached by qualitative means (i.e., interviews or focus groups). The quantitative methodology allows educators to understand the characteristics, opinions, attitudes, or previous experiences of groups in the school community. Researchers often use Likert scales in questionnaires and surveys to capture people's opinions or experiences within an array of possibilities. Examples of such scales include the following: "On a scale from 1 to 5, with 1 being the least and 5 being the most" or "Mark the degree to which you agree with the following statements from 'not at all' to 'completely.'"

Descriptive Statistics

During quantitative analyses, data are crunched using basic mathematical tests that identify characteristics and/or compare one group to another, searching for possible correlations. The purpose of **statistics** is to clarify the variance between data to aid meaning. As a simple example, if a dot is placed on an infinite field, it is impossible to accurately describe its placement. However, if it is placed among a group of dots on paper, then its description becomes its relationship to the other dots and their relationship to the field, in this case the paper, and so on. When employed, statistical analysis techniques aid the discussion of characteristics inherent within and between sets of data.

Research relies on statistics to give solid answers to specific questions such as

- What is the average score?
- Whether and to what extent is an individual or group performing to recognized standards?
- What percentages of any given group need extra help or a different approach in learning a subject?

Descriptive statistics summarize a data set with a few calculations, which PAR researchers find very handy whenever they have to work with a large volume of data, such as the test scores for a school or the district. Descriptive statistics are relatively easy and direct to calculate and include measures of the center points in a data set and calculations of the variance from those points. PAR researchers may use descriptive statistics to discuss the test scores of a cohort of students.

Variance and Correlation

Educators may wish to examine the extent to which two groups are significantly different from each other; for instance, by asking if the scores derived from one variable (say, attendance) differ in relationship to another variable (e.g., gender). In this example, researchers are likely to employ the *t*-test (discussed in Section 3) to determine if the **mean** of one group is significantly different from the mean of the other group on the same variable. The mean is the average score of all the data for one variable. It is determined by dividing the sum of the numbers by the size of the population captured in the data. If the difference of the mean is less than 0.05 or 0.01 (depending on the size of the sample) when compared to the mean of the other group, then educators generally consider the differences "real" (Leedy & Ormrod, 2005; Valentine, 1997).

Inferential statistics are used when looking at a small sample of data, extracted from a larger population, from which the PAR researcher draws some conclusions (makes inferences). Inferential statistics include comparisons and correlations between figures from one group as compared with another. While outside of the realm of this text, PAR researchers find these handy to calculate the differences between a pretest and posttest for two groups of students. For this reason, we have included a brief explanation about *t*-tests. In the example above, while attendance scores reside on a continuous field of possibility, gender is finite. Attendance scores when tracked over time might result in a trend analysis such as seen for economic forecasts in newspapers. Correlations show whether and to what extent one thing links with another in such a way that it increases or decreases in a predictable fashion. A chart of attendance over test scores might show a direct correlation with improved attendance and higher scores. If this was the case, a PAR team might suggest that their school focus on attendance issues as one strategy to address achievement issues (Valentine, 1997).

Complex Questions

Section 1 comes full circle in our discussion of what questions PAR practitioners will answer through quantitative collection and analysis. We return to our previous introduction of Bernhardt (2004) and the continuous school improvement movement. Table 6.1, derived from Bernhardt, discusses how different types of educational data can be mixed to develop holistic answers for various questions. Each line has been expanded to include mixed methodological data collection possibilities that would allow a PAR team to attack the complex questions they face.

REFLECTIVE QUESTIONS

- When have you used informal and formal observations as part of your work in education?

Table 6.1 Types of Data and Corresponding Questions

<table>
<tr><th>Type of data/instruments</th><th>Questions answered with both types</th><th>Questions answered through an overlap of three or more types of data</th></tr>
<tr><td>Demographic data mixed with surveys and anecdotes on community perceptions gathered through focus groups</td><td>Are subgroups of students experiencing difficulties? Do new students feel welcome?</td><td rowspan="2">What school processes and programs are perceived as working to greatest benefit for specific populations of students?
What school strategies and procedures foster a safe and welcoming environment for new students?</td></tr>
<tr><td>Demographic data and school process data derived through surveys and archival evidence (school records) mixed with observations</td><td>What are the patterns of school involvement?
What behavior patterns cause students to be suspended?</td></tr>
<tr><td>Student learning data comprised of tests and portfolio evaluations mixed with community perception data derived from surveys and focus groups</td><td>Is there a correlation between perception and reality about student learning? Where are they in agreement and where do they differ?
Does leisure reading done outside of school affect student performance in reading comprehension on the state assessment?</td><td rowspan="2">What are the impacts of school programs on student learning?
What effective strategies can be implemented to help English language learner (ELL) students increase their academic achievement (Francis, Rivera, Leseaux, Kieffer, & Rivera, 2006)?
How does the implementation of an incentive program affect the amount of English spoken in the ELL classroom (Allers, 2004)?</td></tr>
<tr><td>Student learning data comprised of tests and portfolio evaluations mixed with school process information derived from surveys and observations</td><td>Are the school programs making a difference in student achievement?
Do students who attend school regularly perform more proficiently on teacher-made tests and/or state assessments than students who do not attend school regularly?</td></tr>
</table>

SOURCE: Adapted from Bernhardt (2004).

- What methods or training did you need prior to making your observations?
- What surveys or written assessments have you developed?
- What was successful or challenging in these processes?

SECTION 2: QUANTITATIVE DATA COLLECTION

Quantitative data collection takes place during the diagnosis or measurement steps and relates to the variables and local measurement columns on the logic model as shown in Figure 6.2.

Observations

We discussed qualitative observations in Chapter 4. Comparing the two types of observations shows a similar reversal in breadth and scope as the comparison between qualitative and quantitative evidence. Qualitative observations focus on small populations and are designed to gather a wide range of evidence. Quantitative observations capture a small number of events across large populations.

Observation checklists capture whether the observer saw the behavior occur in a specific period and displays this evidence in a manner that leads to mathematical analysis. For instance, a PE teacher may wish to track whether and to what extent girls aggressively participate in football games. Scales are employed to judge a range of participation characteristics, with each category in the range distinguishable from the others. An individual with an observation checklist might have three columns: one for girls who were not active in the sport, a second for students who played but would appear uncomfortable, and the third column for girls who played comfortably, engaging with the boys at all levels of the game. Other examples of observable tasks include evaluation of performance skills such as solving a math equation, writing an essay, or swinging a bat (Leedy & Ormrod, 2005).

PAR groups assist each other to develop observation checklists for the behaviors they wish to study. As with the creation of qualitative observation checklists, PAR teams should plan first to discuss and define the behaviors to be studied. Step 2 is to draft a rough checklist to collect data. The third step is to pilot test the draft. This is done by going to the location and measuring the population to be studied using the instrument that has been developed. It is a good idea to have more than one person test the instrument and then discuss the results. The final step is to talk about what made it easy or difficult to use.

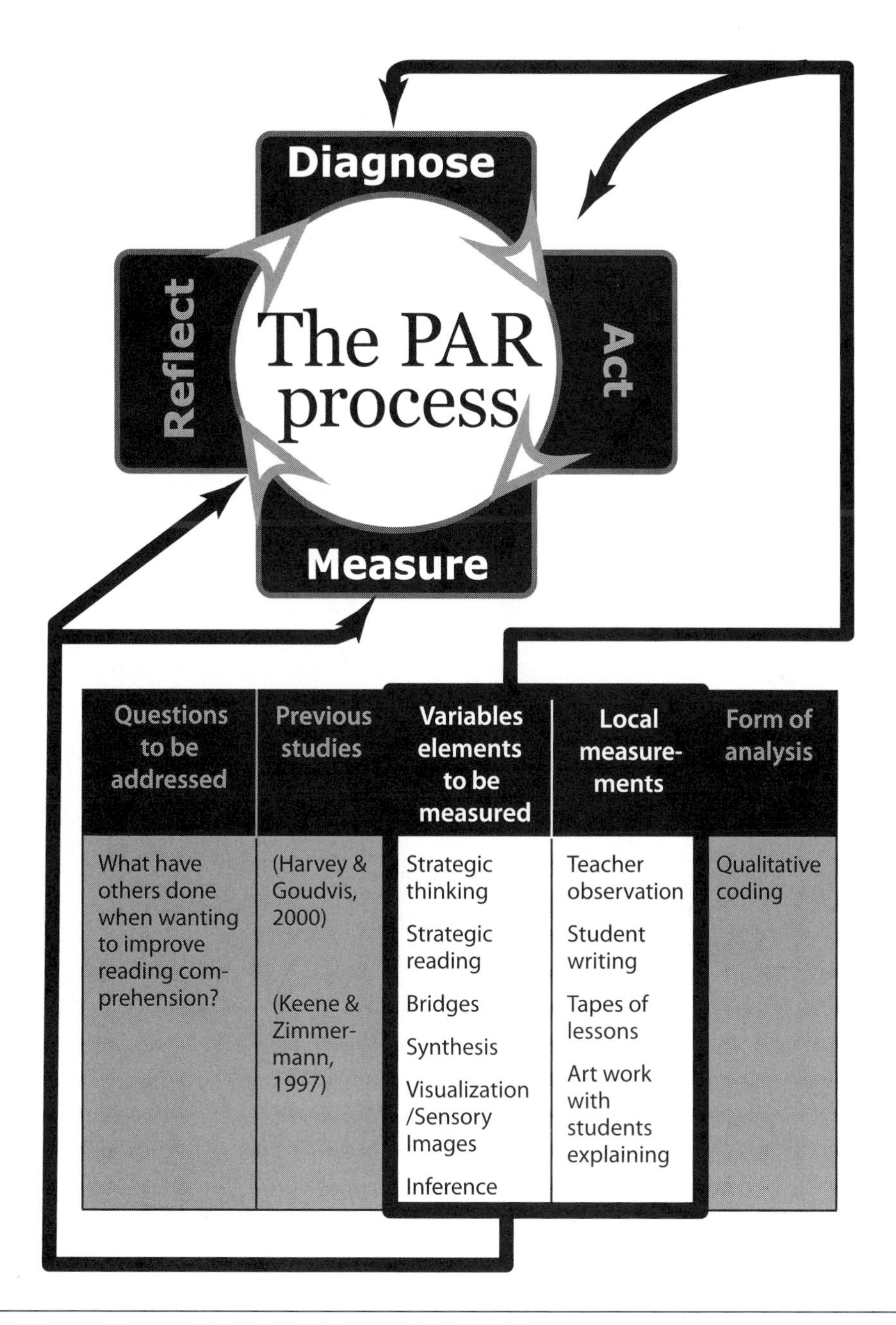

Figure 6.2 Chapter 6, Section 2's Stage of the PAR Process

Several iterations of this process will result in a usable quantitative tool. Then it is important to collect a series of observations over time in order to uncover potential influences on the behavior in question (McKernan, 1996). PAR teams act as critical friends throughout the development of any/all research instruments like observation checklists. The central question is whether and to what extent a person using the instrument is actually measuring what the research team wants to measure. Ambiguity in definition of any category causes confusion. For instance, in the example above, would another word be easier to evaluate or be more meaningful than the term *comfortable*?

Leedy and Ormrod (2005) mention that to maintain objectivity, the following strategies are beneficial:

- Develop a precise definition of the behavior so that the specific behavior becomes easily recognizable.
- Divide any period of observation into small segments of time (30 seconds to 15 minutes, depending on the behavior and likelihood of observation).
- Use precise rating scales when gauging a range of behavior.
- Engage multiple observers to rate the behavior during the same period.
- Train the observers in use of the checklists and scales prior to starting the observation process.

Questionnaires or Surveys

Surveys are methods of asking questions with a predetermined range of answers. The methods most often employed in PAR studies include both written questionnaires and verbal surveys of a subpopulation on a particular topic. These techniques often query parents or teachers about either experience with, or ideas about, situations in their schools. Researchers tabulate and summarize the answers in frequencies, for a snapshot of people's opinions across the wider school community, at that particular point in time.

Building good questions, free from both vagueness and redundancy, is the challenge of survey question writing. It is not enough to say that questions are (a) brainstormed, (b) written, (c) tested by a diversity of people who comment on them, and then (d) rewritten and reformatted for easier completion. Good questions are carefully designed and provide consistent measures in comparable circumstances (Fowler, 2002). Therefore, PAR practitioners need to focus on designing statements and questions not as they would conversational elements but as measures.

The issue arises of question reliability in addressing if people in similar situations respond to questions in identical ways. Several problems impact question reliability. First, in a population's primary culture, people intuitively learn to view events from different perspectives. Second, people's memories of past incidents diminish with time. Third, respondents will tend toward vague answers rather than specific ones. Finally, ratings will mean different things to different people. What some respondents rate as "good," others rate as "fair." The goal, after all, is to "ensure consistent meaning to ALL respondents" (Fowler, 2002, p. 81).

Piloting a survey is helpful prior to full implementation of the instrument. This decreases the likelihood of confusion as to meaning that would render a question invalid. For instance, sentence structures that create difficulty include optional wording, as evidenced in the following: "Did you (or anyone you know) experience bullying behavior?" The data derived from this question would not give a clear count of the extent of bullying, as the tally could not be separated into direct experiences versus those experienced by friends. In addition, without a time delimiter such as "within the last school year," the results do not quantify whether the behavior in question happened in the recent or distant past. If the school population is mobile, educators will also want to add a phrase such as "in this school." Because of the many considerations involved with surveys, we recommend that PAR practitioners who wish to build a precise instrument investigate authors such as Fowler (2002) and Kent (2001), who have written extensively on this topic.

A Likert scale, as discussed in Chapter 3, is a scale of answers on which respondents to the survey indicate their levels of agreement or disagreement with a series of statements. Simple statements scaled from 1 (complete disagreement) to 5 (complete agreement) offer a means for PAR researchers to gather opinions. Using the example above, "I feel this school is unsafe due to bullying" with a Likert scale from 1–5 could measure the responses of the student population and avoid some of the issues related to definition of terms, as mentioned above. Researchers may choose to use a 1–4 scale, the advantage of which is that it avoids the neutral position and forces the respondent to take a positive or negative position. Likert 1–4 scales are also advantageous, as then, depending on the breakdown of results, PAR teams may report the cumulative total of 3 + 4 responses compared to 1 + 2 responses.

Since surveys are frequently used to collect all types of data, the public has become adept at avoiding them. Completed surveys with "nonresponse" answers place a study in jeopardy. Valid evidence is obtained only when a credibly large majority of a cross section of survey respondents submits evidence. For this reason, we suggest either that people with authority in the school, such as the principal, help engage in the appeal or that research practitioners use incentives for survey completion. Fowler (2002) suggests the following to reduce nonresponse answers:

- Personally appeal to respondents rather than rely on letters of explanation.
- Make the survey visually appealing and easy to complete. On the instrument, use boxes to check, numbers to circle, or equally easy tasks with few or no items that require writing.
- Be respectful of people's time. Keep the survey short.
- Use appropriate incentives.
- Remind respondents several times of the importance of the evidence.
- Personally appeal again to nonrespondents, delivering a second survey as necessary.

Samples

PAR practitioners must ask themselves if their selected respondents adequately represent the total population who will be affected by potential changes resulting from the PAR study. For instance, to what extent do the students who responded to the survey represent the entire student population in age, ethnicity, socioeconomic status, and so on? An adequate sample is one where the results of any/all data collection efforts are considered valid, credible, and reliable to PAR educators, their teams, and their stakeholders. This may be decided through group discussion about when the evidence adequately represents the people being surveyed, or it may be done by statistical means.

The easiest sample to implement is the convenience sample, where PAR practitioners ask people who are available to fill out the survey. However, it is unlikely that a convenience group represents the whole population. Use of convenience samples are appropriate when the PAR practitioners want general background information about their topic but do not care about whether, and to what extent, the sample mirrors the larger population.

The gold standard in choosing participants for a data collection effort is the random sample. Randomness means that every given person in the population has an equal chance to be selected as part of the sample or to be passed by. Pure chance must dictate the choice to be included. A simple random sample can be set up by pulling participant names out of a hat or using the Internet to pull a random selection of numbers and then matching student IDs to that random list. A third method is to place surveys in seats around an auditorium prior to it being filled for an assembly. The people who sit in those seats are asked to complete the survey. Statistically, random samples go the furthest to ensure that data delivered through such methods are most likely to match data from the entire population. There are many subcategories of random samples. Two that might be used to aid PAR practitioners, stratified or proportional samples, ensure that all opinions are measured. To give an example of each, educators may need to implement stratified random samples to ensure that a balanced percentage of respondents from each grade answered the questions. Proportional random samples might be used to ensure that opinions were balanced across ethnicity.

Time Series

Once PAR practitioners have decided what representative group of people will be observed or asked to fill out a questionnaire/survey, they need to decide if and how the time element is part of their research design. For instance, a teacher might decide to take snapshots of data throughout the semester or to divide observations to represent both genders during the school day. This type of evaluation of educational results or outcomes requires that the PAR practitioners consciously adhere to a schedule for data collection over time (Bernhardt, 2004).

Time series data can be seen daily; weather forecasts and stock market reports are two of the most common examples. With these illustrations, we can understand the practice of predicting future results. Educators use time series data when they expect student behavior issues to change or escalate, as with the anticipation of a holiday break and the end of the school year vacation (Hand, 2002). An advantage with time series designs is that this methodology requires only one group rather than large numbers of participants. Rather than worry about sampling issues, everyone available for the intervention or curriculum is tested. Though multiple measures can be time consuming, this design has the advantage of minimizing the effects of history and context due to short intervals between measurements (Creswell, 2002).

Creswell (2002) considers a time series approach as a solid experimental design when the researcher has access to only one group and can study them for a period of time. PAR practitioners should consider every opportunity for multiple types of pretest and posttest measures. For instance, can the group be tested, observed, and studied qualitatively prior to an intervention or the introduction of a curriculum? Can the researchers collect the same types of data at the midpoint and at the end? Though time series typically are utilized for quantitative evidence, there is no reason a mixed methodological approach would not prove to be valid, credible, and reliable for use in PAR studies.

In Figure 6.3, a teacher (a) measures the reading level of a class, (b) implements a reading strategy, (c) measures the results at three equal intervals, and (d) gives a booster lesson and measures two additional times. During a time series study as illustrated, it is important that measurements are timed at even intervals and both before and after important events such as the implementation of a new strategy or the booster lesson that followed.

REFLECTIVE QUESTIONS

- On a scale of 1–10, what is your level of comfort in understanding mathematical calculations?
- What methods do you use when performing calculations? Will your methods of calculation be adequate to work with the amount of data in your study?
- Who is available to act as a critical friend and to support your analysis efforts?

SECTION 3: ANALYSIS AND STATISTICAL INFORMATION

Quantitative data analysis takes place directly after the diagnosis or measurement steps and relates to the forms of analysis column on the logic model as shown in Figure 6.4.

Analysis begins by describing collected data. First, the number of people studied in each subpopulation is counted. Next, the numbers of participants who were sent a survey or were available for observation are recorded. These numbers are then compared with the number of people who actually responded or were observed. Data are entered into spreadsheet programs, such as Microsoft Excel, and whether, and to what extent, all questions were answered is tabulated. Two programs aid PAR researchers in the analysis of data, making it relatively easy for people with only a basic statistical understanding to run a few tests. Microsoft Excel is a common software program, and SPSS would be available to individuals who have access to computer labs or bookstores on university campuses. When initial results appear to produce significant findings, we recommend that PAR researchers request support from statisticians in their school districts or a local university.

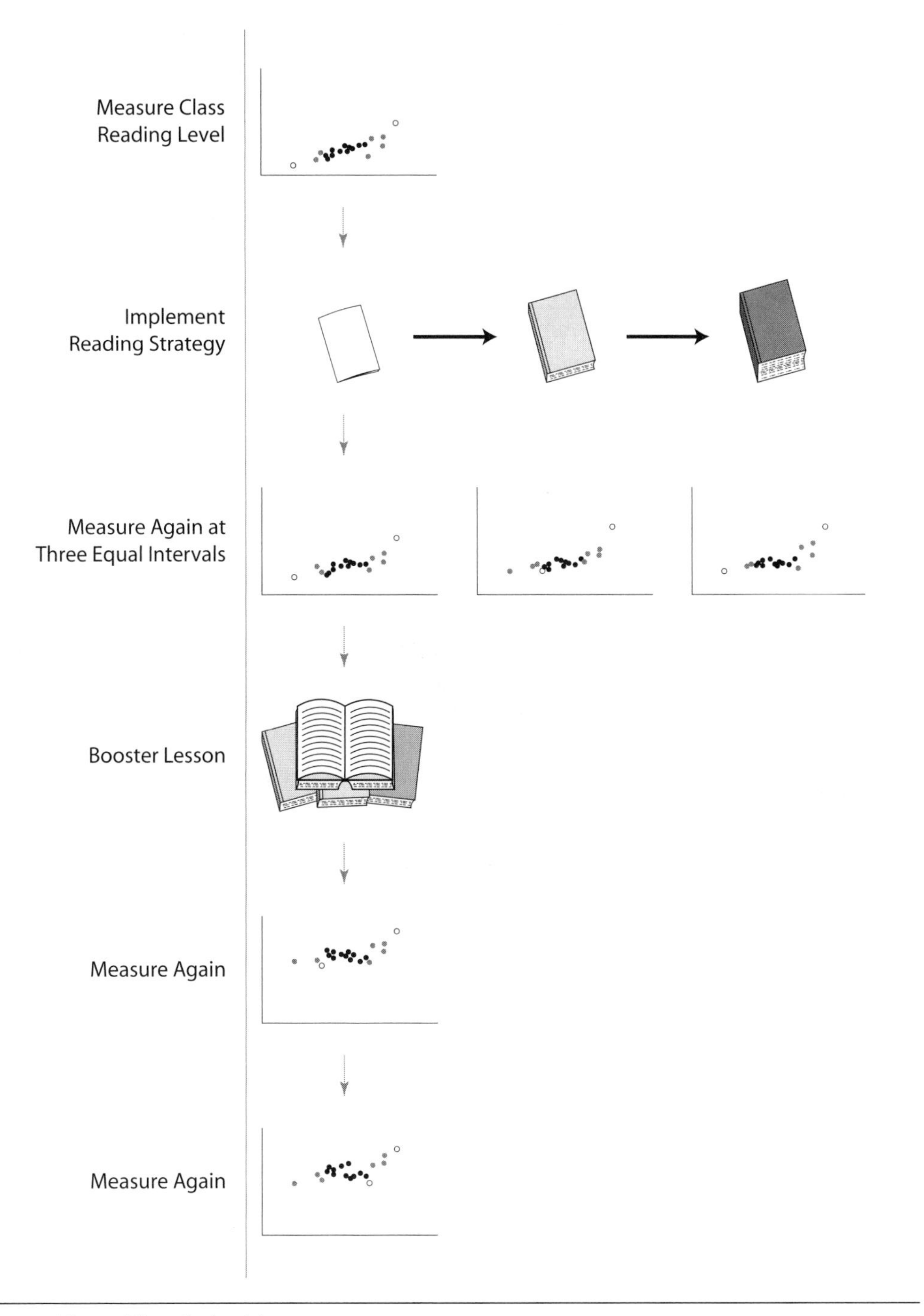

Figure 6.3 Time Series Measurements

SOURCE: Alan Bucknam/Notchcode Creative, 2006.

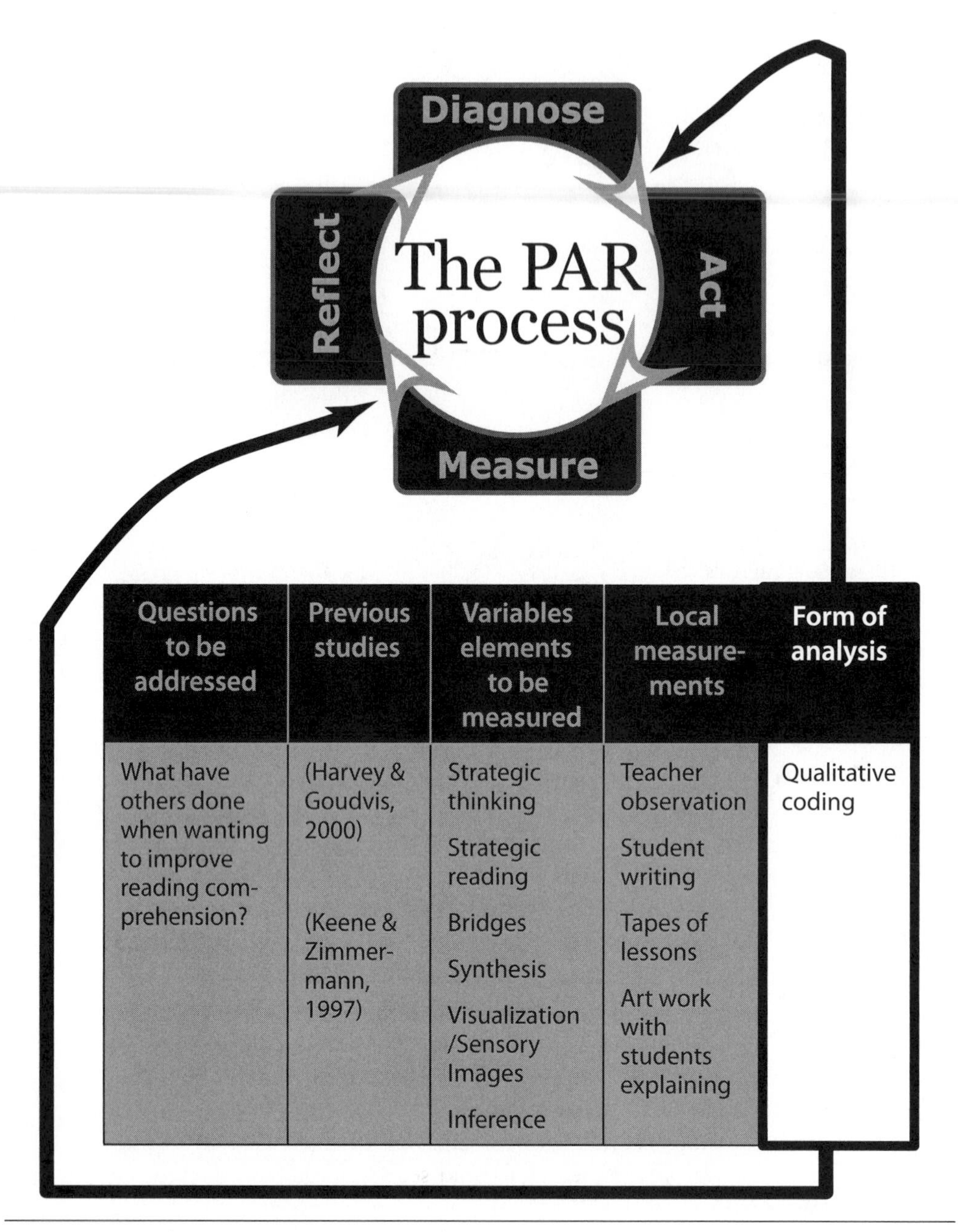

Questions to be addressed	Previous studies	Variables elements to be measured	Local measurements	Form of analysis
What have others done when wanting to improve reading comprehension?	(Harvey & Goudvis, 2000) (Keene & Zimmermann, 1997)	Strategic thinking Strategic reading Bridges Synthesis Visualization /Sensory Images Inference	Teacher observation Student writing Tapes of lessons Art work with students explaining	Qualitative coding

Figure 6.4 Chapter 6, Section 3's Stage of the PAR Process

Descriptive Analysis

Researchers no longer need to spend hours calculating data with complicated formulas. The statistical techniques required by most educational PAR teams are readily available with computer software. Which methods researchers select to analyze quantitative data depends on what they want to do with the evidence. When PAR practitioners need to characterize the population and the resultant scores, they use "descriptive" statistical methods, which include the following:

- Mean—the average score, computed by adding all the scores and dividing by the number of people who answered the question or took the test.
- Percentages or frequencies—measures the frequency within the overall population that answered a question in a given manner, reported as a percentage of the whole.
- Standard deviation—measures how much the scores deviate from each other—the range of the curve from the center point. This is reported both in figures and as a chart showing whether, and to what extent, students' scores fall within one standard deviation of the mean.

The more complicated statistical measures, known as inferential statistics, are used when researchers want to measure the degree to which their measures of a small population will generalize to the larger whole or the differences between two or more samples. Each question requires a specific experimental design, for which we refer readers to one of the many excellent statistical texts available (Jackson, 2003; Ramsey & Schafer, 2002).

Frequencies

Simple frequencies and percentages are important measurements for observations. For instance, a PAR team wanted to investigate pushing and fighting on the playground before school, during lunch, and after school to make recommendations about the amount of adequate staffing needed to supervise students during those times. Table 6.2 shows their data.

By looking at the resulting table, they could see that time periods before school and lunch required the greatest amount of supervision. Nevertheless, how consistent were the playground incidents to warrant supervisory duty by multiple staff? For this, they needed to know how often there were more than four incidents in one time period. More than eight? Or more than 12? Excel

Table 6.2 Table of Incidents on the Playground

Date	*Before*	*Lunch*	*After*	*Totals per day*
11 Feb	6	10	2	18
13 Feb	4	6	0	10
18 Feb	8	5	4	17
20 Feb	6	6	4	16
25 Feb	3	3	1	7
Total times	27	30	11	

calculates the ranges of 0–4 incidents, 5–8, and 9–12 into what they call a bin. By using the Data Analysis tool found in the Excel Tools menu, choosing a Histogram, entering the ranges of the cells of their data and the bins, the PAR team generated the frequencies as shown in Table 6.3.

In this example the PAR team used frequencies to learn that in one observation time, there were no incidents, and in a total of eight incidents, there were four or less. In a similar fashion there were seven instances where there were more than four incidents (6 in the range from 4–6 and 1 in the range from 7–12).

Table 6.3 Frequencies of Playground Incidents

Bin	*Frequency*
0	1
4	7
8	6
12	1
16	0
More	0

Survey Analysis

In survey designs, questions may be worded in various ways to prevent subjects from responding with only one answer. Therefore, researchers must reverse the order of the results to ensure similarity of answers. To do this, researchers first code an "answer" sheet to indicate the answers' relative closeness to a positive outcome. For instance, in a survey that questions whether students found the school welcoming, one question might read, "When I first entered the school, I found the office staff helpful and friendly." For this question, a 5 (strongly agree) would be the most positive outcome. Another question may have been written to achieve an opposite result such as, "My first day in XYZ high school, no one talked to me." For this second sentence, a 1 (strong disagreement) would be the most desirable outcome, and this question needs to be reversed to compare results between the two questions. Once researchers have sorted the questions so that the answers work on a comparable scale, in a comparable direction, they proceed to draw basic conclusions as described below.

Percentages and Mean

Let's suppose that the questions on the fictitious survey described above focused on a welcoming atmosphere in the school, as experienced by new students within the first few days of their enrollment. The two questions described were responded to on a Likert scale of 1–5, the results of which are listed in Figure 6.5.

Table 6.4 shows the frequency of each answer in the first question for a population of 50 students ($n = 50$) as well as the resulting percentages for each answer.

Table 6.4 Student Responses to Question #1

Answer #	*Frequency*	*Percentage*
1	0	0
2	8	16.0
3	26	52.0
4	14	28.0
5	2	4.0
Total	50	100.0

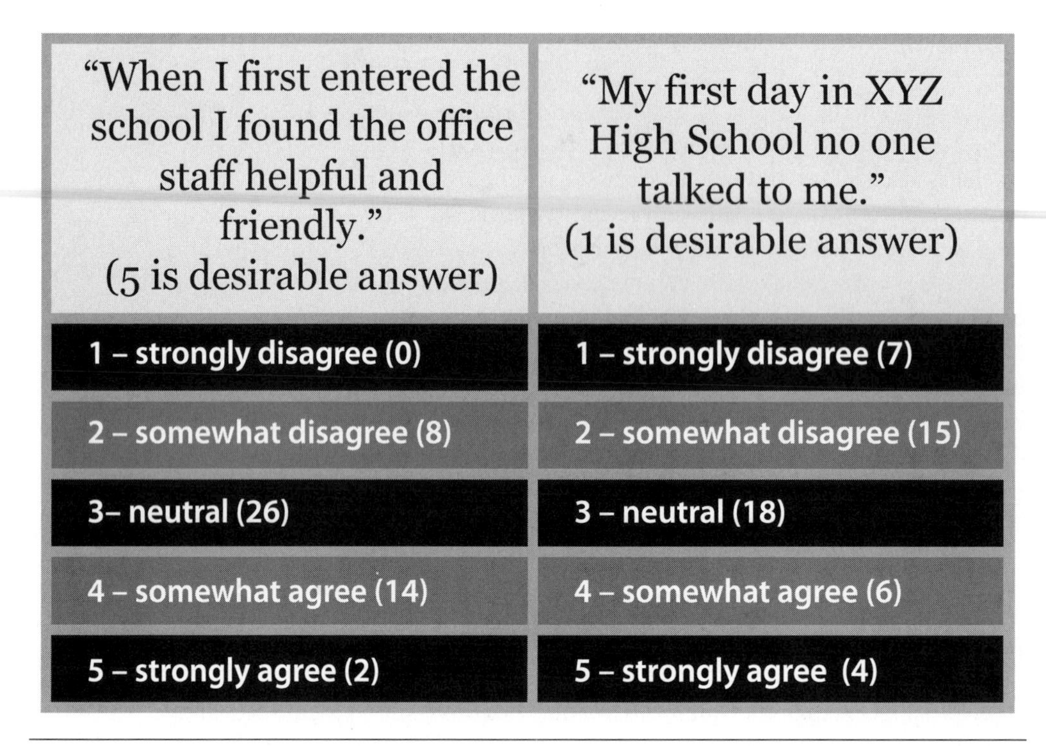

Figure 6.5 Responses on a Likert Scale

SOURCE: Alan Bucknam/Notchcode Creative, 2005.

Table 6.5 lists the same information for the second question.

Table 6.5 Student Responses to Question #2

Answer #	*Frequency*	*Percentage*
1	7	14.0
2	15	30.0
3	18	36.0
4	6	12.0
5	4	8.0
Total	50	100.0

What can be said about the welcoming environment in the school from these data?

Neither statement demonstrates a high degree of welcoming to new students, nor does the school seem overwhelmingly unfriendly.

Thirty percent (almost one third) of the students found the school friendly enough to rate their experience a 4 or a 5. That can also be seen as a little more than two thirds who found the school neutral or somewhat unwelcoming.

The results are more mixed for the question about others speaking to new students. Forty-four percent had the experience of being spoken to, with only 56% (as opposed to 67%) neutral or worse.

These scores show room for improvement by putting simple procedures in place to make the school seem more welcoming to new students enrolling midyear.

Standard Deviation

Standard deviation from the mean is an important measurement for educational leaders. As a statistic that characterizes dispersion within a population, it demonstrates how far some groups of students fall outside of the norm for the school population. In statistical terms, standard deviation measures the *variance;* in lay terms, it measures whether and to what extent a bell curve of the data would show a curve that was tall and thin or short and wide.

Suppose we have the following data for student response to Question 1:

8 students chose #2 (16)
26 students chose #3 (78)
14 students chose #4 (56)
2 students chose #5 (10)

To derive the mean, add the figures derived by multiplying the number of scores with the score itself (in parentheses above). Then divide by the number of students who participated. Fifty students answered the first question above. Find the mean by adding the calculated scores (16 + 78 + 56 + 10 = 160) and dividing this total by the number of students (50), which yields a mean of 3.2 (160/50 = 3.2). Table 6.6 shows the mean.

Simple calculations, using appropriate software, show the standard deviation as 0.76 for the first question shown above. This tells us that anyone whose score was greater than 3.2 (the mean) plus 0.76 (the standard deviation), or anyone whose response was above 3.96 (i.e., #4, #5), deviated from the norm. The same would be true of anyone who chose a score less than 3.2 minus 0.76, or anyone whose response was below 2.44 (i.e., #1 or #2). Any score falling two standard deviations from the mean (or greater than 3.2 plus 1.52) would be outside of

Table 6.6 Graph Illustrating the Mean

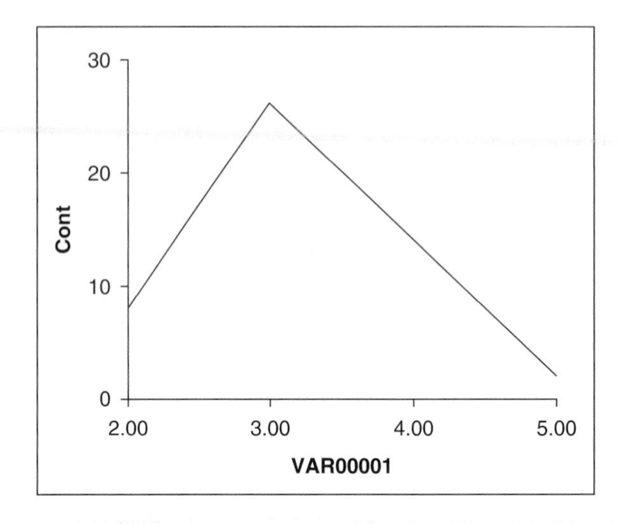

the norm. This said, it could be inferred that the two students who found the office staff very helpful (reporting an experience of a 5) were not at all the norm of the experience.

The power of what the standard deviation measures is made obvious in charts. Figure 6.6 shows a "normal" bell curve distribution, with the positive and negative standard deviation shown in dark gray. Any score outside the dark gray range is outside the norm for that population. Those scores in the lightest gray are far out of the norm, as they are two standard deviations away from the mean.

The t-Test

In simplified terms, the *t*-test is useful to educators in PAR teams when they find themselves needing to infer the similarities, differences, or degrees of correlation between small groups of data. One such question would be whether or not boys in the seventh grade were more or less likely to be caught truant from school. Microsoft Excel has three methods, accessed through the Data Analysis add-in (an advanced Excel feature that comes standard with the program but may require advanced installation) that might prove useful to school-based researchers. The first tests two samples with the assumption that their standard deviation is about the same. The second tests two samples and the standard deviation is unequal. The third tests samples that have been paired for mean scores (Nelson, 2002). As of the writing of this book, a simple Web search

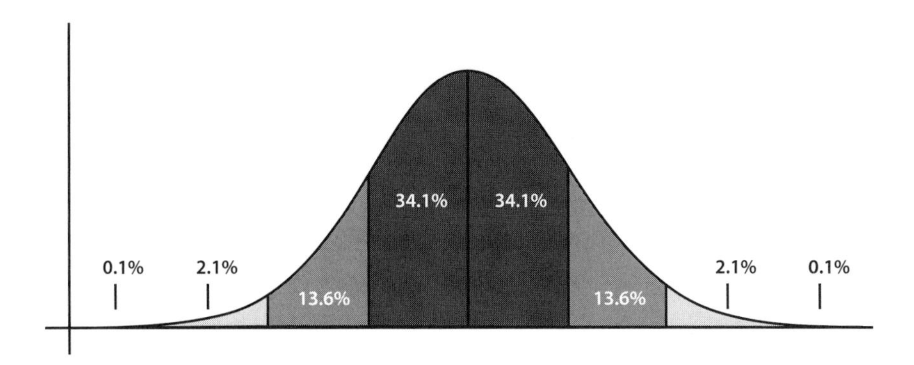

Figure 6.6 Standard Deviation

SOURCE: Alan Bucknam/Notchcode Creative, 2005.

brought up a Web site, available through Vassar College, in which people can enter the data from two groups and tests will be run.

Since most PAR researchers with whom we have worked do not use statistics in their daily work, they often forget the specifics of what they have learned in their statistics classes. Similar to the teacher in the example below, they have data and they know conceptually what they want to accomplish. As an example, a teacher had two classes of one subject that appeared to be fairly equal in their academic understanding of his subject. He decided to try out a new program (Variable 1) to help students in one class, but taught the subject with the standard curriculum (Variable 2) to the other class. After a reasonable length of time, he tested both groups. Their test scores are shown in Table 6.7.

By using Excel, entering the scores in two columns, and then going to Tools/Data Analysis/*t*-Test Paired Two Samples for Means and entering the cell range for both tests, the software generated the chart shown in Table 6.8.

Based upon the evidence shown in rows A–D in Table 6.8, the teacher decided that

- Although it first appeared that one class did much better on the test, the mean scores (Row A) between the classes differed by less than 0.7.
- The class with the higher mean also had the larger variance (Row B) between the high and low scores on the test.
- Both classes had the same number of students (Row C) take the test.
- There was little/no correlation (Row D) between the scores, which was appropriate, because this teacher was not testing two variables (such as

Table 6.7 Test Scores From Two Classes

Class 1	*Class 2*
6	5
10	2
8	7
6	9
3	9
10	4
6	6
12	6
6	4
3	8
2	5
10	6
4	4
4	4
8	8

Table 6.8 *t*-Test Results for Test Scores

t-Test: Paired Two Sample for Means		
	Variable 1 *New Program*	*Variable 2* *Standard Curriculum*
A. Mean	6.533333	5.8
B. Variance	9.266667	4.314286
C. Observations	15	15
D. Pearson Correlation	–0.21916	

gender and test scores) to ascertain whether and to what extent there was a correlation between them.

- He did not need the numbers of students or the coefficient of correlation in this case, but he found the difference in means and variance interesting. Some students in his first class had improved their scores with use of the new curriculum (hence the higher mean), but other students had not grasped the new concepts adequately and had fallen behind.

Correlation

While correlation was not interesting to the teacher in our previous sample, it will be beneficial to PAR teams that test whether and to what extent certain test results correlate with other characteristics, such as attendance. Creswell (2002) defines a **correlation** as "a statistical test to determine the tendency or pattern for two variables (or more) or two sets of data to vary consistently" (p. 642). Leedy and Ormrod (2005) go on to say,

> Correlational research looks at the surface relationship but does not necessarily probe for causal relations underlying them. For example, a researcher might investigate the relationships among high school seniors' achievement test scores and their grade point averages their first year in college. (p. 108)

A correlation exists to the extent that one measure goes up or down in relation to another.

There are many obvious correlations in education, as students typically grow a year in skill for every year in age. A scatter chart, shown in Figure 6.7, is an easy way to plot correlation and might show that relationship.

To say that two measures "covary" means that a prediction can be made about the likelihood of one variable based upon another. Skill improvement over time is an excellent example, and it is likely that most students progress about a grade level each school year, but educators also know that student learning is not continuous and that personal situations can impact any particular student's growth. For this reason, most PAR teams working with smaller populations should leave the more complicated correlation statistics aside.

Should our readers be working with data derived from larger populations and suspect that they could use statistical support, the following information outlines a few other statistical measures to investigate. The Pearson r (named after the man who first worked with it) conceptually equals the degree to which the two variables vary together, divided by the degree to which they fluctuate

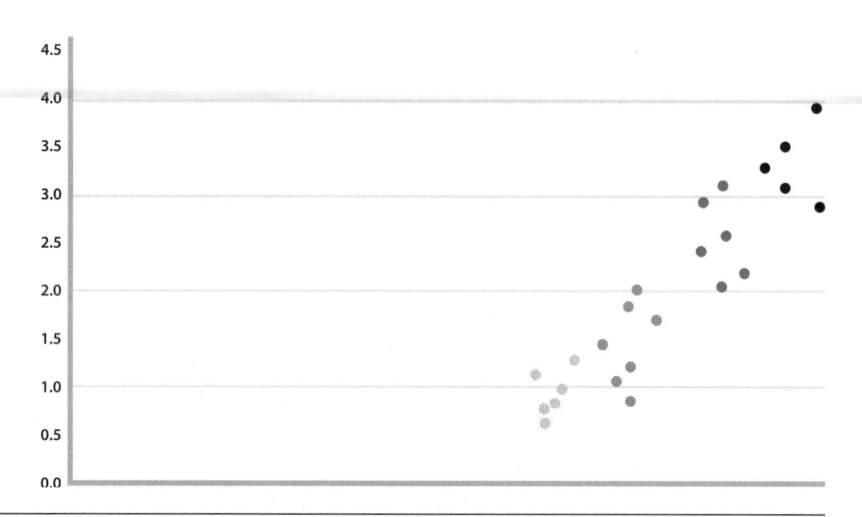

Figure 6.7 Scatter Chart Showing the Correlation of Variables

SOURCE: Alan Bucknam/Notchcode Creative, 2006.

separately. This test can be run in Excel and is accessed through Tools/Data Analysis/*t*-Test. The Pearson *r* is used to determine the magnitude of association between the two variables and is shown with a + or – sign to indicate the nature of the relationship. Educators may be interested in using the Pearson *r* to show the test/retest reliability between one administration of a test and another or to show the internal consistency between the scores in a single test. More important, for most PAR studies relating to educational leadership, the Pearson *r* may be used to confirm a hypothesis that when one action, event, or behavior occurs, educators are likely to see a consistent response. An example of this would be that if students attend summer school, their grades are likely to improve. Running the correlation statistical processes provides educators the opportunity to interpret the strength of the predication. For instance, one guide (Cohen & Manion, 1994, as cited in Creswell, 2002) shows that correlations of 0.66–0.85 equate to a solid prediction that one variable relates to another.

Reporting Results

At the end of each cycle of PAR, practitioners should take the time for a preliminary analysis of their increased understanding resulting from the cycle. We refer our readers to Chapter 10 for an in-depth discussion of the issues involved in reporting evidence. It is always wise for PAR practitioners to know which format they are responsible to as they wrap up their analysis of one cycle and move on to the next.

Task 6.1: Preliminary Quantitative Analysis

The purpose of this task is to help individuals and teams using PAR methodology to capture their increased understanding that resulted from the collection of quantitative data.

Procedure

1. In a separate word processor document, record the following information:
   - Today's date
   - The purpose of the data collection effort
   - The type of data collected (observations, surveys, etc.)
   - The date(s) of collection
   - The size of the population of respondents approached or observed
   - The number who contributed to the data
2. Reflect and attach notes on how the data furthered your understanding of the situation you are studying. Ask yourself
   - What was learned?
   - What data contributed to that learning?
   - What conclusions can you draw?
   - What further evidence do you need?
3. Collect and organize all returned surveys and observations. Separate completed forms for analysis sheets. Place forms in a locked file or another type of secure location.
4. File data analysis with 1 and 2 above.

CONCLUSION

Quantitative methods address many types of questions and have the advantage of providing information from larger groups of individuals than can be collected solely with qualitative methods. Quantitative evidence can also be used to refute or confirm qualitative results. By implementing data collection techniques such as observations of incidents within groups or surveys or questionnaires, PAR practitioners build solid, mathematically based answers to questions about the variance and/or correlation of factors within a group. These questions address issues of classification, progress, opinions, or levels of satisfaction and outcomes.

Strategic use of mixed methodology allows PAR teams to uncover and address patterns of achievement or failure, school processes, and school/community relations. By mixing the power of the human experience, through data gathered qualitatively, with the responses of a larger group using quantified evidence, researchers build a broader understanding of the situation they currently face.

PAR most often makes use of observations and surveys to gather quantitative evidence. Both types of instruments are difficult to design, as each methodology requires specificity and cross-cultural understanding for wide implementation. PAR teams help with creating adequate methods through multiple iterations of writing, testing, and rewriting. This process continues until researchers are satisfied that the instruments are valid (testing what they are intended to test) and reliable (where diverse representatives of the population are shown consistent results across measures). When PAR practitioners also address what segment of the population they need to study (the sample) and how they use time over the course of the project to show measured results, they produce evidence that is convincing.

CHAPTER 7

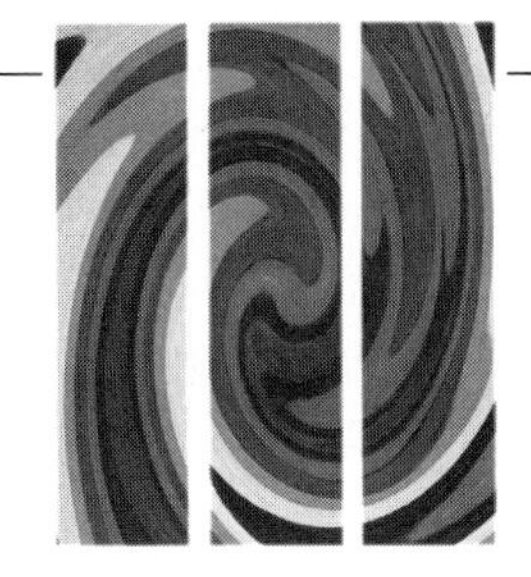

Taking and Measuring Action

The reader may wonder why the second step in the PAR process, taking action, is left to the seventh chapter of the book! It is usual for PAR teams to take few or very small actions during their first cycle of research, especially when they are involved in a systemic change process and need to hold off on taking action until the situation has been completely studied. Therefore, the first cycle is usually dedicated to diagnosing the situation, measuring the exact status quo, and reflecting on the complexities involved in the issue. During this initial stage, the teams of educators and community members also update research skills, interview people who are affected by the systems that need change, and learn to code and analyze qualitative data.

In our experience, the action in the PAR cycle creates both excitement and anxiety. There are two traps to watch out for, each causing either "underaction" or "overaction." PAR practitioners may either become absorbed with the research methods and learning new information (and research their topic exhaustively for the year) or they take actions prematurely, without considering the measurement of the actions (which leads to less than stellar results).

How do PAR practitioners move from diagnosis to determination of the course of action? This chapter discusses the process of deciding what actions are appropriate. We introduce three continuums of outcomes on which actions usually fall. Real stories follow to illustrate types of actions taken by educators who employ the PAR process. To prepare practitioners for the challenges they may face during a complex change process, Section 2 covers the challenges faced by inertia and defensive reactions. As shown in Figure 7.1, Sections 1 and 2 focus entirely on the second PAR step, that of action. The logic model is reintroduced in Section 3, with a discussion of measurement of actions.

REFLECTIVE QUESTIONS

- Remember a time in your life or that of someone you know well that you distinguish as a period of rapid growth. What characteristics come to mind?
- When entangled in solving a problem, how do you know what actions to take?
- What strategies or steps guide your actions throughout a time of change?

SECTION 1: HOW TO KNOW WHAT ACTIONS TO TAKE

At any given time, the most appropriate course of action for each study is guided by the determined purpose of a particular study and the data that have been collected. Actions taken must logically lead toward the final purpose of the study. What did the researchers wish to ultimately accomplish: improved educational practice or whole-school systemic reform? Data, reflections, and the understanding gained from the first steps in the process also steer decisions about what actions to take.

The guidelines for action are as follows:

- Design action to change the situation under study in a positive manner.
- Take small steps.
- Be certain the steps are completely under your control.
- Plan how you will measure each step before you proceed.

Three continuums of positive outcomes of action follow. These give novice PAR researchers a frame of reference for the actions they choose to implement.

Three Continuums of Action

PAR produces positive outcomes in a variety of settings. Results generate discussion within PAR and AR literature about the types of outcomes practitioners work to attain and the methodology proven efficacious in measurement (Hollingsworth, 1997; Noffke & Stevenson, 1995). Kemmis and Wilkinson (1998,

Questions to be addressed	Previous studies	Variables elements to be measured	Local measurements	Form of analysis
What have others done when wanting to improve reading comprehension?	(Harvey & Goudvis, 2000) (Keene & Zimmermann, 1997)	Strategic thinking Strategic reading Bridges Synthesis Visualization /Sensory Images Inference	Teacher observation Student writing Tapes of lessons Art work with students explaining	Qualitative coding

Figure 7.1 Chapter 7, Sections 1 and 2's Stage of the PAR Process

as cited in Woolhouse, 2005) discuss PAR as "that which aims to help people investigate reality in order to change it" (p. 30), thereby creating new realities. Across the literature, outcomes resulting from PAR actions fall along three tangential continuums: emancipatory to professional, individual to the organizational development, and personal to political. While we will not discuss the third type at length, we believe (along with Noffke & Brennan, 1997) that all actions taken by individuals are ultimately as political as actions taken to effect the broader political environment.

The Continuum of Actions From Emancipatory to Professional Development

Educators may have a burning desire to save the world, or they may simply want to improve the educational practices in their sphere of influence. Both are appropriate motivations for the PAR process. The *Encarta Dictionary* (n.d.) defines *emancipation* as setting someone free from restrictions. Used in the context of the PAR process, the definition is most often applied to outcomes from practitioners whose actions produced social justice for underserved populations (Hollingsworth, 1997; Smith, Willms, & Johnson, 1997). We believe, however, that the personal emancipation of practitioners who enthusiastically take charge of their lives and work is equally important and valid. Examples of emancipatory outcomes caused by local community members who participated in both research and action teams include the following:

- The development of adult literacy in Brazil in the 1960s, tying literacy of the peasant class to political activism (Freire, 1986).
- A teacher and her students in Santa Ana, California, who recruited community-based organizations in PAR projects to bring about change in their community, ultimately making great strides in pedestrian safety (Wolk, 2001).
- Educators in Gambia studying the reasons girls were not attending primary school, ultimately leading women to start a communal farm from which the produce sales helped to pay for the school costs of girls (World Bank Participation Sourcebook, 1996).

Rosas (1997) reports on a project with educators in Mexico that is both emancipatory and develops professional expertise of educators. Her case study discusses teachers working together in cross-district groups on four types of improvement: academic, community-school relations, teacher-parent relations, and the development of values. She concludes that the importance of the project was to allow teachers to see themselves as creators of school reform.

PAR has deep roots as a method of professional development for educators. A list of 300+ studies done in Madison, Wisconsin, for instance, included topics from *A* such as "Assessment and learning styles" (Brodhagen, 1994) to *W* on "The use of workshops to improve writing skills" (Blessing, 1996). The continuum of outcomes varies from those for gifted and talented students (Houghton, 2003) to changes in educational practices in schools that serve homeless and highly mobile students (James, 2006b).

Our bias is that "it is all good." When people become more involved in their lives, become passionate about what they can accomplish, and set out to make changes, the world improves. In this outlook, we agree with a remark attributed to Margaret Mead: "Never believe that a few caring people can't change the world. For, indeed, that's all who ever have."

The Continuum From the Individual to the Organizational

The conversation related to the appropriateness of personal practice research versus broader "scientific" study holds broad implications for the development of education, only some of which will be touched on here. Is research valid when individual educators grow in their subjective understanding of their world and their influence in it? Or do PAR practitioners need to worry about whether and to what extent their work develops the field of education? Educators at Bath University believe individual research is sufficient and have developed the theoretic basis for this personalized research, known as "living theory" (Whitehead & McNiff, 2006). Jean McNiff and colleagues (1996) point out that "in action research there is an emphasis on your deliberate intention to intervene in your own practice to bring about improvement. This concern needs to be stated in a special way. Action research questions should be of the type: How can *I* improve . . . ? because action research should be about your action, not the action of others" (p. 17).

At the other end of the continuum, Tomal (2005) emphasizes an organizational development view about PAR methodology. He describes a whole-school project that takes on a typical strategic planning tone more than a project characterized as personalized research or "living theory." Coghlan and Brannick (2001), who work in the field of industry, facilitate projects that are aimed to increase organizational efficiencies, similar to the whole-school project depicted in Tomal's book.

Individual growth need not be mutually exclusive from organizational development. It is our recommendation that all PAR practitioners address the way in which their personalities affect the outcomes of their studies, and vice versa, within their reflective journals. A question worth asking is "To what extent do my personal preferences influence the way in which the issues under study have developed?" These data provide a window of opportunity for personal growth that may result in actions that, in turn, augment the organizational issues contained within the study.

Examples of PAR to Foster School Improvement

The following cases are true, culled from a number of public sources, attaching personal, place, and school names where they were available. These stories are merely a snapshot of the extensive international work done both by people in individual practice (AR) and as part of a group (PAR). They tell of actions that are professionally or personally emancipatory, falling on the continuum between individual to organizational in their significance. Finally, by reading between the lines, they express the difficulties researchers have in measuring the outcomes of their actions.

Some of the following stories may elicit a response similar to "But I work on improving my practice in much the same way, and I don't call it action research!" Educators are by nature somewhat reflective and somewhat critical—consistently striving to improve their practice. PAR does not change any of these characteristics but rather enhances them. As Stevenson (1995) points out, "Action research has the same intent. It seeks not to replace what practitioners normally do, but to enhance the way they do it by helping them work through the problems they encounter" (p. 197).

Teachers or Support Staff in a Classroom or Whole-School Setting

A social worker in Akira Toki Middle School in the Madison (Wisconsin) Metropolitan School District studied what she could do to increase staff buy-in for a schoolwide bullying and harassment prevention project (Rabenstine, 2002). Rabenstine used AR as a methodology to uncover staff attitudes about bullying and harassment. Part of her study was to produce trainings to support staff who would eventually implement a selected bullying and harassment prevention curriculum. Rabenstine surveyed staff prior to receiving training materials about the new curriculum. Following the training, each teacher partnered with another staff person to cofacilitate student lessons throughout the spring semester. At the end of the school year, pre-/posttest results showed a 20% rise in understanding the necessity to focus on bullying and the ability to handle bullying incidents. Results also showed a near 100% agreement, which leads staff to believe that, in the end, their intervention would save instructional time and improve overall safety in the school. Six primary schools clustered around Victoria, Australia, representing diverse physical environments, partnered with a local university to improve science education in their schools (Gough & Sharpley, 2005). The authors condensed the experiences of these schools to six case studies using coordinators' journals, observations, and interviews with both teachers and students as data. In summary, their results showed consistent emancipatory-level improvements in attitudes from teachers about the science curriculum. These changes were engendered because the project (a) increased motivation for learning science in students when it became personally meaningful and they studied their local environments, (b) involved students as researchers, and (c) engaged students in positive environmental outcomes to improve their local environments. The authors conclude that the PAR process stimulated effective teaching and learning in science as well as offering a space through which environmental education emerged.

PAR studies exert broader influence within a school than might first be obvious (Clements & Chao, 2004). A teacher and a literacy coach worked together to increase the degree to which homeless and highly mobile children felt welcome in Westminster Elementary School in Westminster, Colorado. By holding a voluntary Lunch Bunch meeting three times a week, they not only increased school bonding for educationally disadvantaged students but also exposed students' general perception of lack of safety in their school. Data confirmed the issue through a schoolwide assessment. As a result, faculty and PTA provided support to transform the atmosphere. Final data showed a significant change in the development of welcoming school culture.

In response to a poor UNESCO report on the quality of mixed grade-level classrooms on the island of Cyprus, the island's ministry of education centered its attention on these classrooms. To better use local knowledge in their efforts to bring about school improvement (Fullan, 2001a, 2001b), they focused this project on modifying practices to include a teacher-as-researcher model, known as collaborative AR (Angelides, Evangelou, & Leigh, 2005). Two teachers and an academic collaborated, ultimately using reflective journals as data. Teachers' individual practices became more objective about their impact on the curriculum and relationships with parents (Angelides et al., 2005; Wenger, 1998).

Principals

A principal intern at Thoreau Elementary School in Madison, Wisconsin, used PAR methodology to connect her mentoring assistance with an area of concern relevant to the classroom teachers, that of adequate time for curriculum planning

(Watson-Peterson, 2000). Finding great disparity in the varied use of planning time by grade-level teachers, Watson-Peterson used survey, midyear assessment, and observational data to negotiate the tension created when administration raised schoolwide issues that cut into teacher planning times. While no particular actions were conclusive, she ends with admonitions for school administrators to be aware of and keep all-school issues to schoolwide venues and grade-level issues to that smaller group of teachers, thus saving everyone's time.

Elizabeth Soffer (1995) studied her disciplinary practice as a principal in 1990, when the seriousness of behavioral incidents sharply increased. In the first round of research, she examined how staff perceived her discipline practices, reflected on whether and to what extent she agreed with those perceptions, and proceeded to examine the literature. During her first action cycle, Soffer designed forms to track the consistency and persistency of her discipline actions. She introduced elements of self-responsibility into her disciplinary process and changed the administration of consequences. In her final cycles, the principal focused on the few boys whose behavior was consistently difficult.

Whole Schools or School Districts

Tomal (2005) reports on a schoolwide PAR effort at an elementary school in northeast Illinois. The broad study design worked to overcome low teacher and staff morale, conflict, mediocre student test scores, disciplinary problems, budgetary concerns, and inadequate instructional programs. The project initially looked at general strengths and weaknesses in the school. Specific assessments measured curriculum, safety, communications, morale, technology, facilities and transportation, student centeredness and performance, leadership, and community involvement. PAR teams developed in several areas: multiculturalism, facilities, student achievement, school improvement, parent and community relations, safety, human resources and organizational development, and technology. An action plan emerged that was then implemented and measured. Short-term effects included an increase in student test scores in basic reading comprehension and math skills, improved efficiency in several organizational areas, and improved morale.

Madison Metropolitan School District, as cited in a 1998 report, had evidence of almost 300 staff who conducted research on their own practices (Caro-Bruce & Zeichner, 1998). This program accepts proposals during the spring semester for the following school year in which the research will be conducted. PAR participants choose research topics to fit their current professional concerns. Teachers receive release time and supplies. Their projects receive greater recognition in their local school/community forums through reports at meetings or local television coverage. Caro-Bruce and Zeichner point out that the program has influenced the way the research participants see themselves and their practice. They report increased confidence, analytical processing, collegial involvement, and group learning that accelerated the individual projects. Caro-Bruce and Zeichner conclude that, while the greatest influences from the PAR projects were on individual and classroom practice, that data also show positive professional growth on school culture as a whole.

REFLECTIVE QUESTION

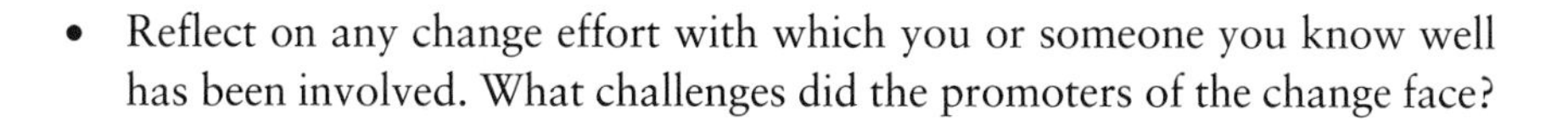

- Reflect on any change effort with which you or someone you know well has been involved. What challenges did the promoters of the change face?

SECTION 2: EFFORTS AT CHANGE

It should be mentioned that not all PAR action steps proceed smoothly. Change is difficult in educational institutions, many of which have layers of institutional history to overcome before new modes of practice can be embraced. This section briefly discusses the challenges of inertia and defensive behavior—providing two methods that may help PAR practitioners address these issues.

The Challenge of Inertia

Usually, educators' actions are consistent with their beliefs about what is best for students. Each educator's position can be placed on a continuum of belief about any topic. For instance, is it better for children to have tightly structured disciplined environments or open, nurturing environments? Because educators are already acting in a way believed to be good for students, schools can become deeply entrenched in current patterns and procedures. Change may require battling a state of inertia, and facilitators must appeal to underlying belief systems while demonstrating that results will be measureable in improved student outcomes. Sagor (2000) reports that the introduction of data pointing to a need for improvement creates the necessary discomfort or **cognitive dissonance** and will propel people to reevaluate their actions. Cognitive dissonance is defined as a condition of conflict or anxiety resulting from inconsistency between one's beliefs and one's actions.

Inertia may be a valuable asset to a PAR study if viewed from the perspective of inquiry. Why are some educators or community members resisting changes? Perhaps they sense a concern with the implementation plan but have lacked the opportunity to express their perspectives. Although combating inertia may appear troublesome to practitioners who are convinced of the efficacy of their solutions, we recommend using the inertia to decelerate the process of change, allowing the implementation plan to include even the most conservative ideas. This slower process may ultimately result in an improved iteration of the research questions and greater focus of a study.

In Figure 7.2, the forces between change and inertia are stable and the situation is stuck at the status quo.

PAR practitioners can use the concept of cognitive dissonance to propel change by employing a tool derived from the work of Lewin (1951). "Force field analysis" allows educators to plan actions that aim to tip the balance between forces that create change and individual and organizational inertia. To achieve change toward a goal or vision, three steps are required:

First, the proponents of the change need to mobilize the driving forces to break through the restraining forces. This includes the broadcast of data pointing to the tension between the ideal and the status quo, or discussing the fact that the behaviors seen are not as widespread as imagined (Braxton & Caboni, 2005).

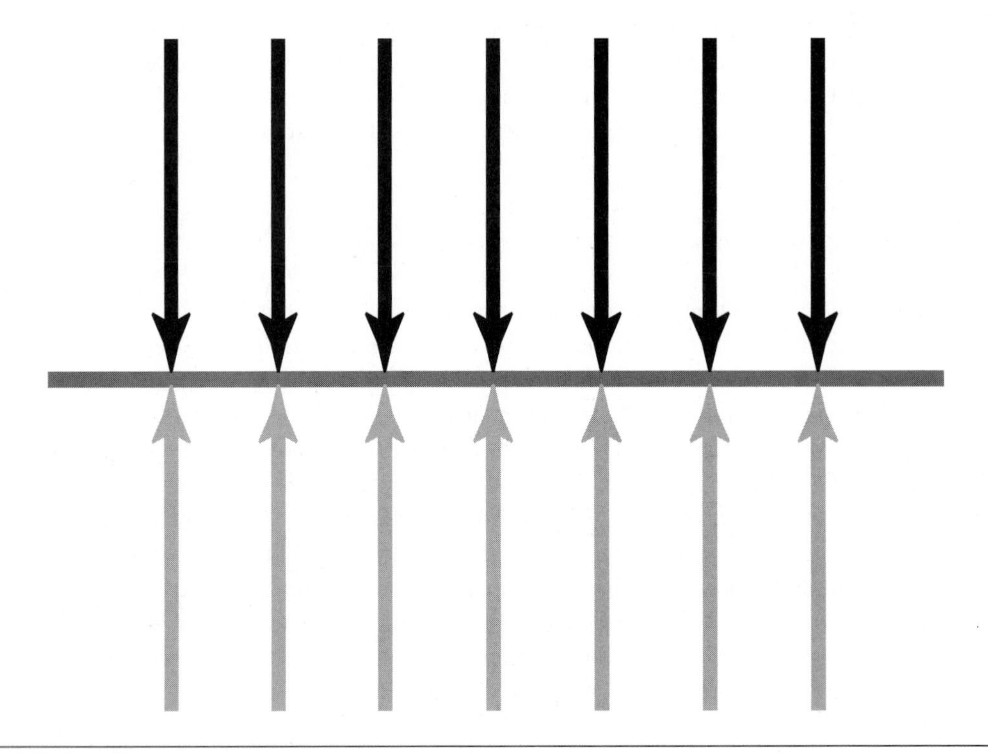

Figure 7.2 Section 2 Forces Between Change and Inertia

SOURCE: Alan Bucknam/Notchcode Creative, 2005.

Second, a series of imbalances are introduced to the situation to enable the change to take place. In PAR these imbalances are data and actions. This is shown in Figure 7.3.

Third, once the changes move forward, are measured, and demonstrate efficacy for students, policies and other stabilizing influences are established to stabilize the situation at an improved level.

In his book *The Tipping Point: How Little Things Can Make a Big Difference,* Gladwell (2002) points out that many types of circumstances and various roles of people aid the creation of the imbalance that will destroy inertia. The PAR team is a natural environment through which educators can work with their communities to mobilize the positive influence of community leaders toward shifting public opinion, connecting the work of the team with broader resources, and broadcasting its success so that it is adapted by others.

AR texts address the issue of moving past inertia with slightly different viewpoints that are worth consideration. Sagor's (2000) strategies use the mechanics of program development to suggest that PAR practitioners can accomplish this tipping mechanism by (a) presenting the data; (b) establishing a pilot

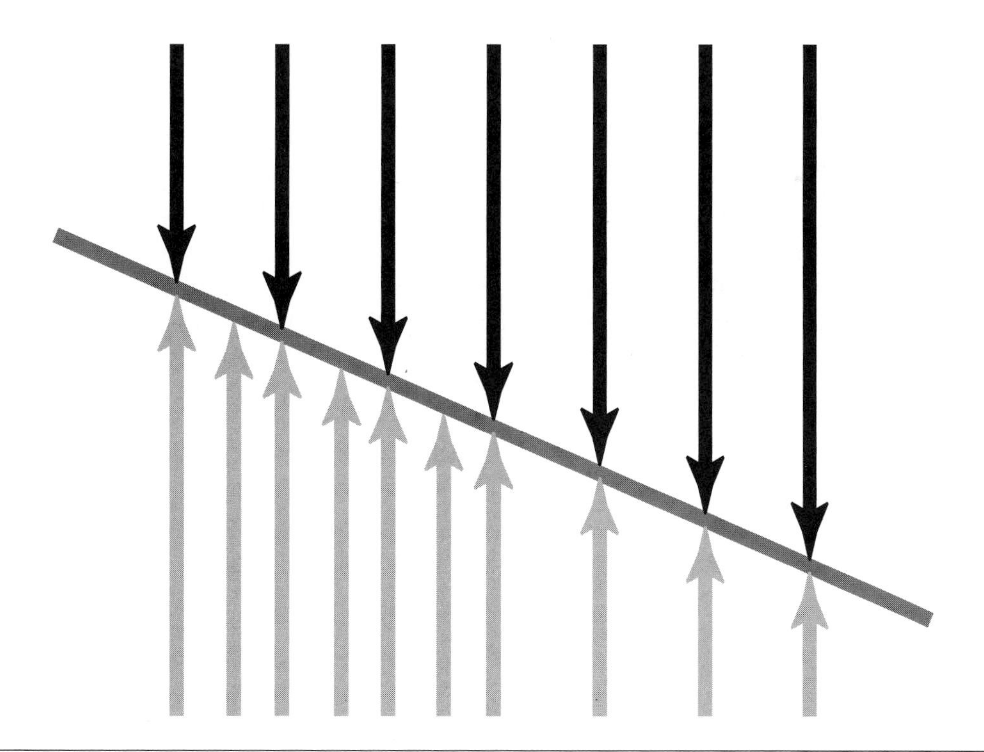

Figure 7.3 Tipping Diagram

SOURCE: Alan Bucknam/Notchcode Creative, 2005.

program; and/or establishing competing pilot programs; (c) using the research as educational specifications to define, understand, and brainstorm new alternatives; and (d) proofing new action proposals. On the other hand, Calhoun (1994) believes that the tipping is best guided by the value-driven question, "Should we act differently? If yes, how?" (p. 89). These questions drive the initial data collection after which PAR practitioners are instructed to ask, "Knowing what we know now, should we act differently?" Calhoun notes that inertia often comes in the form of focusing on collecting data rather than moving to action.

We believe the PAR process itself mobilizes a holding environment through which educators can manage their unease during systemic change. Since the field of education is one in a current state of flux, this holding environment mitigates distress. PAR teams who experience resistance due to inertia and defensive mechanisms from school and community members may consider inviting these individuals to participate on the PAR teams. Conservative points of view can benefit a study, and major detractors for an initiative can transform into the strongest advocates when engaged from inside the process.

Defensive Behaviors

Cognitive dissonance may not be enough to push human behavior in a new direction. Frequently, change is seen as a threat to power and authority, and this increases the likelihood that PAR practitioners will encounter defensive reactions, both within themselves and from others. As practitioners have ideas about which they feel strongly, the PAR process enables them to unfreeze, surface, change, and refreeze their ideas or mental models. Adept practitioners understand that during these moments when they believe a situation to be "wrong," they may be operating upon the assumption that everyone shares their perceptions about the situation. Therefore, to cull out diverse and multiple perspectives related to the issue, further investigation is required.

Overcoming defensive behaviors is discussed by Argyris, Putnam, and Smith (1985) in their treatise on action science. They suggest that a method in creating action is confronting that which does not want to move. Confronting is a process by which social actors are forced to confront themselves and others explicitly by pointing out (and inquiring into) defensive reactions while analyzing the consequences of giving in to them. Argyris and colleagues point out that while not all defensive reactions have negative consequences, many are the cause of groups that cycle endlessly between conflicting demands. Greenwood and Levin (1998) counter this by suggesting that PAR studies are successful when they confront opposition and resolve conflicts.

Argyris and Schön (1974) and later Senge (1994) work with the ideas of defensive behavior in the creation of what they call the **ladder of inference,** which is a problem-solving strategy in systems thinking (adopted here to discuss choices made with data) used to help understand the development of inferences. Shown below in Figure 7.4, this model describes potential escalation of defensive mechanisms. PAR practitioners can use the tool to analyze how thoughts, assumptions, beliefs, and actions may be based first on data but quickly evolve (or de-evolve) into something originally not intended. This devolution creates the defensive behaviors that Argyris and colleagues (1985) and later Greenwood and Levin (1998) suggest need to be confronted. PAR presents an excellent format with which to confront defensive behaviors due to its reliance on the first rungs of the ladder: observation and data.

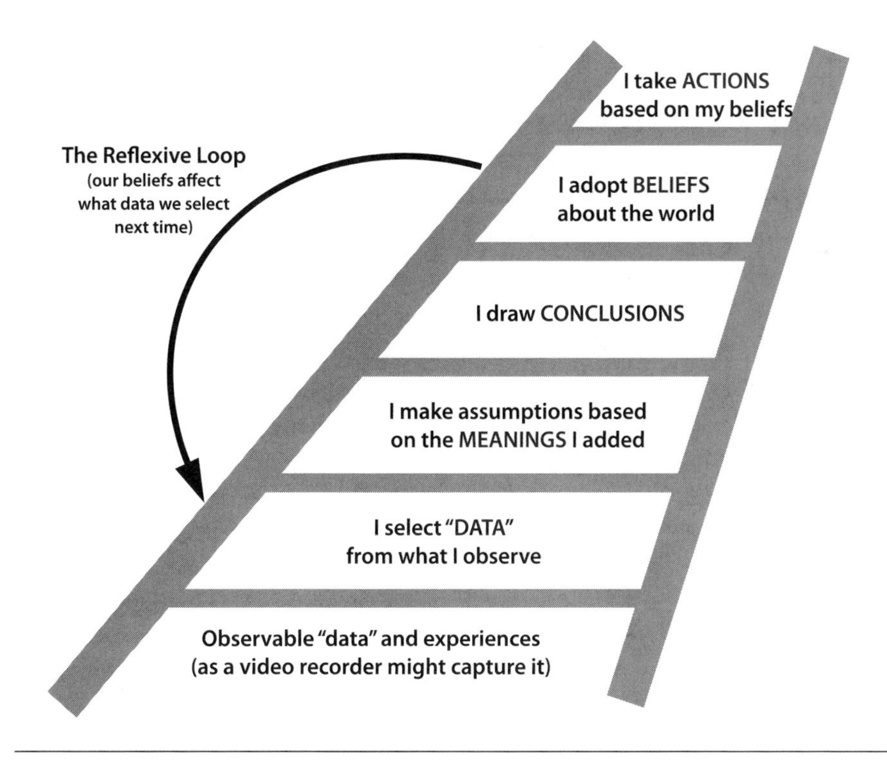

Figure 7.4 The Ladder of Inference

SOURCE: Alan Bucknam/Notchcode Creative, 2006. Adapted from Argyris & Schön (1974) and Senge (1994).

Task 7.1: Analyzing Force Fields and Defensive Behaviors

The purpose of this task is to aid PAR practitioners in confronting their own inertia and defensive reaction through reflective note taking. This task can be done easily by either individuals or groups.

Procedure

On a piece of paper draw a diagram similar to the first one in this chapter shown in miniature here.

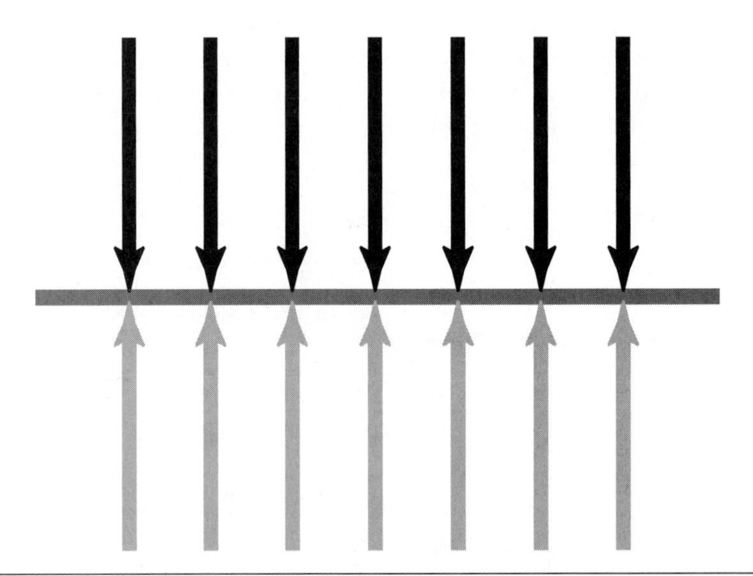

Figure 7.5 Task 1 Forces Between Change and Inertia

SOURCE: Alan Bucknam/Notchcode Creative, 2006.

1. List the forces that work for change in the situation under study by the PAR group and those that work against it.
2. Brainstorm other data, communication systems, or actions that can be added to create a tipping point that propels change to occur.
3. List the major stakeholders, including yourself.
4. Reflect on the areas of action or change in personal and institutional behaviors that are likely to cause defensive behaviors.
5. List possible underlying motivations and ideals for education that can be enlisted to ease defensive behavior.

6. Note which motivations may be driven by an assumption. Do data exist that challenge the assumption?
7. Brainstorm ways to confront potential defensive mechanisms both in yourself and in others.

REFLECTIVE QUESTIONS

- Imagine an action that you wish to take to improve upon the educational situation you are studying. What measurements do you readily have that express the status quo?
- What components of the current situation should change because of the actions you intend to implement?
- What additional measurements will be needed before, during, and after the implementation to demonstrate outcomes?

SECTION 3: MEASUREMENT

We conclude this chapter on action by discussing the measurement of short-term actions and change. For this discussion, we move to the wisdom developed in the past 30 years in the field of program evaluation, particularly evaluation designed for use in the social sciences. Two considerations bear discussion: formative versus summative work, and determining the focus of the evaluation.

PAR practitioners decide upon how their actions will be measured before they act, and then they implement research methods to capture pertinent data from which they analyze outcomes. As shown in Figure 7.6, Section 3 corresponds to the act and measurements steps when PAR practitioners focus on measurement during and after each action they implement to create the desired change.

Formative Evaluation

There are two recognized types of evaluations: formative and summative. The first, **formative**, contains a variety of ways in which practitioners measure short-term results *with the purpose of making course corrections while the program continues*. **Summative evaluation**, on the other hand, measures outcomes close to or at the end of the project. For our purposes, measuring the results of any individual action cycle within a PAR project falls under the heading of formative

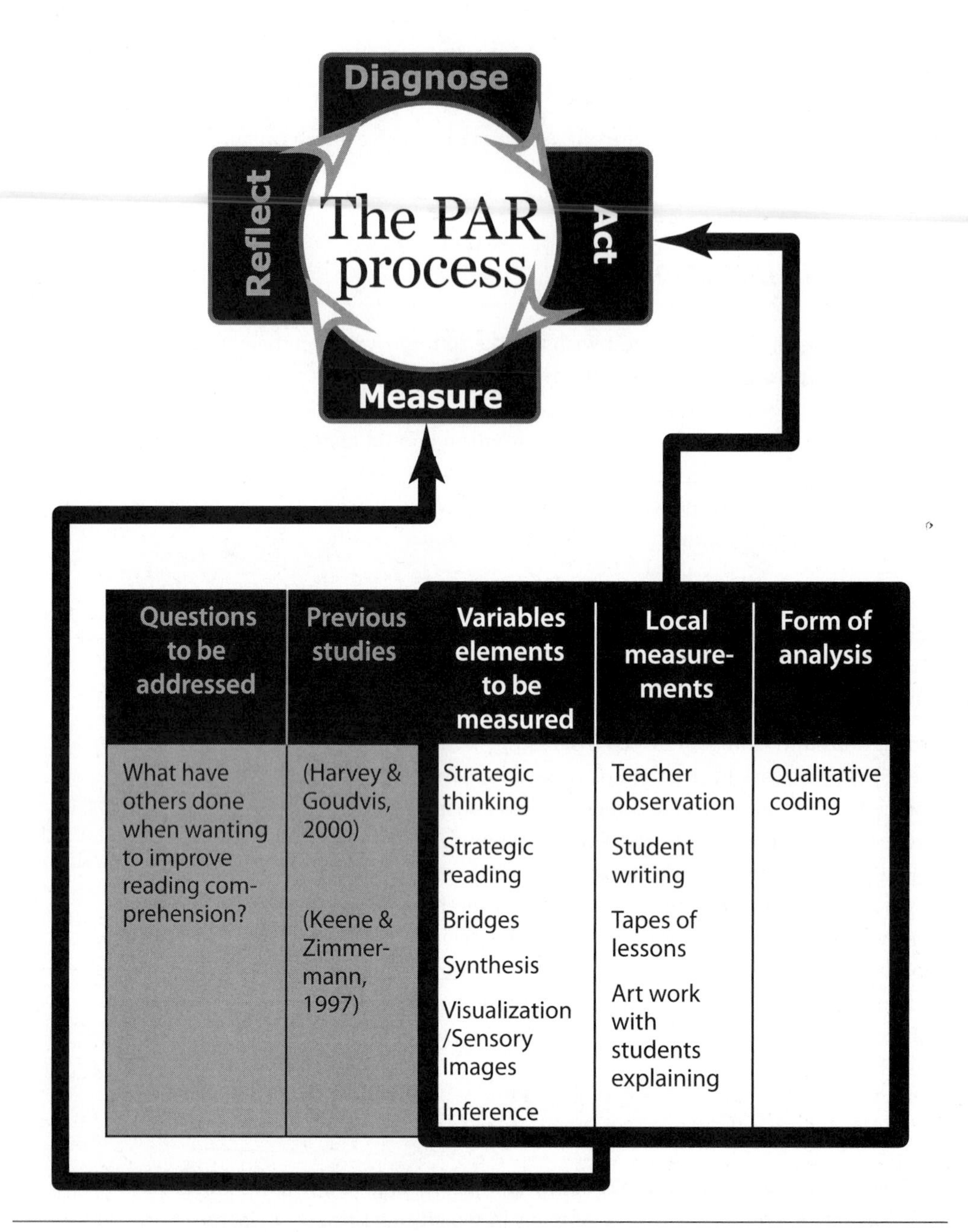

Questions to be addressed	Previous studies	Variables elements to be measured	Local measurements	Form of analysis
What have others done when wanting to improve reading comprehension?	(Harvey & Goudvis, 2000) (Keene & Zimmermann, 1997)	Strategic thinking Strategic reading Bridges Synthesis Visualization /Sensory Images Inference	Teacher observation Student writing Tapes of lessons Art work with students explaining	Qualitative coding

Figure 7.6 Chapter 7, Section 3's Stage of the PAR Process

evaluation. This is theoretically important because this type of evaluation acknowledges the PAR practitioners' understanding that the outcomes they measure may or may not remain valid at the end of the project and that outcomes from each successive cycle will be used to suggest new directions for future work (Fitz-Gibbon & Morris, 1987; Herman, Morris, & Fitz-Gibbon, 1987).

Focus and Responsiveness

There are two standards for program evaluation: focus and responsiveness. Focus refers to considerations that drive the researchers' approach, the questions they ask, and the people of whom they ask questions (Stecher, Davis, & Morris, 1987). Focus covers the variables and local measurements sections of the logic model and sets the standard that local measurement of short-term outcomes of action cycles should be "goal oriented" (p. 27). By this we mean that the focus of the evaluation of an action is to determine whether and to what extent the actions aided the PAR practitioners in addressing the issue they are studying. As an example, Principal Soffer, whose study on disciplinary consequences was discussed in Section 1, examined whether the actions she took diminished the numbers of students being sent to her office after each cycle of actions.

The second standard focuses evaluation of short-term outcomes in a way that is responsive. Stecher and colleagues (1987) define "responsive" as that which is "guided by the belief that the only meaningful evaluation is one that seeks to understand an issue from the multiple points of view of all the people who have a stake" (p. 36) in its outcome. The participatory nature of PAR conveys the belief that education is served best by the inclusion of all the voices of local concern. Consequently, a responsive focus would dictate that research practitioners employ qualitative measures as they seek to understand the reality of the people involved in both delivering and receiving project actions.

Determining Variables With Which to Measure Short-Term Outcomes

The PAR team first decides what short-term outcomes will result from their actions. These outcomes need to be measured against the goals of the action and the purpose for the study as a whole, using variables derived from previous research when possible (Fiester, 2001; Fitz-Gibbon & Morris, 1987; Herman et al., 1987). We suggest the following steps in determining which local measures to use:

1. Separate the actions into multiple lines of cause and effect. In the Soffer example, she increased the number of staff on the playground to decrease the number of behavior incidents. Therefore, she could measure the behavior before, midway, and after a few weeks to note whether and to what extent there had been improvements.
2. Note potential mismatch between desired outcome and the action(s) taken and revise variables accordingly.
3. Use the PAR team to brainstorm imaginative yet credible ways to detect both student-level and organizational goals. Note all variables that might change during the implementation of new actions and decide whether and to what extent they relate directly to the purpose of the project and should be included in measuring the effect of the change.
4. Match measurements to the purpose of the project.
5. Focus data collection methods on outcomes that are observable and can be gauged using local measures.

Measuring the outcomes of actions in PAR is similar to measuring the outcomes of feasibility studies in other types of evaluation (Herman et al., 1987). For instance, a PAR group may have in mind multiple actions that they believe will address the challenges they are studying. First, they decide which actions to implement and measure. Then they divide the work among them, testing their ideas with a limited amount of the school population. By restricting the work to a smaller population, they quickly gather preliminary data with which to inform the next reflective and diagnostic PAR steps.

Measuring Outcome Steps

PAR practitioners should be wary not to derive too much meaning from any specific short-term outcome. For instance, the first step for students to turn in homework is to have the knowledge of the importance to complete the homework. Knowing about homework and its importance, however, does not necessarily mean that students will change their behaviors.

In the **stages of change model,** behavior change does not happen in one step. People tend to progress through different stages on their way to successful change and progress at their own rate. The model describes a person's growth from awareness to taking action. These stages help to illustrate possible areas for measurement. Referring to the work about changing addictive behaviors (Prochaska, Norcross, & DiClemente, 1994), social scientists widely agree that change can be viewed along a continuum. At one end is "no knowledge of a situation or the desire to take action," and at the other is "full knowledge of the situation with successful outcomes of sustained actions over time." The scale established by the stages of change outlines specific, measurable steps using interview, focus group, or self-report survey data. Though it may not characterize every educational program, it can be massaged as a guideline for growth.

Precontemplation: at this stage the stakeholders (teachers, students, etc.) either do not have the knowledge or the intention to take action. *No* action is expected within the next 6 months.

Contemplation: the stakeholders feel they have the knowledge they need and they intend to take action within the next 6 months.

Preparation: the stakeholders intend to take action within the next 30 days, and some measurable, behavioral steps have been taken in this direction.

Action: Beginning measurable outcomes have been achieved. An example at this stage would be a student whose work shows progress but has not yet increased significantly, such as a grade level of growth.

Maintenance: the equivalent of this stage in education would be the successful completion of the actions as designed, or academic attainment equal to anticipated grade level, for more than 6 months, and so on.

Termination: The PAR practitioners possess full knowledge of the issue and feel that they sufficiently advanced the educational practice in their school while solving the problem researched throughout the study. The team is completely confident that there is little chance of reoccurrence.

Once a PAR team has decided upon the variables that measure the actions and logically lead to the desired improvements, they implement standard research practices to capture evidence. A final checklist, as an overview from previous chapters, reminds them to

- Simplify all data collection methods whenever possible.
- Create flexible procedures that take the culture and relative sophistication of the school population in mind.

- Build a multilevel flow of communication throughout the project between teachers, students, parents, and administrators.
- Ensure confidentiality to all participants.
- Document the full stories of people as much as possible.
- Record changes resulting from actions taken in various cycles.
- Develop communication feedback loops throughout the process.
- Determine the scale against which to evaluate success.

CONCLUSION

In PAR and AR literature, three continuums of action are discussed. The continuums from emancipatory actions to professional development, from the individual to the organizational growth, and from the personal to the political all provide rich theoretical material for discussion. Multiple examples of successful PAR projects undertaken by teachers, groups of teachers, principals, entire schools, and school districts illustrate advancements in local educational practices. While PAR research studies vary as to the amount of data that support results, the participants engaged in these projects consistently agree that it is the action cycle that makes it worth their personal investment of time and energy (James, 2006b).

Taking action necessarily promotes change. In turn, the change is likely to create reactions. The two most common challenges when promoting change are inertia and defensive reactions. Two methods discussed in Section 2—force field analysis and the ladder of inference—were developed as means with which to discuss issues of organizational development (Argyris et al., 1985; Schön, 1983; Senge, 1994). PAR practitioners can implement both methods as a way to understand and plan around the forces that ultimately could impede the outcome of their work.

Measuring each action cycle has much in common with formative evaluation practices. PAR practitioners focus on measuring whether and to what extent actions contributed to the positive resolution of an educational issue and the extent to which all stakeholders are responding to the changes involved. Short-term measures will not determine conclusively if the actions are successful in helping the PAR team meet their goals. Nevertheless, it is useful to measure each action against a predetermined scale of possibility. The scale derived from the stages of change introduced in 1994 by Prochaska, Norcross, and DiClemente may provide a system to measure early action cycles as participants learn about the change, determine to take action, test the modification, and decide to adopt it.

CHAPTER 8

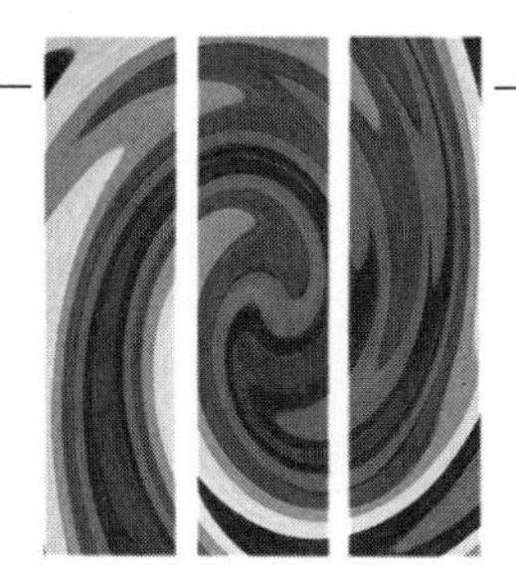

Cycles of PAR

The Power of the Iterative Process

The power of the PAR process lies in its iterative cycles, because implementing multiple cycles causes people to advance beyond knowledge gain to understand the issues they face.

PAR is distinguished from other strands of research by its multiple cycles of diagnosis, action, measurement, and reflection in the context of organizational change (Coghlan & Brannick, 2001; Coghlan & Coughlan, 2003; Dick, 1998a, 1998b).

"To my mind the *cyclic* nature of action research is part of its special strengths . . . to be both *flexible* and *rigorous*" (Dick, 1998b; emphasis added).

Cycles "allow the integration of the conscious and deliberate thinking and knowing of reflection with the less conscious and deliberate knowing and thinking of action" (Dick, 1998b, p. 1).

Educational leadership employs these cycles to build discernment and become well armed to create change.

As shown in Figure 8.1, this chapter focuses attention on the second, third, or fourth cycle of PAR, where the team of practitioners move into multiple layers of their logic model.

The spirit of PAR, and therefore of the content of this chapter, is captured in Figure 8.2, which demonstrates the increasing energy and multiple outcomes created through continued study.

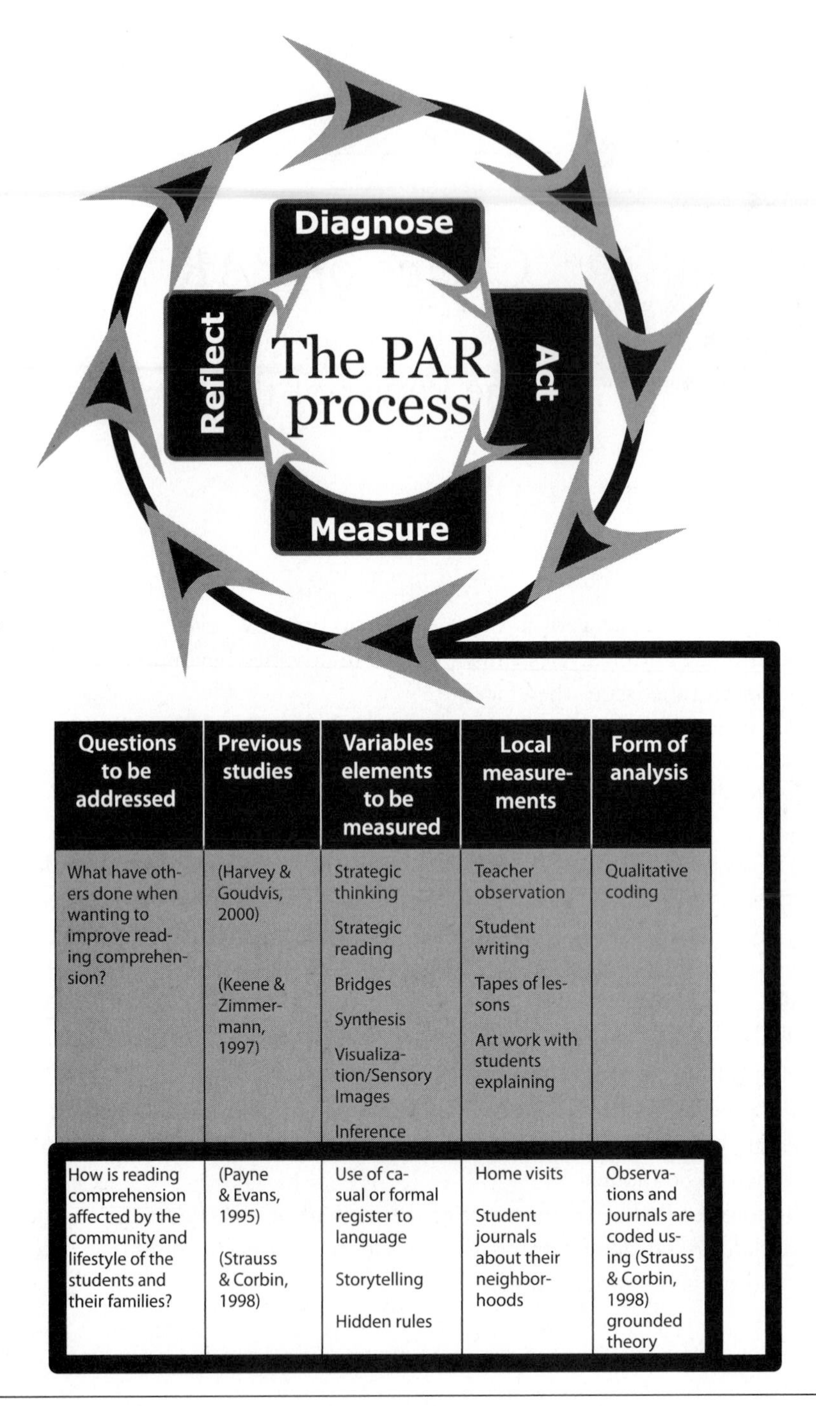

Questions to be addressed	Previous studies	Variables elements to be measured	Local measurements	Form of analysis
What have others done when wanting to improve reading comprehension?	(Harvey & Goudvis, 2000) (Keene & Zimmermann, 1997)	Strategic thinking Strategic reading Bridges Synthesis Visualization/Sensory Images Inference	Teacher observation Student writing Tapes of lessons Art work with students explaining	Qualitative coding
How is reading comprehension affected by the community and lifestyle of the students and their families?	(Payne & Evans, 1995) (Strauss & Corbin, 1998)	Use of casual or formal register to language Storytelling Hidden rules	Home visits Student journals about their neighborhoods	Observations and journals are coded using (Strauss & Corbin, 1998) grounded theory

Figure 8.1 Chapter 8's Stage of the PAR Process

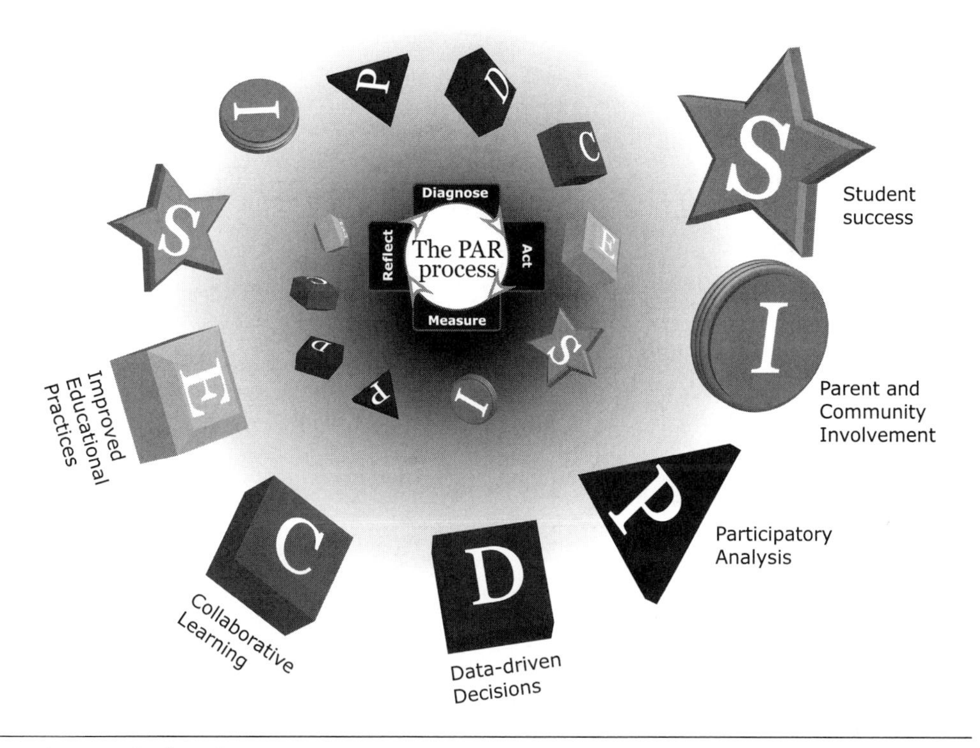

Figure 8.2 Cycles of PAR

SOURCE: Alan Bucknam/Notchcode Creative, 2005.

Through multiple iterations that ideas and actions mature, McTaggart (1997) points out:

> PAR starts small by working on minor changes which individuals can manage and control, and working towards more extensive patterns of change. These might include critiques of ideas of institutions which might lead to ideas for the general reform of projects, programs or system-wide policies and practices. (p. 4)

The most important aspect of the cycles to research is the manner in which they increase rigor by forcing the practitioner to build on evidence gathered in previous iterations (Kock, McQueen, & Scott, 1997). These authors conclude that the strength of data collection and analysis over multiple cycles of PAR increases rigor because "disconfirmatory evidence in further iterations" aid practitioners in correcting distortions created by personal assumptions, historical memory, and so on (p. 2). For example, a small-town principal, interviewing parents, found that part of their appreciation of the school lay in how well they perceived their children to be doing. Teachers of the same children reported that they were behind. The distance between parent and teacher understanding created a future round of research to uncover methods to bridge the gap (Pflug & Watson, 2004). PAR cycles allow projects to be both flexible and rigorous. The iterative process, combining research and reflection, allows educators to understand their topics and the systemic mechanisms that position them to create sustainable change.

REFLECTIVE QUESTIONS

- In your experience, when does change proceed in a linear fashion and when is it more likely to be complex or messy?
- What types of issues or challenges cause strategic plans to go awry?

SECTION 1: MESSY CYCLES

While the initial presentation of the four steps in a single cycle of PAR methodology may have suggested to practitioners to expect their research studies to progress in even, linear cycles, it is rare for the process to be orderly. Figure 8.3 describes the many other permutations that are frequently part of PAR cycles. For instance, PAR processes may actually start at a juncture between steps. In a similar fashion, especially in later rounds of research, practitioners tend to go back and forth between diagnosis and action until the implementation of new ideas is concrete enough to measure.

An overview of practitioners writing about their cycles of research shows little consensus about how educators access and move through cycles. Some documents present each step in a predefined educational strategy as a cycle (Loerke & Oberg, 1997), while in other writing the second cycle is not planned until the first is finished, using each cycle to build on knowledge developed in the previous cycle (Soffer, 1995). These adaptations and permutations are to be expected (Dick, 1998b; Kemmis & McTaggart, 1988; McTaggart, 1989), and we have seen both strategies lead to successful student-level outcomes. If an

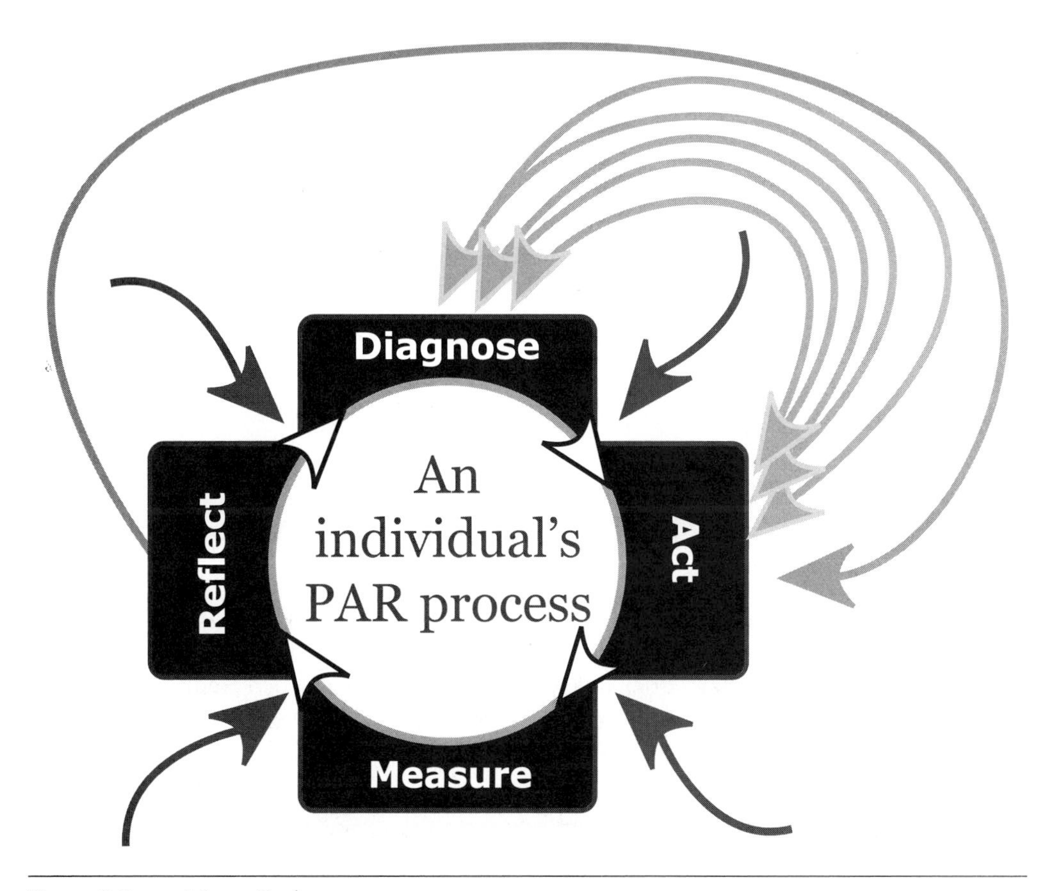

Figure 8.3 Messy Cycles

SOURCE: Alan Bucknam/Notchcode Creative, 2005.

educational strategy is predetermined, the PAR team must maintain a willingness to be flexible and change directions if and when discordant evidence emerges. It is equally important that group process be maintained and the entire participatory team agree to the logic of steps as they move forward. The following four points provide useful guideposts to ensure the work of PAR practitioners remains on target.

1. Focus on the overarching purpose(s) of the project.
2. Build the synergistic process of the PAR team.
3. Involve the stakeholders and constituency whenever possible.
4. Listen carefully.

REFLECTIVE QUESTIONS

- Think of a time when you learned a new skill. What part did repetition play in that process?
- What new kinds of awareness develop with repetition?
- How do these ideas apply to your PAR process so far?

SECTION 2: ITERATIVE GROWTH

The PAR steps shown in our familiar figure evolve through multiple iterations (see Figure 8.4).

Diagnosis

Diagnosis is generally made up of two parts: raising questions and collecting data. While Hughes and William (2001) believe that the questions raised become "less fuzzy" or change with time and greater understanding, it has been our experience that an equal portion of educators have strong driving questions

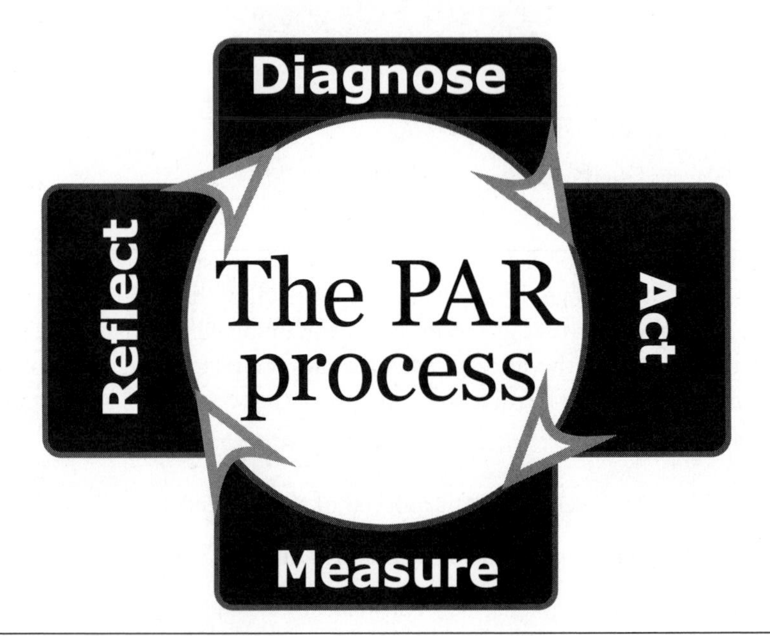

Figure 8.4 The PAR Process

SOURCE: Alan Bucknam/Notchcode Creative, 2005.

right from the beginning (James, 2004). When this is the case, the diagnosis of the underlying issues and the PAR practitioners' actions mature with each cycle.

In an example of questions maturing with process, two teachers studying the experience of homeless and highly mobile (H&HM) students first asked what information their districts could provide. In their first round of research, they discovered that both the teachers' schools and the school districts were unaware that any of the students could be considered homeless, so the answer to their first questions was "None." During their second round, they studied H&HM students' experiences enrolling in school. For this round the teacher researchers asked students to compare their current experiences to their previous experiences in other schools. When almost 10% of these students stated that no one in the school wanted them around, these teachers began their third round and questioned what it would take to increase the degree of welcome felt by new students. Subsequent cycles informed other teachers about the students' perspective of an unwelcoming environment, set up practices for the administrative office staff, and established a "new student" buddy system for the following year. Each further cycle built new questions developed through the accumulated understanding of previous cycles (Rahn & Skrobela, 2004).

Three principals in the same study started and ended their PAR project asking, "What can schools do to stabilize H&HM families?" Their project took them through many steps: interviewing families and teachers, setting up relationships with outside resources, initiating programs in the school to address the needs families expressed, and so on. Throughout each step, the principals tracked the relative satisfaction and stability of the H&HM families in their schools. These administrators concluded that while all their steps, made a positive impact, nothing in the long run could combat the chaotic conditions faced by much of their student population who experience high mobility or homelessness (Cook, Heintzman, & McVicker, 2004).

The distance between diagnosis and action may be blurred from the beginning of the project. Herr and Anderson (2005) point out that "just raising the question and designing a way to study it is often already an intervention into the setting" (p. 108). The nature of educators is to want to help from the moment a student expresses a need that may result in immediate action.

Action

The actions of research teams mature as individual cycles of the study grow in complexity. The cycles of a whole PAR team, or group of teams within a school, overlap and integrate. This totality of their combined efforts can be viewed as "meta cycles" (Coghlan & Brannick, 2001). There appears to be a relationship between the roles of the PAR participants as individuals and the increase in productivity during the action cycles because of the accountability these practitioners feel to the larger PAR team (James, 2006a). As an example, in an adult literacy project in a homeless shelter, Kalinosky's (1997) group produced consistent results in recruiting "recalcitrant" residents as long as both her curriculum and the research project were guided by the suggestions of residents. As soon as the curriculum was changed to meet the needs of shelter staff, attendance of residents in the literacy classes dropped to pre-PAR levels. This link between PAR group process and improvement also plays a role in outcomes as shown in Timmerman (2003). In this study, prospective teachers experienced a cycle of teaching while collaboratively planning, implementing, and analyzing math lessons. The researchers conclude that the peer support contributed to both the teachers' and the professors' professional development as their objective analysis of each other's work provoked mature responses in the new context they faced.

Measurement

Individual and metameasurement as well as analysis advance through multiple cycles as well. Discussion of the logic model discussed in Chapter 2 is best updated toward the beginning of each research cycle or as a bimonthly process—whichever makes the most sense (Hughes & William, 2001). Regular team conversations about the use of these two methods helps measure sustained focus on the study's purpose, allows for spontaneous celebrations of the progress, increases the specificity of planning for the next round of data collection and analysis, and increases rigor (Kock et al., 1997).

Similar to the metacycles of learning as discussed by Coghlan and Brannick (2001), multiple cycles of measurement can be analyzed both by individuals and across teams. The underlying principle of **meta-analysis** is that many small studies can blend to show an accumulative effect. Meta-analysis is defined as a method designed to increase the reliability of research by combining and analyzing the results of all known trials of the same product or experiments on the same subject. While each individual study may show only small or moderate outcomes, as a collection of studies their educational implications can be significant (Wampold, Ahn, & Kim, 2000). While the term *meta-analysis* applies to a specific set of statistical processes that allow multiple studies to be analyzed as a group, the principle of blending and coanalyzing data can also be of value to those involved in schoolwide, districtwide, or national PAR projects.

Reflection

In simple terms, reflection is the motor that makes the PAR cycles turn. Firmly rooted in the theoretical underpinnings of adult learning (Bray et al., 2000), reflection can be viewed as both a cognitive and affective process. During the reflective cycle, the PAR practitioner acknowledges the growth in wisdom that accumulates through every cycle. Coghlan and Brannick (2001) point out that reflection not only advances the topic under study but also the group process as a whole—bringing about organizational change as a result. To the extent that PAR teams work together across the various departments within the school, they represent different departmental views and realities—becoming essentially intercultural.

> It's phenomenal—one of the greatest journeys you can embark on—I feel like a professional. Reflection helps me go so deep into what I do as a teacher, and the job does not become monotonous. Every day I pay attention and I reflect—it helps me grow and life is all about growth. It also teaches me that I have to make mistakes—this allows our humanity and then I move on. (James, 2006c)

Time Line and Group Process for Significant Success

In our experience, a PAR project with the purpose of making a significant change in a school can get off to a strong start within a complete school year. During the fall, the individuals form a team, set up regular meetings, and adjust to the extra work in their schedules. The learning curve during this term includes meetings to discuss the purpose of their project and the review of the literature. Progressively during the fall, team members remind themselves about the rigors of research and begin to carve out time to conduct initial interviews and discuss the project. By the conclusion of the term, they have completed their first round of diagnosis and initiated a small action or conducted additional measurements of the situation under study. The practitioners have also begun their ongoing reflective process.

The spring semester seems to be the time of action, and commonly PAR teams implement two additional cycles of further diagnosis, action, measurement, and reflection before May, when the analysis of project outcomes for the year are finished. If the practitioners have only 1 year to dedicate to the project, their experience may be that they have learned more than originally expected and have accomplished some positive outcomes. Often by spring semester, the excitement about the potential for further growth has increased to the point that the PAR team decides to continue the project for a second year.

We generally work with school-community teams, comprised of three team members. However, recently a comprehensive study, one that combined homework and school culture, was conducted by a team of six, inclusive of classroom teachers, the principal, Title I support staff, and a community agency employee. The PAR group process may have its difficulties, but ordinarily tensions that will derail the entire project materialize within the first few months. In a national project during the 2005–2006 school year, one PAR team lost two of its members due to illness within the first 6 weeks of school. Occasionally, we have witnessed situations when one member of a team is just not engaged sufficiently or experiences family difficulties and needs to drop off the project. When this occurs, the group will either replace that person or proceed without the individual.

Group process requires people to respect each other's differences and to see the value of diverse ways to solve problems. Committing to and following through with scheduled meetings seems to be the single biggest key to success. Groups who are excited about learning from each team member and who hold together to the end finish the process more easily than groups whose members are less sure of each other. However, the less cohesive teams do complete their studies, even multiyear projects, as long as working the PAR process happens often enough to become a habit.

Task 8.1: Using the Forward Planner

The purpose of this exercise is to help PAR teams keep on track with their cycles of learning while maintaining intergroup accountability to the project.

Procedure

1. Copy the chart in Table 8.1 on a flip chart so that everyone in your PAR group can use it as a point of discussion.
2. Write your purpose on the top of the sheet so that everyone keeps it in mind throughout the discussion.
3. Write today's date at the edge of the paper near the left-hand column.
4. In the first left column, list the major questions and answers you have used while investigating your topic.

5. In the second column, list short- and long-term actionable steps you have taken or plan to take.
6. In the third column, list the measurements you have used (or plan to use) to test the success of your actions.
7. In the fourth column, use a word or short phrase to represent each of the lessons you have learned through your first PAR cycle.
8. Repeat Steps 4 through 7, strategizing your next steps and ideas for as many future cycles as the group can envision.
9. Finish by giving due dates to each part of the upcoming cycle(s).

Table 8.1 PAR Process Related to Access of Services

Purpose statement for study *To improve access to services for homeless families in order to increase readiness to learn*			
Diagnosis: questions and data	*Actions*	*Measurement of actions*	*What has been learned*
How many students in our school can be classified homeless or highly mobile?/office records and student drawing family exercise	(1) Collected data from drawing family exercise (2) Contacted families about potential for services	(1) Analyzed student drawings for information about families (2) Recorded interviews with families about services (3) Tracked service records	(1) Most of the school's families who are eligible for services live doubled up with multiple other families. (2) Readiness to learn may be tied to quality of homework support—a key for future investigations.

One line of Table 8.1 is filled out in a manner typical to what educators in the homeless project would write. In their first round of research, they identified families eligible for services and contacted them. In future rounds, the PAR team will track and measure attendance, attachment, and homework, as well as overall achievement as indicators of readiness to learn.

REFLECTIVE QUESTIONS

- Would you describe yourself as a person of thoughts, a person of actions, or both?
- What personal characteristics do you think contribute to your analysis?

SECTION 3: THEORETICAL UNDERSTANDING BOLSTERS ACTION AND VICE VERSA

Readers in an academic setting may be called upon to discuss the theoretical underpinnings of their PAR projects. The purpose of Section 3 is to offer a succinct explanation of the main theoretical discussions surrounding PAR. We have found that theory, and specifically discussion around positivism, may or may not be inherently useful to educational leaders. Educators who benefit from searching out and understanding explicit theories that guide their design for a course of action may find inspiration from searching out the works cited below:

- In planning, I draw on my explicit theories. In action, tacit theories often guide me. In later critical reflection, I have time to ask if my explicit theories corresponded to the theories implied by my actions (Dick, 1998b, p. 1).
- An important outcome of AR is to produce theory, "whose validity can be tested against publicly communicable standards of judgement" (Whitehead & McNiff, 2006, p. 1).
- Some believe that the only true knowledge is scientific, which they defined in a linear process from inquiry to knowledge. This positivist theoretical doctrine denies the validity of any notion of reality that cannot be measured. This belief creates debate with PAR practitioners on four main levels (Dick, 1998a).
- Rigor in positivist-based research tests the direct linkage from the research question through the reliability of the instruments employed in the methodology to the results. PAR addresses rigor through questions of holism and diversity, encouraging practitioners to investigate multiple avenues in support of the purpose of their project (Dick, 1998a).
- PAR studies occur with local context, whereas a positivistic approach would try to control outside variables associated with the environment in which they work (Kock et al., 1997).
- PAR practitioners actively try to manipulate positive outcomes, and no pretense is made about being neutral observers (Kock et al., 1997).

The metacyclic nature of PAR combats the proponents of positivist theory and leads to confidence in areas of validity, credibility, and reliability of results. A bias of PAR practitioners is that because local educational issues are complex in nature, the issues need to be studied within local environments. The more the issues are studied, the more diverse approaches are implemented, and the more likely educational practice will improve. Kock and colleagues (1997) assert that having diverse local evidence to build on is essential in finding sustained solutions in uncontrollable environments. They stress how a compilation of multiple data collected from various sources and analyzed by a diverse group of people creates the potential for a "desirable form of triangulation" (p. 9). Lessons learned through the practitioners' involvement, as they attempt to construct positive outcomes, are heightened because of the experiential nature of the learning and are confirmed through multiple measures.

CONCLUSION

The cycles inherent in PAR are important because these multiple iterations generate a process through which the practitioners are forced to be both flexible and rigorous. Both of these characteristics increase the understanding of the issue being studied. PAR cycles ordinarily do not progress in a linear fashion. This results in a myriad of approaches.

Each step deepens and matures when revisited throughout the cyclic process. As data gathering broadens, so does the diagnosis of the issue. The complexity of understanding the key issue and emerging solutions grows as actions are taken by individuals within groups and between group members. Each PAR project within a group magnifies the others' results and can be seen in the context of metacycles (Coghlan & Brannick, 2001). Measurement also accumulates, resulting in the development of multifaceted learning through many small projects. Reflection then advances the PAR team into a new cycle. Finally, theoretical understanding increases exponentially, as does rigor, throughout multiple cycles. Complex weaving of research and action in groups and through cycles results in the validity, credibility, and rigor available through PAR studies.

CHAPTER 9

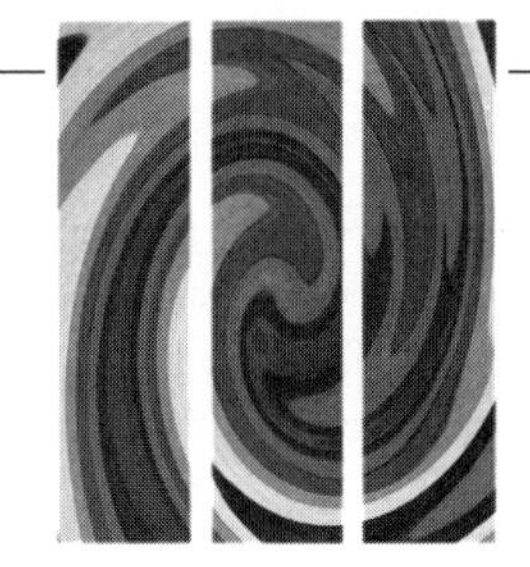

Final Analysis and Results

The expansive topic of final analysis and results requires two chapters. Covered in Chapter 9 is the alchemy of analysis, a search for patterns and themes in the data, and specific considerations entailed in writing quality reports. Chapter 10 contains specific ideas for reporting to different constituencies. The process of writing helps PAR practitioners formulate ideas and make the thoughts "real" and ready for critique by the broader world, schools, and communities. Philosophers would remind us that the more we objectify our reality with words, the less likely our reality represents the reality of others (Schostak, 2002). This "whose reality?" concept or debate is significant. We conclude that writing represents *one* reality rather than *the* reality or *the* set of ideas. Quality analysis represents the broader array of reality and ideas by stating both agreement and disagreement within results. Every concept or idea that builds toward the final analysis also blocks researchers from seeing alternative views. Therefore, these processes are a mix of humble exuberance—humbleness, in that PAR practitioners realize their views are not the only possibility for interpretation, yet exuberant, because the researchers bring their unique interpretation of events and outcomes that engender a liveliness and sense of high spirits.

Professors tell us that they find educators have difficulty sorting through data to find the patterns that create alchemy during the final analysis. There are two strategies that help PAR practitioners gain objectivity: (1) time and (2) each other. Whenever possible, we recommend that the PAR team step back from their research for a short time to talk with people outside the PAR team. Through listening to the way they tell their own story, they will begin to realize the true gems of learning that came from the process. This leads their strategy for final analysis, which is to retell their story with enough data to convince others. When the PAR team meets again, they each offer different conclusions related to the importance of the project. Figure 9.1 illustrates this point in the process with the arrows as it occurs after measurement, during and after reflection.

ALCHEMY

The final analysis of a PAR project is the alchemy that may result in PAR practitioners changing their hard work into pure gold (Blakley-Reid, 2001; Patton & Patton, 2002; Watling, 2002). Ultimately, these efforts will advance the issues they have studied, giving the outcomes of the research a life of its own in the world. As Watling (2002) points out, "Like alchemy, such magic calls for science and art in equal measures" (p. 262). While PAR practitioners have been analyzing their data throughout each cycle, this chapter addresses what it takes to wrap multiple strands of ideas together to make one contiguous whole. During final analysis, the practitioner answers the following questions: "What was learned during this project?" "What do I think others can use of the lessons I have learned?"

Like alchemy, analysis is a cumulative process—one that cannot be completed without the "right" ingredients. At the end of the PAR project, the practitioners must show that the opinions they have formed are logical and accurate, following naturally from data collected during the process. For this reason, as with many other research books (Creswell, 2002; Maxwell, 1996; Patton & Patton, 2002; Strauss & Corbin, 1998; Thomas, 2003), we suggest at the start of the PAR study that practitioners contemplate the types of information they will need in the **final report**. The use of reflective notes on the subject will help keep the project on task, making the end stages of the project less daunting, because Piantanida & Garman (1999) describe the analysis and writing process as "slogging through the stuff" and "managing the stuff" (p. 166). Cumulative records of all the data collected over the course of a multicycle PAR project can be overwhelming if left until the end to analyze.

Reasoning and Writing

Philosophers have debated how people reason, describing multiple paths taken to reach conclusions. Whether by classification, observation, induction, or deduction, different processes trigger different levels of thought and understanding (Garson, 2002). While PAR studies seldom follow the linear progression outlined in scientific methods, conclusions from PAR studies must follow logically from all data collected.

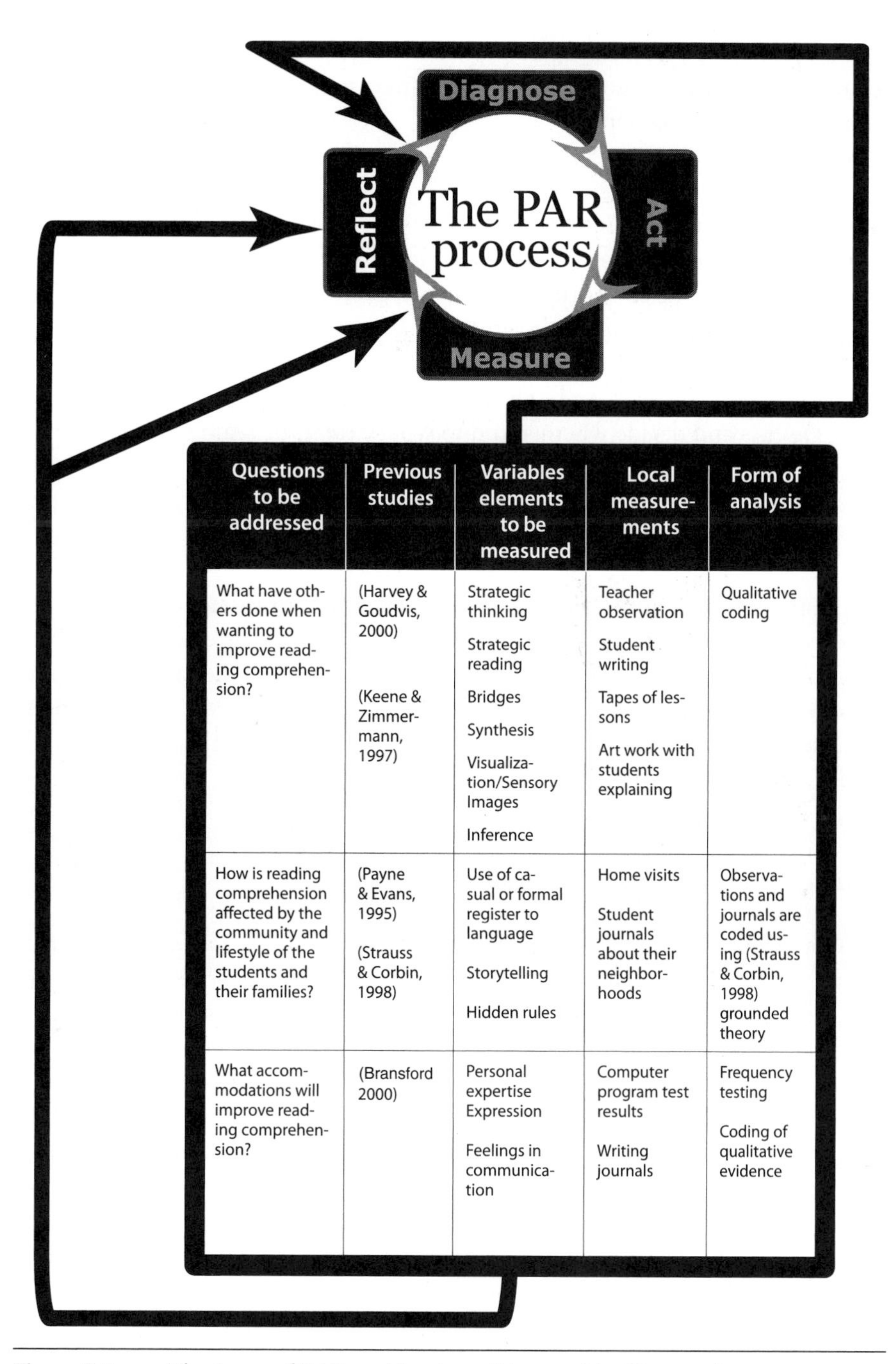

Questions to be addressed	Previous studies	Variables elements to be measured	Local measure-ments	Form of analysis
What have others done when wanting to improve reading comprehension?	(Harvey & Goudvis, 2000) (Keene & Zimmermann, 1997)	Strategic thinking Strategic reading Bridges Synthesis Visualization/Sensory Images Inference	Teacher observation Student writing Tapes of lessons Art work with students explaining	Qualitative coding
How is reading comprehension affected by the community and lifestyle of the students and their families?	(Payne & Evans, 1995) (Strauss & Corbin, 1998)	Use of casual or formal register to language Storytelling Hidden rules	Home visits Student journals about their neighborhoods	Observations and journals are coded using (Strauss & Corbin, 1998) grounded theory
What accommodations will improve reading comprehension?	(Bransford 2000)	Personal expertise Expression Feelings in communication	Computer program test results Writing journals	Frequency testing Coding of qualitative evidence

Figure 9.1 The Stage of PAR and Logic as Discussed in Chapter 9

The following steps aid PAR practitioners to sort through data, code or group it into new categories, and find patterns that hold the essence of the knowledge they have gained.

PAR teams

- Sort their findings into "lessons learned" categories.
- List under each category the data that confirm the lesson.
- Rank order the categories. The top category should be the lesson with the most confirming and least refuting data.
- Discuss whether and to what extent this rank order listing matches what the group considers to be the most important conclusions.
- Discuss and decide whether and to what extent the team members met or exceeded the purpose of the project.
- Outline the most logical way to discuss the project outcomes and the process that led to these outcomes.

The process of writing takes us on a journey into *our* thoughts and what *we believe* about the PAR experience and is therefore inherently empowering. PAR practitioners need to express what is personally and professionally meaningful in order to have their findings ring true to constituents. PAR methodology, because of its reflective component, is innately personal and therefore demands a personal touch in final research reports.

Standards for the Final Analysis

Research practice is typically measured against the standards of validity, credibility, and reliability. However, there is debate in the broader research community about whether and to what extent it is wise to use the same terms across multiple formats of design and analysis. *Valid, credible,* and *reliable* are concepts applied with and beyond the research community. We feel it is important to use these standards throughout all types of inquiry wherever they fall on the continuum from casual to scientific. As discussed in Chapters 7 and 8, the final research and analysis are built upon through all the cycles of the PAR process. Analysis of the early research cycles provides formative results that affect later cycles. Earlier chapters discussed the methods for both qualitative and quantitative data analysis. The concern here is that the final analysis is of a summative nature and concludes what was learned and provides suggestions for future inquiries.

Because PAR studies go on and on in cycles, it is difficult at times to know when a study is complete. The last cycle turns up further areas of investigation or new ideas about potential improvements to the educational process. The short answer to the question of whether and to what extent a PAR study is done is to ask, "What conclusions can be reached and are they valid, credible, and reliable?" Sections 1, 2, and 3 will discuss these milestones.

REFLECTIVE QUESTIONS

- When listening to other people's reports, how do you determine if they have thought critically about their topics?
- What questions or probing thoughts might help people reflect upon their analysis in a critical manner?

SECTION 1: VALIDITY

PAR has two overarching goals: (1) increase practitioner (and community) knowledge about the topic under study and (2) show results through improvements in education that have resulted from the study (Herr & Anderson, 2005). Whether and to what extent a practitioner can demonstrate these two goals determines the validity of a study. A PAR study may be valid in one arena but not in the other.

Herr and Anderson (2005) discuss five types of validity for PAR studies:

1. *Outcome* validity is the easiest to discuss, centering on whether and to what extent actions taken during the study proved efficacious in improving educational practices for students. Summative evaluation is an example of research that focuses on outcome validity.

2. *Process* validity is softer and more difficult to prove, as it asks the question of whether and to what extent the project resulted in an increase in knowledge and systems that improve the overall educational environment that was studied. Reporting on the cycles of PAR and the assumptions that were questioned during the PAR process, in addition to outcome data on increase in knowledge and engagement of participants, all lead to process validity. The story of the elementary school teacher in Chapter 1 demonstrates process validity.

3. *Democratic* validity is proved through data and analysis of increased participation of the underserved in decision-making positions. Democratic validity is illustrated by the community member who involved parents in the design of the program to improve parent involvement in homework at Lowry Elementary in Chapter 1.

4. *Catalytic* validity demonstrated when the project results in greater than could be expected involvement from outside parties in the issue being studied. The example in Chapter 6 of two teachers who started a Lunch Bunch for transient students and ended up by engaging the entire school community population in issues of welcoming culture and safety could be used to illustrate catalytic validity.
5. *Dialogic* validity is the extent to which the PAR practitioner can demonstrate that a diverse group of stakeholders were involved in reviewing data, results, and conclusions and provided input into the final analysis. In participatory work, where the final recipients of the implemented actions are also included in the collaborative body of practitioners, the way the data are reported should be open to agreement by consensus. The documentation of this approach leads to increased dialogic validity (Herr & Anderson, 2005, pp. 55–57).

My "Real" World—or Yours?

Maxwell (1996) discusses the issue of whether qualitative data, limited as it is to small populations of study, can be shown to represent reality in a broader context. He encourages researchers to continually question their conclusions by asking how they might be wrong. In PAR studies, validity is not determined by set procedures or techniques but rather by the rigor through which PAR teams act as critical friends and challenge each other throughout the process. Maxwell states, "It depends on the relationship of your conclusions to the real world, and there are no methods that can assure you that you have adequately grasped those aspects of the world that you are studying" (p. 86). PAR practitioners improve the validity of their studies to the extent that they show evidence of

- Looking for alternative hypotheses, meanings, or conclusions.
- Testing their ideas against data.
- Reporting areas of disagreement or where their actions were not successful.

Most authors of research methodology encourage researchers to follow up any/all incidents, during data gathering, of evidence outside the norm (Creswell, 2003; Leedy & Ormrod, 2005; Maxwell, 1996; Patton & Patton, 2002). In order to claim valid results, any disagreement between the theory of action being proposed and evidence must be thoroughly discussed. The play back and forth between qualitative and quantitative evidence may help here. When faced with discordant evidence during a focus group, smart practitioners might respond by creating survey questions that allow slightly mentioned outlying opinions to be substantiated. To perform these analyses, Maxwell (1996) points out that (a) the data must be complete—use of transcripts or tapes rather than notes, (b) the interpretation of the data is verified by other PAR group members and by the subjects themselves, and (c) the ways in which discordant data were handled must be documented.

Theory Building and Testing

There are two ways of looking at theory. The layperson may use the term in opposition to fact, defining theory as an idea that has not yet been proven. To the scientist or philosopher, the term *theory* is more than an idea; it is a proposition or model that is being proposed as a foundational idea for the work. PAR practitioners vary to the extent that they employ theory as a basis for their studies, and they may use either meaning. However, when a theoretical basis is proposed as a model from which the study evolved, the validity of the study will rest on whether and to what extent the theoretical base is supported by results of the project.

Theory may derive from a localized idea of "how things are around here and what we can do about them" that develops through the PAR process, or the theory may be obtained from published literature. Practitioners test their local theories, report the tests' results, and document the changes made to the theories. Thomas (2003) defines a theory as "an estimate of (a) which components of an event are involved in the event and (b) how those components relate to each other" (p. 147). He continues to suggest the usefulness in defining whether and to what extent the researchers' working theories identify or explain the cause of events or merely classify them.

Reporting the Analysis Process to Others

The last skill that PAR researchers will need to show the validity of their process is what Brause (2000) reports as "sufficient information to enable a reader of the study to envision all the steps which the researcher followed" (p. 118). Lewis and Ritchie (2003) added to this discussion five principles for reporting qualitative data that transfer to PAR projects as educators report the analysis of their qualitative data:

1. There is a liberal use of original qualitative data within the report of findings.
2. The ideas expressed encompass the diversity and display the full range of findings.

3. Theoretical inferences are drawn and their relationship to other educational context is discussed.
4. General findings as well as specific ones are reported, as general findings may be easier for readers to transfer to their own context.
5. The people contributing to the research, as much as possible, have verified any meanings conveyed in the conclusion. (pp. 277–279)

Figure 9.2, "The Final Analysis," demonstrates the goal of a valid argument: to delineate both the qualitative and quantitative data (shown here by the small cubes and spheres); the ways in which the PAR team has sorted and regrouped the data; and the logic from which the regroupings construct new ideas, strategies, or meanings for the field of education.

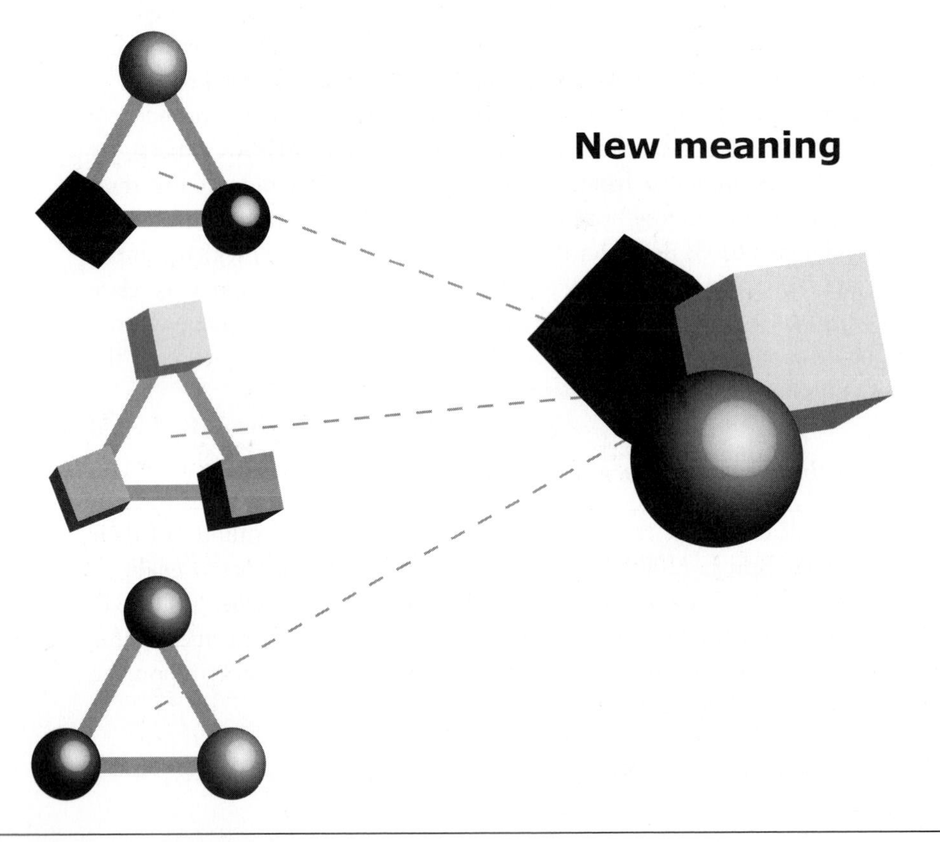

Figure 9.2 The Final Analysis

SOURCE: Alan Bucknam/Notchcode Creative, 2005.

The key elements contained in reports that successfully draw these connections are as follows:

- Identification of the data collection methods
- Description of the method of analysis
- Description of the data sorting process
- Description of the specific elements, including software, methods of coding, and so on
- Description of the quantitative evidence used in the study
- Description of the ethical constraints on use of individual evidence during analysis

Task 9.1: Building a Preliminary Report on the Analysis Process for Others

It is not necessary to report the analysis process to every constituency in a formal document. However, it is important that all readers of a PAR report are convinced about the valid level of critical analysis contained within the report. For that reason, it is a useful exercise for practitioners to put together a formal report of their critical analysis process.

Procedure

Step 1: Make a chronological list of all the methods of collecting data that were used during the project, noting the month and the people involved in each. For ease the list may be sorted by cycles and list the who, what, where, when, and why of what occurred in each cycle.

Step 2: Write a two- or three-sentence description of how data were analyzed. Include assumptions that were challenged and methods of verification, as appropriate.

Step 3: Write two or three sentences about the PAR team or individual process through which data were sorted into overarching ideas and how those led to final conclusions. To the extent that these methods mirror those written about by methodological theorists, make a note of their work as a reference.

Step 4: Write a sentence or two about any/all use of software or other methods during analysis.

Step 5: Describe quantitative evidence separately, making note of publishers of tests, date written, populations to whom it was administered, and the manner in which that population was chosen.

Step 6: Describe the relative use of identifiable individual evidence versus aggregate data. In a sentence or two, discuss the manner in which confidentiality was maintained.

Step 7: Condense all of the above into a paragraph or two describing your process of analysis.

REFLECTIVE QUESTIONS

- When listening to other people's reports, how do you determine if their results seem credible?
- What criteria do you apply?
- Is there a particular method of reporting that helps you understand the relevance of credible results to your own educational situation?

SECTION 2: CREDIBLE INTERPRETATION

Data transformation is suggested by Creswell (2003) as a method through which mixed methodological research makes its credibility apparent to its constituency. Credibility is the degree to which the person reading the report thinks the conclusions make sense. This is a subjective judgment and requires PAR researchers to be cognizant of their audience and context. When applying concurrent qualitative and quantitative strategies, both types of processes enhance the strengths of the other. As an example, qualitative data will be quantified by counting the number of times certain subjects are mentioned or the percentages of individuals who agreed to one side or the other on a debate and so on. In addition, quantitative data can be qualified by discussing key phrases that were written as comments. Both types of data measure specific variables that are key to the discussion of developing theories, as are any correlations that exist between them. Reporting these data require reducing the data and finding patterns between them to compare and contrast.

Brause (2000) cautions that to reach credible results and conclusions, there needs to be an internal connection between these conclusions and a study's original purpose, questions, and literature. PAR practitioners who have regularly completed the various lines of the logic model during each cycle will find this connection easy to discuss. Additional tools that aid the reader to understand the PAR process and to evaluate the credibility of the findings are graphic organizers, compelling arguments, and disclaimers.

Graphic Organizers

Graphic organizers benefit the researchers as well as their audience. PAR teams should consider what relationships they see between data and, on a trial-and-error process, graph these data along the relative axis. For instance, school studies on parent and community involvement often recognize interactive homework as a way to encourage parents to relate to their children's academics. A PAR team that arrived at a similar conclusion could list both quantitative and qualitative data in a chart. Located along one axis would be the data on involvement by parents with homework. Various supports to that process would be situated on the other axis. The task of sorting data into graphic organizers aids analysis. Once the analysis is firm, the same organizer advances the understanding of those reading the report.

Sagor (2000) suggests that PAR practitioners analyze data in a "Triangulation Matrix" (p. 21). The left-hand column of this graphic model organizes the data to be charted by either research question or theme. Each subsequent column to the right is used to indicate sources of data that have relevance to the question or theme. These bits of data are then analyzed for the meaning conveyed. Each piece of data is compared to each other or triangulated. This method of segmenting results helps with analysis for individuals and their PAR team, as well as for the readers of final project reports.

A brief written explanation supports readers to interpret the meaning of figures and tables accurately. The sole use of numbers or phrases can easily be misinterpreted. The challenge for PAR practitioners is to represent data fairly without misrepresentation (Booth, Colomb, & Williams, 2003). Two suggestions aid in this. First, represent all data in every possible manner and discuss, as a PAR team of critical friends, the impressions given by each representation. Second, in the final report, use both words and pictures or charts to support a complete understanding of the issues under study. In most cases, use of a graphic representation *must* support written analysis. Graphics delineate results in clear, short sentences by giving the reader a frame of reference from which to work (Levy, 2002a).

Compelling Arguments

Findings that are surprising may hold the most value to the PAR team and to their constituency (Brause, 2000). Provided the findings are valid and credible, they need to be reported with the process used to establish credibility. Readers will make independent judgments on the relative credibility of these arguments.

Compelling arguments draw upon the credibility of the findings to motivate readers toward appropriate action. Results are credible when presented in clear and unbiased ways. A convincing report with conclusions written in strong and passionate language concludes with a suggested course of action (Roberts, 2004; Thomas, 2003). The study's purpose that drove the researchers to expend time and energy on the project ultimately encourages others to take an interest in their findings.

Disclaimers

Credibility improves when research teams state directly what they do not know or cannot infer. Patton and Patton (2002) point out that there is no such thing as the perfect study; researchers always arrive at the conclusion where questions that should have been asked were not asked and that further verification of the study would be useful. Documenting these issues is part of analysis and the reporting cycle. **Disclaimers** are statements that explain a potential flaw in the findings due to issues with research methodology that may be construed to weaken results. Disclaimers allow other researchers to avoid similar problems.

As an example, in education the ability to translate a survey into different languages will have implications for results in some communities. A disclaimer might be that, due to lack of easy translation, the study did not completely reflect the ideas of an immigrant community within the school. Other educators with similar communities might find the earlier data flawed for this reason and would know to translate first, before attempting their studies.

REFLECTIVE QUESTIONS

- When you listen to reports that describe educational successes, how do you determine whether those successes might transfer to your educational context?
- What information do you need to make that decision?

SECTION 3: RELIABILITY

Education is complex, so results from educational improvements may not dependably transfer across settings, and we do not believe in a "one size fits all" type of solution. That said, we also know the importance of educators learning from each other and completely believing in the reliability of PAR project results, if not to create a model for success, at least to provoke new and innovative ideas in education. For this reason, we begin our discussion of reliability by suggesting that educators can discover valuable insights from PAR studies of other educators. Part of the test of reliability will be to implement a PAR study of their own to test these new ideas.

As previously discussed, PAR studies can be valid and credible in the development of knowledge and/or the improvement of educational practices. PAR practitioners who write the final report need to consider whether and to what extent both the knowledge gained and the actions developed could transfer to other educational settings. The ideal report will explicitly address different aspects of questions such as these: Whether and to what extent can these findings be transferred to other contexts? Is the knowledge transferable? Are the actions transferable? Have the actions been evaluated in a manner that shows dependable results?

Lewis and Ritchie (2003) point out three layers of questions that lead to an evaluation of internal and external reliability of findings:

1. Do the findings from the population queried accurately represent the entire population of which they are a part?
2. Can it be inferred that the findings from this study can be transferred to other locations or environments?
3. To what extent do these findings provoke greater ideas about the larger field of study of which they are a part? (pp. 270–273)

Patton and Patton (2002) discuss cross-case analysis, which is frequently employed in organizational studies (for instance, the highest performing schools in areas of poverty). Suggestions for this type of analysis have implications for people thinking about the reliability of their study or whether lessons learned locally will transfer to other educational settings. PAR teams in these circumstances need to answer the following questions:

- What was learned?
- What results back up these lessons?
- Why is this lesson important and to whom?
- Under what conditions would it be important to an educator in a completely different context?
- Are there themes across the findings of the various PAR team participants?
- Are these themes verified by the population being studied?

- Are these themes verified by literature from other sources?
- Can the process be broken down into steps that would lead other educational practitioners to improve their practice?

Fallacy

To borrow a discussion from the empirical or quantitative side of the toolbox, conclusions must be drawn from a study that logically tests assumptions and is without **fallacy** (Garson, 2002). Fallacy is defined as something that is believed to be real but is based on erroneous logic or reasoning in which the conclusion does not follow from the premises. The concept of fallacy of findings is a view discussed frequently in the social sciences, where researchers may commonly assume that individual-level correlations will transfer to the larger population or that analysis proven true in the larger population will be true for the individual. A common example of this type of ecological fallacy is seen in the correlation between race and illiteracy in the United States. Because large numbers of African Americans live in the South, a geographic region with high levels of illiteracy from all races, the data turn out to be quite skewed. The correlation between race and illiteracy virtually disappears as a predictor at the individual level.

Other debates continue to rage in education that congregate around questions of ecological fallacy. For instance, while it is true that master-level experience in teaching has shown, on an individual basis, to be efficacious, will its benefits transfer to entire populations of teachers? Another equally poignant discussion is whether and to what extent do population-level standardized tests measure increases in learning (Baker, 1997; Essex, 1967)?

The idea of fallacies in research returns us to a previous discussion about what is real. A description in Chapter 4, taken from the movie *Rashomon,* illustrates how the world looks very different from various perspectives, and the reality that makes logical sense from one perspective may be processed from an entirely different angle. What is reality? Schostak (2002) mentions several reference points, each of which PAR practitioners may want to consider when they ask themselves how their findings would reliably transfer to the experience of educators in schools with different contexts. Reality, according to Schostak, can be tested by checking statements against observable facts, but the sense of something being "right" is taught in familial habits and crosses generations within given contexts. Therefore, many versions exist. These are the overarching considerations as PAR practitioners begin to write about whether and to what extent they perceive the personal, contextual, or global findings that their projects uncover. Will they transfer? Are they reliable? Ultimately, researchers or educators who read about the project will decide if they believe the results are reliable enough for them to attempt to build on the foundation of a particular PAR study.

REFLECTIVE QUESTIONS

- What did you learn most during your PAR study?
- To what extent are you able to revise these lessons into simple sentences or brief bulleted points?
- What three words might capture the emotion of these lessons?

SECTION 4: PASSIONATE CONCLUSIONS

While some merit exists in research conclusions that are conservative in nature, it is important that final statements are strong enough that they could be disproved through future study (Garson, 2002). It is also personally important that PAR practitioners be strong enough to stand up for what they have learned and its significance to educational practice. If the project did not demonstrate positive outcomes, this finding needs to be reported just as clearly as findings with stellar results. This degree of accuracy equally adds to the field of education by helping others avoid similar traps.

To sort findings into two or three camps is beneficial as a tool for practitioners to finalize their conclusions. "What do we know for certain versus what results do we suspect to be true but warrant more study?" "Which can be sorted into knowledge gained versus programmatic improvements that were demonstrated?" Finally, "What are the most important aspects of my project from which other educators can profit, and what steps do I recommend others in similar situations take?" When all of these considerations are taken into account, researchers are ready to start writing their final report.

Task 9.2: One Sentence and Three Words

Using a process developed for theater, this task helps PAR practitioners focus on the key thoughts they wish to write at the conclusion of their project (O'Kelly, 2006). This exercise can be done individually, with a PAR team, or with a group of critical friends.

Procedure

Step 1: Reflect for a moment on your PAR project. Write down answers to the following questions:

- What were the most significant moments for you during the project?
- Why were these moments important?
- What would you tell others about the parts of the project that led to the greatest professional growth?
- With what outcomes or results are you most pleased?
- What did you find motivating?

Step 2: Focusing only on the parts you just included in your reflections, write down the answers to the following questions:

- What do I know for certain versus what results do I suspect to be true but warrant more study?
- Which can be sorted into knowledge gained versus programmatic improvements that were demonstrated?
- What are the most important aspects of my project from which I think other educators can profit, and what steps do I recommend others in similar situations take?

Step 3: Condense what you have just written into one coherent paragraph.

Step 4: Tell others what you have learned in one sentence, condensing all of the reflective points you have just made.

Step 5: Craft three words that capture the tone of your project.

Step 6: Work with others in your PAR team to ensure that the conclusion in your report has the clarity and punch of the one sentence and three words you just wrote.

CONCLUSION

The writing of PAR results is a critical endeavor and goes hand in hand with a PAR practitioner's final analysis. Writing embodies two conflicting emotions: humbleness in becoming aware that one's situation can never be exactly the same for others, and exuberance in the celebration of lessons learned and outcomes gleaned from the hard work. PAR methodology is inherently personal, largely because of the reflective portion of each cycle. The personal, as well as professional, meaning of the project should be conveyed for the final conclusions to maintain integrity with the research process. Shifts from professional to personal, from knowledge to results, from suspected information to confirmed data all form the final analytical stages from writing to thought and back again to writing.

The PAR process ultimately produces new knowledge and concurrently seeks educational outcomes. Validity is judged against both measures. Three processes aid in insurance of valid claims. First, PAR practitioners employ the help of others to test their analysis throughout the process. Second, they develop and test theories about what they consider the key components of their findings. Third, and finally, they accurately report their analysis process so others can judge for themselves the validity of the procedure that established published results.

When stakeholders read a final report, they test the results in their minds to decide whether, and to what extent, these results seem credible. This depends largely on their ability to follow the logic from the data, to the findings, and through to the conclusions. Graphic organizers help them do this. Compelling personal stories of lessons learned along the way also provide a reality check and support the study's credibility. The readers' sense of credibility is confirmed as the authors discuss the aspects of their project that they felt were weak or needed more study before being confirmed.

Reliability addresses the ability of the PAR project's outcomes to transfer to other educational settings. While the decision to replicate or build upon a previous study rests with those reading the report, the potential for transference may be discussed by the PAR participants writing the report. The fallacy that inhibits reliability pertains to research conclusions that attempt to either extrapolate population-wide conclusions from data collected from small groups or the reverse, extrapolating individual possibilities from population-wide studies. Because educational environments are complex settings, a complete disclosure of the context of the PAR study, along with a discussion of potential transference to other settings, will aid readers to decide whether and to what extent the project is reliable.

The aim for the final report is to represent the full process and content of the PAR project. When conveying the personal and professional lessons learned during a PAR study, this can be written in the first person or simply covered in a selection of topics. When the PAR team writes the conclusions of the data findings in a logical manner, when the entire project is accurately reported, and when the questions of transferability are discussed, the team can realistically assume that readers will find their analysis and final report valid, credible, and reliable. Figure 9.3 demonstrates the satisfying moment when all the data, reflection, process, and meetings come together to build a solid final analysis.

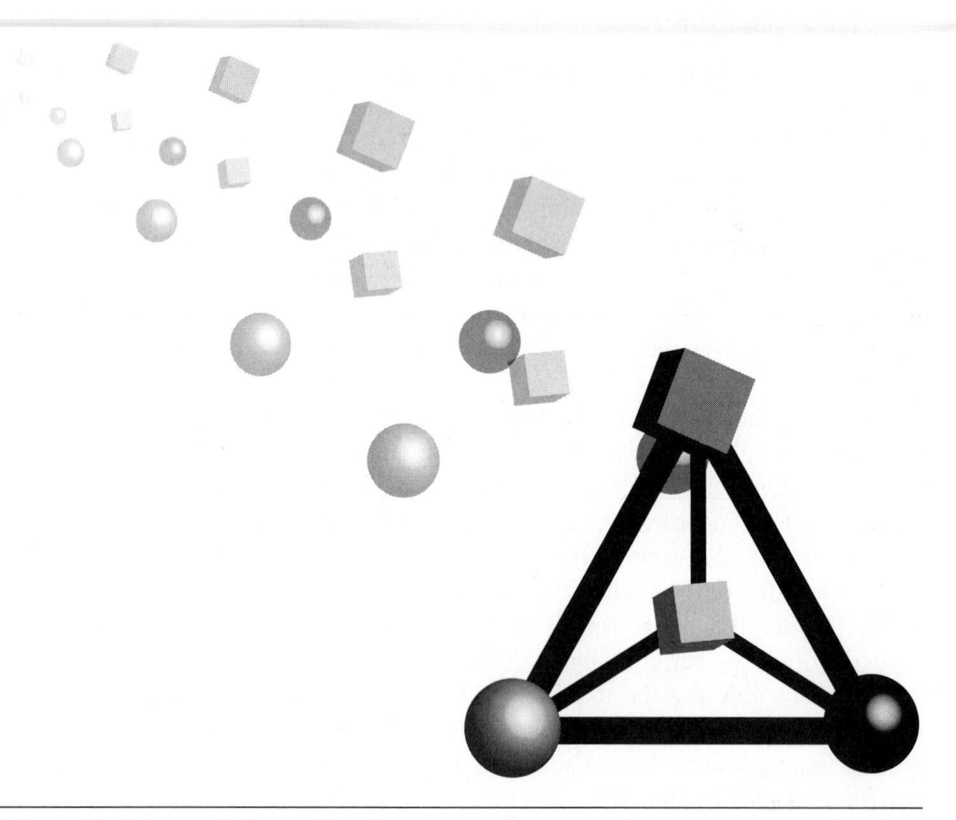

Figure 9.3 The Moment It Comes Together

SOURCE: Alan Bucknam/Notchcode Creative, 2005.

CHAPTER 10

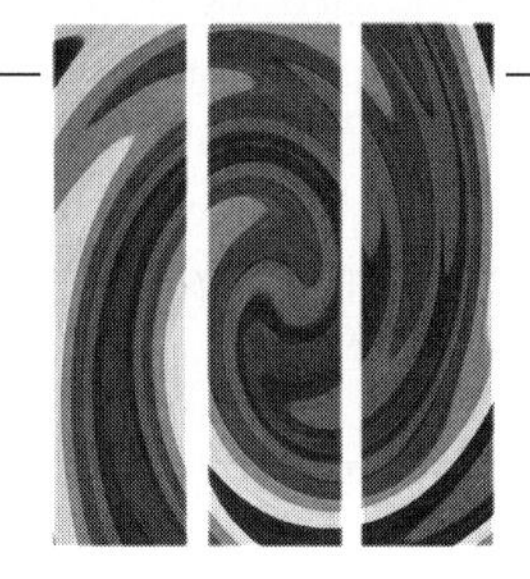

The Final Report

Every constituency has its own requirements for final reports. Different groups of stakeholders diverge on what parts of the PAR project capture their interest. For example, one variance relates to how much the stakeholder groups care about the PAR process. Some will be more interested in the human side of the project, others in the implications for educational practice. While it is important that PAR practitioners report to the specifications of their audiences, it is critical that PAR teams report the totality of a study's results and not solely the evidence to support the expected or desired results. Levy (2002b) speaks of the need for research writing to be "satisfying for the reader" (p. 319). Seeing a new truth, learning of life-changing experiences, and feeling called to action each exemplify a satisfying reaction of a reader to a poignant report. When results do not confirm the outcomes the audience expected or desired, the reported results will still be satisfying to the extent that PAR teams suggest improvements and next steps.

This chapter addresses the considerations that we have found most likely to create success for PAR practitioners reporting to different constituencies. We separate considerations into the various audiences that educational leaders are most likely to address. To help PAR teams position their final report for greatest success, we consider four potential report groupings, as shown in Table 10.1. The formal report is widely used by researchers, and while it may not do justice to the lessons learned in PAR cycles, its common usage allows for clear presentation of the methodology and outcomes of the study. When participatory groups report their findings to formal authorities such as school boards or legislators, they may want to share stories of success to engage their listeners in the meaning of their outcomes to students. Such authorities rarely are interested in research methodology but are driven by the effect of work on people's lives. When administrators or teachers who have not worked with a participatory group do PAR and informally report their findings, it is frequently either to the people who have sponsored their professional development activities or those who have influence on the program development ideas becoming widely disseminated. Both groups have influence and are interested in both the story and the research on which it is based. Finally, there may be a need for an informal community gathering to celebrate results. This works for highly participatory community groups who, because of the diversity inherent in such groups, have a wide range of experiences and outcomes. Such a gathering may also be used as a bid for funds to continue their projects.

Regardless of the style chosen for the final report of the PAR project, the results must be documented in such a way that the audience finds the evidence valid, credible, and reliable. As discussed in Chapter 9, three steps are common for primarily qualitative studies: (1) a statement is made as to a lesson learned, (2) qualitative data are quoted from participants in the study, and, finally, (3) any evidence that triangulates with and confirms these ideas are reported. Triangulated evidence often includes survey data, student work, and so on (Roberts, 2004; Rudestam & Newton, 2001). No matter how these data are reported, two elements maintain the reader's focus: (1) the discussion of the issue studied and why it held the group's attention and (2) evidence about on how the team worked with the data as they reached consensus about the meanings they derived (McTaggart, 1989, 1997).

Writing the final report is a worthwhile process in and of itself. Reports provide a sense of finality or closure to the entirety of the project, and PAR practitioners become more aware of what they have learned through the writing process. Dana and Yendol-Silva (2003), in reporting ideas from Mills (2003), suggest that there are several benefits to the PAR practitioner in writing up their findings: clarification of the issues and the results in the mind of the writer, empowerment and added motivation to take the project to its next level, and its generative capacity, as it finishes the project with a tangible product. All of these culminate in a heightened sense of accomplishment. For PAR practitioners who have not written recently, finding and following examples in published reports from other people can serve as an exemplar, making the task seem more manageable (McKernan, 1996).

Some of our readers may be positioning their reports for academic audiences. These audiences may include older educators who earned their terminal degree at a time when, or from an institution that believed, quantitative scientific research was the sole valid form of scientific inquiry. They may demonstrate a prejudice against PAR or any of its numerous derivations. Stringer (1999) reports having students tell him of professors commenting, "That is not real research" (p. 166). As mentioned, the most important part of the report is its ability to reach the audience for which it is intended. Should the current academic environment of our

Table 10.1 Four Categories of Reports

<table>
<tr><th>The Formal Report</th><th>The Formal Presentation</th></tr>
<tr><td>Contents
Background
Context
Methodology
Results
Discussion
Conclusion
Appendices
Format
Written document or PowerPoint presentation
Audience
Academics
Funders
Publications</td><td>Contents
These same elements (background to conclusion) reported through the story of the PAR project and the cycles of inquiry of the investigation
Format
Presentation
Audience
School boards
Legislatures
Parent groups
Administrative meetings</td></tr>
<tr><td colspan="2">Direct quotes from qualitative evidence strengthen both these types of reports by giving voice to the people who gave their input to the study.</td></tr>
<tr><td>The Informal Individual Report</td><td>The Informal Group Report or Presentation</td></tr>
<tr><td>Contents
Streamlined to audience needs
Format
Speaking engagements
Charts
Presentations
One-page overview with bulleted highlights
Audience
Faculty meetings
School district or statewide conferences
District newsletters</td><td>Contents
Limited
Focus on success
Format
Party
Stories
Awards
Celebrations
Newspapers
Newsletters
Story boards or pictures
Short synopsis for newspapers or newsletters
Audience
Families and community members</td></tr>
</table>

readers not completely support the terminology used in this book, a simple substitution of "cyclic, primarily qualitative mixed methodology" may provide a phrase that is more easily understood. Lack of acceptance of PAR or its variations is an old issue, one that seems to be idiosyncratic to academics in the United States more than in other countries. Hopefully, this lack of acceptance is also a dying issue, as PAR methodology advances the creation of sustainable local educational solutions and generates new applications for research.

REFLECTIVE QUESTIONS

- What are the benefits of the standard research report style?
- In reflecting on research reports, what components engage the reader?
- What components are boring or of less value?

SECTION 1: THE FORMAL REPORT

Every writing has a beginning (one that hopefully reels the reader in), a middle (which is coherent and thoughtful, both raising and answering questions), and a conclusion (which provides the reader with something provocative to remember). Human stories give the writing punch and interest but are lost if they are not subservient to the larger message of the document. Many authors find writing a circular process that starts with the introduction, runs through all the parts to the conclusion, and then returns to rewrite the introduction so that it more completely outlines the chapters within the book. Next, revisions start, first those found by the authors themselves through multiple readings, and continued by one or two external reviewers and editors who help clarify weak portions of text (Booth, Colomb, & Williams, 2003).

When the writing process begins, Hubbard and Power (1993) recommend using the "aha" moments that were experienced during the PAR process as milestones through which to tell the story (p. 114). They also suggest finding a visual metaphor to help hesitant authors envision themselves in the starring role to motivate their writing. Hubbard and Power's students have seen themselves "standing on bridges, walking on tightropes and nurturing babies" (p. 116). These metaphorical images help the PAR practitioner decide the tenor of their final reports, allowing them to negotiate the difficult task of framing their writing. Perhaps other, more robust, authors will find the image of storming the gate, convincing the audience, or creating the lifesaving solution as the image through which to moderate the fears they face once they begin their final report.

The Formal Academic Report

One of the advantages of the formal academic report of findings is that it can be used for peer-reviewed journals and as a basis for papers presented at national and international conferences. Because of its consistency, readers know how to approach the paper, search out key elements, and make decisions about whether or not the research bears closer study. To engage readers using this style, the authors need to consider the constituency to whom they write and target each section in an engaging manner.

The first section is generally the *background* and establishes the purpose for the study and any necessary context so that the readers understand the motivation and general environment for the project (Coghlan & Brannick, 2005). Through reading the background and context section, readers will first become engaged in the study being reported and make decisions about whether and to what extent this study is likely to contain findings that are seen as reliable or can be transferred to wider settings (Dana & Yendol-Silva, 2003). While the purpose of the study is always included, details about the context may be shaped to the audience for which the report is written. Rural educators, as an example, may wish to emphasize that aspect of their context so that other rural educators can see the reliability of their findings, thus adding to that subset of educational research.

The *methodology* section outlines the how of the research to the audience of the report. Therefore, this section will vary as widely as the audience to which the reports are written. Academic audiences use this section to test the rigor, validity, and credibility of the findings. For some reports this section is simplified, if addressed, and contains two parts: first a discussion of the philosophy behind the choices and then a step-by-step understanding of what research strategies were followed (Coghlan & Brannick, 2005). If well done, the audience fully understands not only the intentionality behind the decisions made by the PAR practitioners but also comes to the same conclusions as the authors. This happens to the extent that the PAR practitioners have demonstrated thoroughness as they tested each result in multiple ways, designed new actions that reflected the outcomes of prior cycles, and used reflective practice to hone the decisions they made.

The *results* section tells the story of what took place throughout the investigation. Coghlan and Branick (2005) suggest that practitioners write up the story of the cycle's events in chronological order. Then as the story develops, so does an understanding of how each cycle of research led to the whole study. The story proceeds to the wider discussion of overarching issues and solutions that were addressed during the study. In the final analysis, the synthesis of the learning contains the seeds from which other educators can learn. At the beginning of this book, we told the story of Tobey's first year using PAR methodology.

Her outcomes demonstrate a synthesis that combined the first cycle, which addressed lifestyle issues of homeless students, with the second cycle, which measured the extent to which these students perceived her class as a welcoming environment. She finished with the understanding that her students who experienced homelessness needed to have their lifestyles included in the mix of readings to be motivated and ultimately needed to improve their reading skills. Tobey's measurement of this synthesis made Tobey's report exciting to read.

The *discussion* builds on the momentum of the results toward the claims or outcomes as seen by the practitioner. Whether the PAR practitioners write the discussion section to demonstrate (a) the cycles of research or (b) as a more standard research article, the way in which they analyze the measurement of their ideas is dependent on the audience for which the report is written. Audiences whose constituencies include students and families (such as school boards or legislative audiences) will likely be engaged in the individual story of the research and the stories of the people who provided the data for the study. Academic audiences may care personally for the stories of the people involved but will need the report to be balanced by the progression of methodology to findings to conclusion.

If the reporting of your reflective data and its impact on the study as a whole requires special notice or explanation, due to the nature of the study or its intended audience, then Coghlan and Brannick (2005) suggest that reflections be contained in separate boxes or sidebars. These allow the PAR practitioners to reflect publicly, show their train of thought, and share what they plan to do next and why. This technique provides a mechanism for having accounts of your own reactions, interpretations, and action planning beside the factual narrative in a format that does not confuse the two. The readers can see the story's progression by viewing the boxes to learn what you thought, how you interpreted the unfolding situation, and the logic of your actions. This is a tool for inserting first-person narrative alongside the second-person narrative (p. 129).

The conclusion is the place for the passion of the PAR practitioner to come forth. What is the meaning of this research to the researchers personally, to their practice and the practice of others in their community and district? Does this research have broader implications in the field of education? If so, what are these implications and how does this research justify the conclusion? While this section may be composed reflectively, it may also be written as a more scholarly treatise, again dependent upon the audience to whom each practitioner reports. Coghlan and Brannick (2005) address a common complaint about any of the varieties of AR by pointing out that critics say AR studies do not produce or address the theoretical implications that have impact on the field of education. This issue may exist when local researchers find it difficult to either see or believe in the efficacy of their findings to the field of education as a whole. PAR practitioner groups can play a role as critical friends by supporting each other to test and believe in the valid, credible, and reliable nature of their work. If these three standards have been reached, then we believe that PAR written reports should be evidence of the standards and the authors deserve to postulate the importance of their findings to other educational contexts.

To the extent that these reports are intended for other educators who learn from the PAR experience, appendices become useful tools. We recommend two types: (1) a full disclosure of the survey, focus group, and interview instruments and (2) a step-by-step list of the steps through which other educators could duplicate similar results. A full disclosure of instruments will prove helpful to other educators who would like to test their school populations to see if they obtain similar results. This systematic process will allow educators who may not be interested in the research angle to implement similar programs. Sagor (2000), who suggests designing a graphic organizer or table with the questions or purposes behind your study, presents another form of appendix with the various data sources listed along the top. The table is completed with the synthesis of the lessons learned from each data source about each question—thus visually outlining for the reader the level of agreement between sources. Graphic organizers as described may be embedded in the report, if space allows, or can appear in an appendix.

REFLECTIVE QUESTIONS

- What style of presentation allows the group to report not only their findings but also their individual contributions to the whole?
- What key considerations come to mind when thinking about reporting to people who have authority over policy or protocols that influence the subject that was researched?

SECTION 2: THE FORMAL PRESENTATION

PAR practitioners may choose the presentation over written reports, which may not be the most effective way to catch the attention of those who possess the authority to sustain PAR projects or support them with policy or resources. To illustrate, the PAR groups studying H&HM students, with whom we work, occasionally need to present their findings to school boards. These verbal reports purposely encourage districtwide policies that support effective practices uncovered in their studies. Two considerations intersect when a PAR group presents in the described scenario: (1) how to design the presentation to demonstrate the entire group's participation in the study that will add weight to the seriousness of the findings and (2) how to organize a powerful presentation communicated succinctly. Often educators find that it is difficult to get on the agenda for school board meetings, which are frequently overscheduled, and that a concise presentation is best.

Any group presentation should allow for both information sharing from the researchers to the community, and reaction from the community to the researchers, even if it is simply a question-and-answer section at the end. Designing a two-way interaction as part of the presentation will help the stakeholders for whom the presentation is written become more engaged and interested in the topic. Likewise, participation by the entire PAR team should be planned to increase the impact of the findings.

Rehearsing presentations ahead of time to a neutral audience improves the likelihood that PAR teams will hold the attention of their audience. Critical friends listening to practice sessions want to be alert to places the information seems dense or they lose interest. If using PowerPoint slides, dense areas can diminish when key phrases are highlighted or enlarged. Verbal emphasis also helps to focus interest on key components.

Prior to Beginning

Sorting out the following will give a PAR team a firm foundation on which to build their presentation:

- What are their roles in relation to the people to whom they are presenting? Employee? Colleague? Student? Community member?
- Will their audience perceive the PAR team as the expert on this topic?
- Does the audience care as much about the topic as the presenters?
- Are there sensitive topics? How much can be dared without risking alienation, given the political context in which the presentation will take place?
- What are the explicit values on which the presentation is based?
- What actions (if any) is the audience to be motivated to take?
- How explicitly should goals of motivation or funding be stated (Garmston & Wellman, 1992)?

By discussing these issues as a group, the PAR team comes to consensus on their roles during the presentation, thus freeing up higher levels of spontaneity and support.

Constraints

As mentioned earlier, it is rare for presenters to have what they consider "enough" time. The following questions aid PAR teams in realizing the constraints they need to consider when designing their presentations:

- How much time will be allotted for the presentation?
- Will that time be rushed due to discussions earlier in the agenda?
- When a presentation is not the main agenda topic, what unique elements of the PAR presentation stand out from other topics to capture the interest of the audience?
- Will the PAR group members who speak be credible to the audience with their presentation (Garmston & Wellman, 1992)?
- If credibility is not a given, how can it be established?

When faced with the dilemma of too much to say and not enough time to talk, Garmston and Wellman (1995) remind readers to go back to their purpose in designing the presentation as a whole. People who present frequently concur that short and engaging are guidelines for most presentations. Short keeps the minds of the audience from wandering, and while stories and pictures are engaging and data are convincing, appropriate fast timing is essential.

Openings and Closings

The audience is likely to remember two parts of a presentation—how it opened and the emotional response experienced as it closed. Therefore, both must be crafted to have the maximum effect on the audience for whom the presentation is written. If the opening presents a problem, then the closing should either present the solution or ask for support in finding solutions. When the beginning tells a story, referring back to it at the end creates a feeling of closure. Presenters who take the extra time to decide what emotional response they want from their audience and consciously craft words, pictures, and documentation to build a desired response have a high likelihood of influencing their audience in the manner they desire.

Content and How to Present It

A presentation by its nature will not contain the level of detail contained in a written report. Therefore, PAR teams may want to augment their presentations with data handed out as they finish their presentation. PAR practitioner groups design these elements as they decide the following:

- What are the three main points of content that they wish to convey?
- What stories, pictures, data, and so on are the most convincing evidence through which to lead the audience to those conclusions?
- Can these be covered in the time allotted? If so, fine. If not, what can be conveyed in another way or at another time?

Regardless of the format of the presentation, the story model still applies. The PAR team needs to draw people in, show them the actions, reactions, conclusions, and changes that occurred during the project, and then summarize.

REFLECTIVE QUESTIONS

- What would be the pros and cons of various report formats in K–12 school settings?
- What is the value of eliciting educators from other schools to participate in a similar PAR project?

SECTION 3: THE INFORMAL INDIVIDUAL REPORT

While the formal report may covertly add sections that hint at actions in which the writer/speaker hopes to engage the audience, the advantage of informal reports is the ability to encourage action. Sagor (2005) suggests that future presenters begin with a reflection about what they themselves have found interesting and useful when they were the audience in a similar situation. Generally, the content of all informal reports will include (a) the context, (b) the purpose and anticipated outcomes, (c) actual outcomes, and (d) next steps and requests for help or resources.

The informal or individual report may also be adapted for updates or as a formative evaluation of the knowledge gained during the process to date, before summative or final analysis is complete (Herman, Morris, & Fitz-Gibbon, 1987). It is important to keep all stakeholders abreast of results. Memos and e-mails are also beneficial and serve, when transferred to the larger body of evidence, as reflective data. Face-to-face meetings, as another form of informal report, allow PAR practitioners to judge whether and to what extent their project is engaging to others. In all these cases, the knowledge gained from an informal report may transfer to other report forms later.

There are several formats for the informal report:

Presenting to *faculty meetings* (McNiff, Lomax, & Whitehead, 1996; Sagor, 1992) is one method in which administrators and teachers can keep their colleagues abreast of their work. A series of reports, increasing in length, can be used to engage faculty in an issue. For instance, communicating with a three- or four-sentence update every few months can set the stage for a 15-minute presentation at the end of the school year. Likewise, a presentation at the conclusion of the school year can set the stage for a half-day workshop the following year if implementation of the project is planned schoolwide.

School district or state-level conferences offer opportunities for the PAR group to discuss the implications of their study for the field of education. Teams may also use these initial local presentations of this type as a stepping-stone to more formal presentations at national conferences. Should the PAR project continue to multiple years, conferences provide the opportunity to meet colleagues who may want to engage in similar and supportive activities.

District or school publications offer opportunities for short explanations of lessons learned and the potential impact on local education. It is important to write even short documentation of the project to the audience for whom it is intended. PAR projects are more easily sustained when they attract stakeholders from a variety of subgroups within a community (Sagor, 1992).

Reporting through *personal contact* may take several forms. McNiff, Lomax, and Whitehead (1996) recommend sending copies of the final report to a variety of educational stakeholders to introduce the study and the results that were obtained. The authors suggest that PAR practitioners offer to come and meet with these stakeholders if there are additional questions. Finally, the practitioners request that the report be passed on to others, as appropriate, and that the PAR team would be available for additional talks. To the extent that the study has impact from the wider perspective of educational leadership, the use of stakeholder networks may prove to be the fastest and most efficient way to broadcast results.

Finally, PAR practitioners may consider speaking to local service clubs or faith-based organizations in the community. Often such groups have an interest in educational issues and may prove to be valuable resources should the PAR team wish to expand their work (McNiff, Lomax, & Whitehead, 1996).

REFLECTIVE QUESTIONS

- When is a celebration more effective than a report of findings?
- What purpose(s) could any of the strategies mentioned here serve in your community and school?

SECTION 4: THE COMMUNITY REPORT

Knowing your audience is critical when the PAR team wants to secure community support. Hubbard and Power (1993) tell a story of a principal who reframed a very modern reading and writing curriculum into "back to basics" language. He reworded the process as "reading from current literature when it was time to read and writing when it was time to write" to ensure that his conservative community embraced the concepts and supported the practices at home (pp. 117–118). This is an example of how appropriate reframing will make the difference between reports to the community being well received or not.

As with informal individual reports, informal PAR group reports disseminate in a variety of venues.

PAR groups may choose to host an event to celebrate their successes and to broadcast proposed next steps while having fun. The team may throw a party, inviting both friends and current or potential strategic allies as well as the students and families who participated. Stakeholders might then have a chance to mingle with the beneficiaries of the project and discover for themselves its relevance.

PAR teams might also choose to contact newspapers or the editors of local newsletters. McNiff, Lomax, and Whitehead (1996) point out that while the newspaper is looking for short, sharp, focused, and topical writing, a newsletter format dictates that articles be relevant to a selected subject and contain practical ideas. Again, by targeting the writing to the specific audience, the group has the opportunity to bring sustainable wide-range support to their PAR project.

While some academic conferences may host poster sessions through which researchers display their work process and outcomes, this strategy is also appropriate for PAR groups in an informal setting (Dana & Yendol-Silva, 2003, p. 145).

CONCLUSION

The report format the PAR group chooses is dependent on the audience they wish to reach and the impact they desire their report to have. This chapter has divided those possibilities into four main types: the formal written report of findings, the formal presentation, the informal individual report, and the community report.

The report of findings has the advantage of being a format that is known to its audience. To the extent that PAR practitioners satisfactorily advance the validity and reliability of their claims using this format, their findings are seen as credible by many types of authority. While rigorous in its structure, the writing of a formal report of findings aids PAR practitioners in understanding the strengths and weaknesses of their project.

The formal presentation allows the PAR group to use the force of their diverse perspectives to add power to the consensus of their findings. Containing much of the material as the formal written report, these presentations focus on no more than three main points. It is recommended that presentation formats should consciously include consideration of the teams' position relative to their audience, any constraints they face, and the emotional impact they strive to achieve.

Informal individual reports can be written or spoken, disseminated as a document or shared in person, and may come before the project is finished as well as when it is completed. A series of small informal reports are advised when PAR practitioners wish the project to obtain wider recognition or support for the issues they study. By updating the stakeholders on the project, it is easier to obtain a longer venue at the end of the project.

This chapter discusses a variety of venues for both informal individual and community reports. Each type of reporting might be considered by PAR teams as methods to obtain recognition for the educational efficacy of the issues they study and sustainable support for worthwhile programs that may develop from these studies. Planning and executing an event to conclude the project offers increased understanding and closure to the PAR team, as well as honoring the participation of the students and families who were involved. PAR research-practitioners advance the local development of educational practices and support other educators and community members to endeavor similar challenges in the future.

CHAPTER 11

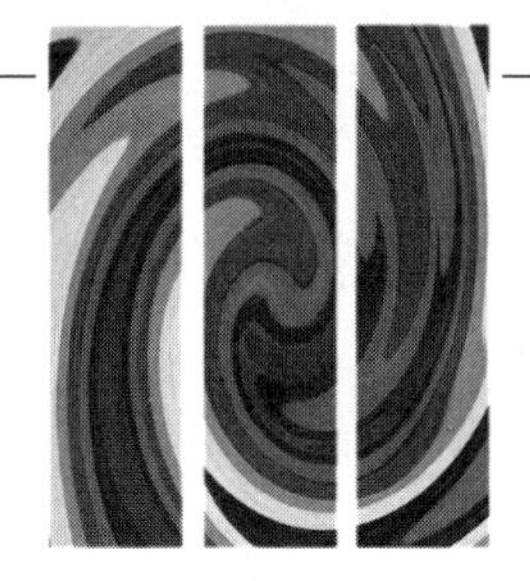

PAR for Educational Leadership

No one knows what public and private schools will look like in 50 years. Educational leaders struggle with issues of home schooling, multilingual education, magnet schools, and online learning as well as ubiquitous test scores or changing financial and demographic patterns. All these issues will play a role in the overall adaptation of education. With each new wave of theories, initiatives, and programs, the complexity of education increases. Formal and informal educational leadership are learning to work together to face the challenges in coordinating these efforts to achieve maximum benefit to students.

After the PAR project is complete and the report is written, educational leadership takes time out to reflect. This is represented in Figure 11.1. Likewise, we conclude this book with a similar reflection on educational leadership and the role of PAR to help facilitate involvement and change.

How to lead through complexity has captured the attention of many writers. Fullan (2001b) sees a series of steps. First, leadership uncovers issues requiring deeply seated situations to change, and then they experience these changes evolving along diverse, seemingly contradictory lines. This moves on to distinctive phases of a change process, each requiring different facilitation skills. Finally, the advice they receive from their administration or other experts often comes in the form of suggestions or guidelines rather than steps to follow.

Other schools experience complexity more in the realm of survival. One elementary school had a fluctuating "average" enrollment of 520 students, sometimes exceeding 580 and in other months dropping below 500 at any given time. During the course of the school year, 30%–40% of a student population would change, resulting in sixth-grade classes of 89 students, where only 15 youth started their education at the school in the fall. Nearly 90% of the school's student population received free/reduced lunch (James, 2006c).

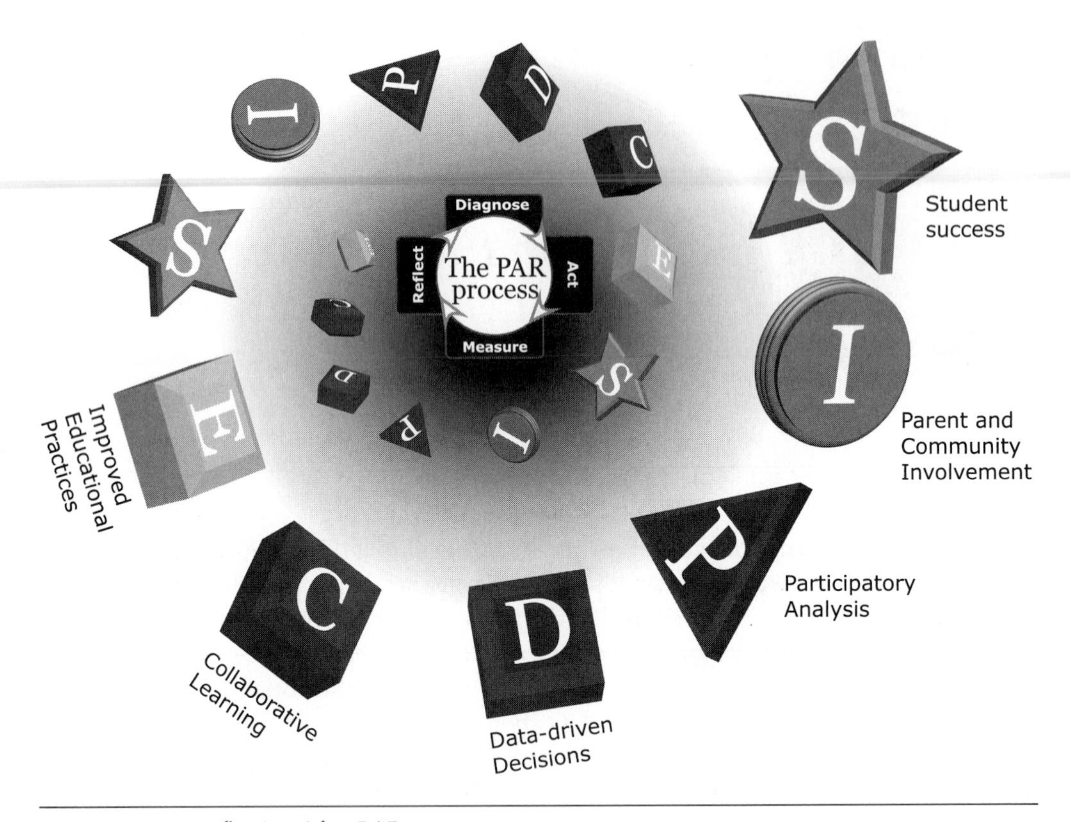

Figure 11.1 Reflecting After PAR

SOURCE: Alan Bucknam/Notchcode Creative, 2005.

Few principals and administrators are strangers to the realms of chaos and complexity. School problems, traumas, and events occur daily in both rural and urban school communities. A working understanding of both the theoretical issues and organizational development that underpin the diverse complicating factors of school operations is essential for educators today to understand and reflect upon.

REFLECTIVE QUESTIONS

- What elements add to the complexity and chaos of the educational setting of which you are most aware?
- What part do formal and informal leadership play in diminishing the tension created by these elements?
- What exacerbates the tensions created?

SECTION 1: A CREATIVE TOOL IN ENVIRONMENTS OF CHAOS AND COMPLEXITY

> An examination of the "new sciences" offers insights into new approaches to school improvement and provides practical methods and ideas for school refinement that can lead to improved learning for all students. The new sciences reveal to us that we live not in a world of either/or but in the dawning of a world of both/and. Chaos and order are part of the same. (Garmston & Wellman, 1995, p. 6)

Complexity science is not a single theory; rather, it is an interdisciplinary approach to consider the question of how systems learn and grow and is viewed as overarching principles that transcend disciplines. Emerging in education, as well as the stock market, business, and the biosphere and ecosystems, complex adaptive systems are diverse and contain multiple interconnected elements that hold the capacity to change and learn from experience (Waldrop, 1992). Issues of complexity explain the experiences of both joy and frustrations inherent in educational leadership.

Traditional leadership approaches to organizational development discuss the difficulties that school and district leadership face as a matter of the size of the school or district in question and how it is organized, rather than as an interplay between constantly changing forces. Chaos and complexity theory requires leadership to focus on small and large issues and the interplay between both types.

Likewise, the traditional use of AR projects relates to professional and curricular development (Elliott, 1991; McKernan, 1996; Stenhouse, 1983; Zuber-Skerritt, 1992). Authors based in organizational development suggest that for coordination of schoolwide or districtwide efforts, the leaders employ strategic planning and increase management to keep systems running smoothly (Stringer, 1999; Tomal, 2005). This idea develops from a mechanistic view of leadership, and most schools are too complex for this strategy to remain successful for a long time. Therefore, what is the role of PAR in long-term educational reform?

Small-scale participatory projects aimed at professional development can be a prime asset in the complex or adaptive leader's toolbox. On an individual level, engagement in a project may inspire educators to improve their practice. Smart leadership links professional development to outcomes they want to achieve. Therefore, we recommend that formal authority suggest a range of project purposes and support PAR teams to investigate changes that synchronize and support the whole improvement effort. In this way, seemingly small, chaotic elements move forward in a steady manner, sustaining locally driven endeavors. Madison, Wisconsin, is an example of a school district that invested in AR for professional development, establishing a culture within the school district that exemplifies "lifelong learning." What is less clear is whether and to what extent the PAR projects are managed to address the complexities within the district.

Counteracting Educator Mobility

Since 1990 Peter Senge railed against the traditional view of leader as hero: the "knight on a white horse" or "general leading the cavalry." Educational leadership literature currently includes several stories of such leaders who have made dramatic short-term impacts. Often when these educational leaders left the positions they held when they became famous, their notable endeavors devolved.

Two of the hundreds of stories to which we could point include Cile Chavez in Littleton, Colorado, who led her school district to embrace performance-based assessment—only to fall quickly and dramatically to the conservative forces within her district as the school board changed. Another similar case on a larger scale is Anthony Alvarado, superintendent of New York City Public School District #2, who worked to build a sustainable learning community in one of the most complex educational settings in the United States. His successors effectively dismantled the innovations built during his leadership.

Similar stories abound at the school level, where a shift of principals is similarly common. Nothing guarantees sustainability during change in leadership, but we believe that a commitment to ongoing PAR projects builds an infrastructure that creates stability through transitions. PAR empowers all participants as they collaborate through the project. Community resources are often embedded in both the process and the outcomes. Both elements lead to the sustainability of the outcomes from PAR projects.

Inclusion: Both/And Rather Than Either/Or

What, then, does complexity science add to the discussion of educational leadership? The study of chaos and complexity in the natural sciences has uncovered many startling results. Two of the most pervasive are the fact that

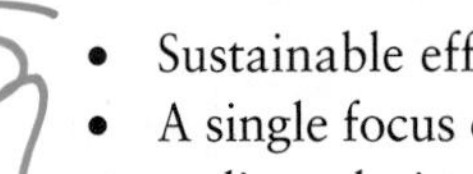

- Sustainable efforts are those with the greatest flexibility.
- A single focus or specialization will experience greater pressures than generalist solutions.

What this means to educational leadership is that flexibility requires leaders to focus on *both* sides rather than one *or* the other (Fullan, 2001a; Garmston & Wellman, 1995). Again, we see the advantage in schools using PAR to focus on building both knowledge and actions, content and purpose, culture of the school, and the outcomes of assessment.

The Need for Flexibility

In the past, schools adjusted to the specific needs of constituencies and the ideals of the societies in which they developed. For instance, the manner in which desks are placed in classrooms strongly resembled the placement of workers in a factory. In some ways, little has changed in education since the early 1900s—especially when compared to the dramatic types of change that have recently occurred within the greater society. Greater flexibility is required to appeal to both a population who travel and who have the vast information resources of the Internet constantly available. Current educational reform efforts aim to help schools become adaptive and flexible as they suddenly compete for students with schools in the private sector, home schooling, and, at times, with other schools in their own districts. Complexity science would applaud these efforts as being adaptive to new environmental stresses while cautioning that specialist answers will fall under the greatest pressures (Garmston & Wellman, 1995).

To be as flexible as needed, wise leaders take care to ask the right questions. Educational systems that have valid and reliable answers to the wrong questions fail; therefore, some authors remind us that the greatest task lies in seeking relevance in the questions rather than in the correctness or validity of the results (Mayer, 2003). In complex situations, it is difficult to know what questions we should be asking. PAR collaborative teams, studying the issues they consider important in schools, offer the leadership of their schools and their districts an additional lens through which to view education. Like five men describing an elephant, each man's perspective contains some truth and some misunderstanding. PAR helps local educational leaders sort out which is which for their own environments.

Prediction: The Study of Outliers

The study of the **outliers**, cases within a sample that may be extreme and aggravate the chaos in a surrounding environment, can assist educators to advance the entire system further. In research, it is important to study the incidents lying outside the main body of evidence. Similarly, when honing leadership skills, it is important to build alliances with individuals whose voices or conduct raise disturbing questions (Creswell, 2003; Heifetz, 2000). Schools are a complex dance between those who currently follow the main thrust of order and the outliers (both teachers and students) who do not follow the norm.

When the teaching staff generally feel that the educational systems are under control, outliers represent no threat and seem to offer diversity, adding a creative spice to the school atmosphere. An example is the creative students who dress and speak outside the norm within an otherwise upper-middle-class school. Within other educational environments, however, outliers may disrupt an already tenuous situation. This typically leads to their marginalization and suppression (Stanton-Salazar, 2001).

Students who are experiencing H&HM may create such a disruption when they enroll midway through the school year. To the extent that they have moved frequently, their assessment scores may vary greatly from their peers. Figure 11.2 graphically displays a school, showing both the diversity and clustering of activity within the main influences of the staff and student populations and the few instances where entirely different forces are at work. Leaders at all levels within complex environments such as this illustration continually need to evaluate the questions presented by individuals on the fringe (Wheatley, 1992, 1999; Zohar & Marshall, 1994). When education best meets the needs of students who face the most rigorous challenges, it increases the educational efficacy of the entire school (Waxman, Gray, & Padron, 2004). Outliers may also indicate the start of an important trend. Imagine how strong the academic potential of a school that created a robust ESL department as immigration emerged in the neighborhood rather than waited until the challenge became overwhelming. Education abounds with examples of school and district leadership that implemented programs for small, growing populations, positioning them for excellence within a few years.

Feedback Loops

The last principle from quantum physics to be discussed in relation to PAR and educational leadership states that all matter is influenced by the act of observation (Garmston & Wellman, 1995). In classrooms, teachers typically use this principle to encourage students to pay attention to details by marking a chart when students behave in an appropriate way. The tension created by being explicitly different from the norm sets up the cognitive dissonance that causes the students' behavior to change. At the school building level, the use of feedback loops increase effective communication and encourage leadership to make appropriate changes (Senge, 1990; Senge et al., 2000). The PAR process naturally sets up communication with its four cycles of diagnosis, action, measurement, and reflection. These feedback loops help the adaptive leader be

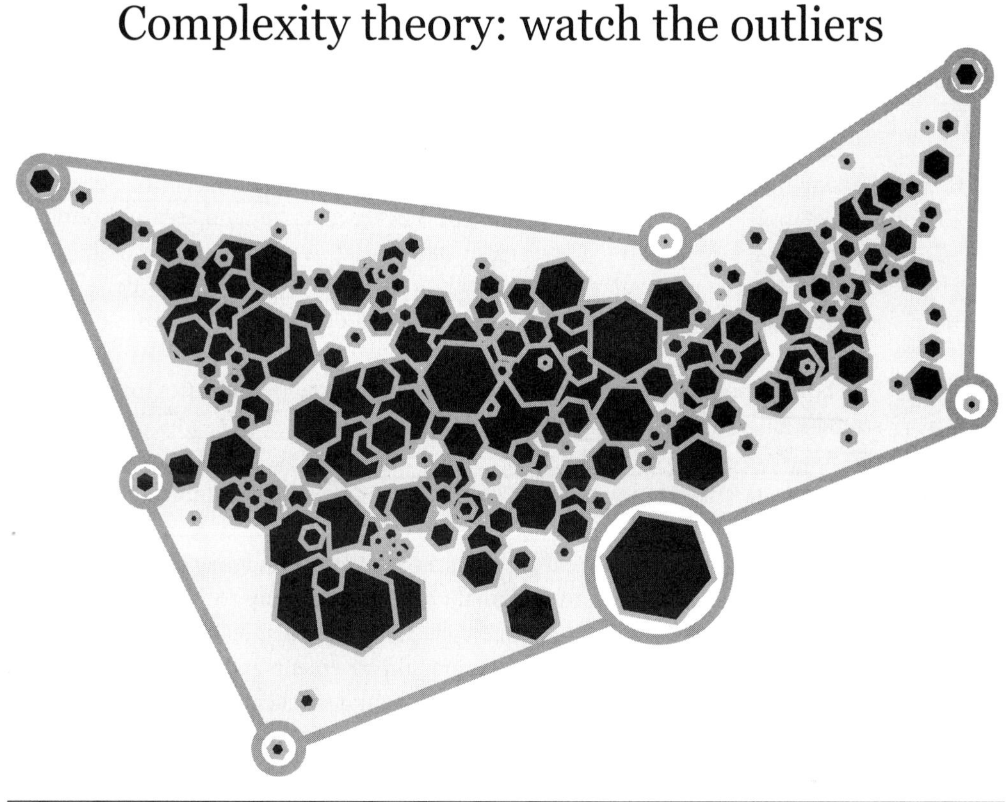

Figure 11.2 Watch the Outliers

SOURCE: Alan Bucknam/Notchcode Creative, 2005.

inclusive, flexible, and predictive. Finally, the PAR process supports the adaptive leader in creating a holding environment to help staff feel secure as they work toward change. As mentioned in Chapter 1, a holding environment is a situation set up by a leader of a group facing a difficult and complex set of issues to diminish discouragement as the team addresses the situation.

REFLECTIVE QUESTIONS

- Reflect on a time when you tried to make a big change in your life. What support systems, including people and processes, were helpful?
- How did you manage the tension created by this change?

SECTION 2: A TOOL FOR ADAPTIVE LEADERSHIP

> Disorder can be a source of order . . . and growth is found in disequilibrium, not in balance. The things we fear most in organizations—fluctuations, disturbances, imbalances—need not be signs of an impending disorder that will destroy us. Instead, fluctuations are the primary source of creativity. . . . The most chaotic of systems never goes beyond certain boundaries; it stays contained within a shape that we can recognize as the system's strange attractor. . . . Throughout the universe, then, order exists within disorder, and disorder within order. (Wheatley, 1992, pp. 20–21)

The role of leadership is to focus the energy of the organization in ways that strategically aid significant growth and change while at the same time keeping the focus on the primary business of learning (Heifetz, 2000; Roberts, 2004; Wheatley, 1999). Adaptive change requires that pressure be administered to keep conscious attention on the difference between the ideal and current reality. To accomplish this intentional effort requires an acknowledgment and consistent interplay between formal and informal types of leadership. A holistic and adaptive approach to educational change calls for principals, teachers, and community members to assume roles in propelling improvements (Chrislip, 2002; Fullan, 2001b). We have heard school administrators and teachers who work with community members state that

> [Using PAR] as a professional development experience—you live it, you don't forget it. Our interaction [is what creates our success]—our team is tight—we raised awareness in school, out of school, and overall interaction. (James, 2006c)

Formal and informal leadership both have a role. Informal leadership has the advantage of keeping a single-minded focus, while formal authority needs to focus on the good of the whole community. Formal authority must remain somewhat conservative to mitigate the needs of the general population. For these reasons, the two types of authority must work together to create sustainable substantive change (Heifetz, 2000). Targeted PAR projects become the foundation of this communication because teamwork on data-driven projects engages people who might not be otherwise involved in adaptive issues (Greenwood & Levin, 1998; James, 2006b).

PAR creates a dramatic rise in engagement with difficult issues and creates opportunities for the teams to become leaders. This became evident during the first cohort of a PAR project when multiple school teams around the state were studying issues concerning H&HM students. Of the 17 participants in that study, 88% (15) became noticeably engaged in the improvement of education for their students by midyear. This contrasts with the experience of school professional development efforts where the faculty appear engaged at the beginning of the year, but by midyear visits, enthusiasm wanes.

The motivation to participate in a PAR learning community as a form of professional development is often *healthy dissatisfaction* with some element of the educational process. Addressing issues that create dissatisfaction challenges educational leadership due to the feelings of unrest and discomfort these concerns engender. When issues are ones that do not have easy answers, due to the complexity of both causes and solutions, people require leadership to invoke a process that will alleviate the pressure to allow them to proceed. Otherwise, they are lost before they begin.

Heifetz (2000) calls an environment that allows people to continue facing the "un-faceable" a holding environment. He describes it as one that supports people through sustained periods of disequilibrium during which individuals confront the contradictions inherent between their values and ideals and the realities they face. The PAR process has proven itself to create such a holding environment for educators studying disadvantage (James, 2005a, 2005b).

Creating a Holding Environment

Introducing PAR as professional development will not guarantee the development of a holding environment. The role of the administration is to support and be engaged in the use of PAR as a portion of a lifelong learning environment until such a time as the process takes on its own momentum and no longer requires this support.

Hargreaves and Fullan (1998) agree with Heifetz that an ideal holding environment maintains a healthy level of distress that people will find motivating, without allowing a high level of discomfort and upheaval. Tension and stress within systems leads to adaptive change; although too much anxiety may lead to rebellion. Too little stress may lead to complacency. Adept school leadership must harmonize risk with feelings of safety for the staff and maintain healthy levels of uncertainty and insecurity. This will deter complacency. At the same time, this skilled facilitation will manage pressures to keep situations from deteriorating into frustration, anxiety, and burnout.

Avoiding Implementation Failure

Facilitating professional development work in public schools draws out stories of curricular or strategic implementations that have failed. Because change efforts fail or run out of support before they become sustainable, trainers frequently hear staff ask, "Why should we believe in your process or curriculum when so many others have come and gone?" How do new implementations avoid failure?

In his book *The Logic of Failure,* Dietrich Dörner (1996) concludes that management in complex situations is prone to several types of error. These errors could be avoided through a network of teams employing PAR to study situations and collectively finding local solutions to the issues. According to Dörner, leadership must first understand the internal dynamics of the issues, which in current school environments translates to a reliance on data to sort out information on how to proceed. As a data-driven effort, PAR's diagnosis and measurement steps support leaders in their review and comprehension.

Second, Dörner (1996) tells us that new implementation must proceed in small steps and each must be measured for the necessary course corrections to be made. Again, the PAR steps help educators do this as they diagnose, act, measure, and reflect in each cycle. Third, the process demands flexibility for both small and big plans, for without the ability to correct the course of a plan, systems will fail. We propose that because PAR provides both the necessary holding environment and multiple avenues for feedback, groups have the ability to highlight potential failure and to suggest course corrections before failure occurs.

REFLECTIVE QUESTIONS

- With what types of educational reform are you familiar?
- How do you judge the relative success of these reform strategies?
- What components of educational leadership do you find the most successful?

SECTION 3: PAR AND EDUCATIONAL REFORM EFFORTS

PAR has long been documented in its efficacy as a tool for professional development (Elliott, 1991; McKernan, 1996; Stenhouse, 1983; Zuber-Skerritt, 1992). Along with the increased attention on professional mastery in the teaching profession, resulting from the implementation of the No Child Left Behind Act of 2001, evolved the understanding of PAR and its value in school improvement and staff development. While Zeichner (2003) reports that few studies have systematically studied both the systems under which the research was conducted and its impact, his findings agree with ours:

- Educators report that they view PAR valuable and transformative.
- They demonstrate increased confidence in the area of study.
- They become more proactive in addressing educational issues.
- Their perception is that educational practices improve and that students benefit from these changes.
- Their enthusiasm increases for their roles in education.

Increased personal and professional capacity can play a part in whether, and to what extent, educators have the skills they need to take up the mantle of leadership they are offered in their roles within schools. These will differ, depending on the type of school reform effort subscribed to within local schools and school districts.

Distributed leadership refers to many recent developments in the field of education that create the awareness that a one- or two-person administration will lack the capacity to lead complex organizations such as schools. Moving away from hierarchical administration, there are many types of distributed leadership. When reviewing their characteristics, Bennett, Wise, and Woods (2003) reported only three consistencies: (1) leadership emerging from some type of group dynamics, (2) leadership having more or less open boundaries and being predisposed to shared responsibilities and/or power, and (3) leadership that is inclusive of as many ideas as possible to create increased flexibility within the organization. Distributed leadership can be found at the core of many ideas in education that align with issues of leading complex adaptive systems such as schools.

Professional Learning Communities and Communities of Practice

Many models exist that focus on collaborative professional learning or "cultures of inquiry" (Earl & Katz, 2006, p. 28). The professional learning community (PLC) model of Rick DuFour and others (Eaker, DuFour, & Burnette, 2002) and communities of practice (CoPs) (Wenger, 1998; Wenger et al., 2002; Wenger & Snyder, 2000) share characteristics with PAR groups. Both are discussed as one central idea with small permutations. Each of the three processes are self-organizing communities demonstrated to benefit participants by increasing professional capacity as well as creating organizational outcomes of merit (Altrichter, 2005; Eaker et al., 2002; Wenger, 1998, 2004). All three models require a cultural shift to be implemented in school environments. Last, leadership is distributed within the teams and throughout the school (Bennett et al., 2003).

Writings from members of PLCs, CoPs, and PAR groups point to a degree of shared identity that develops as the teams mature and their work is successful (Eaker et al., 2002; Wenger & Snyder, 2000; Zeichner, 2003). This is not surprising, for endeavors where members engage in joint activities, help each other and share information, and so on in order to improve their context likely create a pride of ownership that correlates to shared identity. These forms of people working together are not soft. Because of their proven effectiveness in a range of organizational types, these three processes provide participants with a sense of power to bring about change. All have demonstrated, through case study research, their ability to drive strategy, start new ways of doing business, solve problems quickly, transfer best practices, develop professional skills, and help recruit and retain talent (Eaker et al., 2002; James, 2006b; Wenger & Snyder, 2000; Zeichner, 2003).

PLCs, CoPs, and PAR groups share similarities, as they involve acquiring knowledge and orchestrating improvements. The primary difference lies in the context that defines each of the three. For instance, PAR is usually construed as a method of professional development and is implemented for a limited time to study a single issue. PLCs are initiated with the intent to change a school's management structure. PAR also has the highest likelihood of financial incentive for participation (James, 2006a; Zeichner, 2003). CoPs often begin in an ad hoc fashion, and although they may be supported by the official management of the organization, they are similar to PAR as a specific issue or context draws participants together (Wenger, 1998). Both models are dissimilar to PAR, for they are rarely time limited, although CoPs have cycles of growth and disintegration (Eaker et al., 2002). While all three are likely to use data, PAR alone, with its defined steps, has specific levels of requirement for both data collection and analysis and the use of reflection as data.

What Is Required

What should educational leaders who plan to commingle PAR with other forms of distributed leadership keep in mind? The literature suggests three concepts for educational leaders to remember: (1) the management of group dynamics within supportive contexts, (2) the holistic nature of education, and (3) the maintenance of an atmosphere conducive to partnership.

Group dynamics within schools need specific kinds of support and clear leadership. Stevenson (1995) found that successful and transformational AR groups took place *within supportive contexts*. To reach a transformational potential requires supportive school cultures, similar to those attributes described by Eaker and colleagues (2002), who recommend alignment between the words and actions of top administration through the values as described in the mission and vision to the behavior of teachers and staff—all maintained in a consistent and persistent manner. Stevenson (1995) goes on to recommend that private reflections be shared within groups to maintain an ongoing interplay between leadership, values, and culture. Together these create feedback loops of ideas and values between layers within the organization and set up the necessary contexts for transformative work.

The personal aspects of learning also need to be supported within systems that are changing. Basile (2004), in *A Good Little School,* speaks about *the holistic nature of education,* serving and inspiring not only the intellectual but personal issues as well. In order to help students in this manner, schools need to provide personal, social, and professional as well as intellectual stimulation for teachers and staff. Teachers and staff deserve to feel professionally nurtured through training that is meaningful to them and to work in schools free from physical or mental abuse at any level. Noddings (2003) discusses meeting these needs through consciously building home environments in our schools that are supportive of the various needs of both students and adults. By employing an ethic of care, schools are also likely to diminish turnover.

Active inquiry benefits from conscious modeling on the part of school administration (Barell, 2003). Because active learning also requires taking intellectual and social risks, the *atmosphere* needs to be one of *partnering* with each other in inquiry rather than taking a patronizing tone. PAR groups may expand the ways and create possibilities for schools and communities to work together on issues such as parent involvement. Epstein's (2001) work on this subject points out that, given authentic work to aid school improvement, parents can become strong partners in these efforts. A PAR team in Westminster, Colorado, found this to be true when parents came to the aid of creating a safer and more welcoming school environment after their research uncovered specific needs (Clements & Chao, 2004).

The Development of an Inclusive Leadership Structure

Learning networks, combined with formal coaching practices that incorporate the principles of critical AR, may provide the right ingredients for radical and sustained change to occur in practitioners' practices: in schools and in school systems (Robertson, 2004, p. 1).

Robertson's model of coaching, based on Kolb's (1984) adult learning theory, utilizes components very similar to the PAR model discussed here as providing a structure for the development of school leadership. As mentioned earlier in the chapter, our research concludes that PAR is a powerful tool for creating adaptive leadership, aiding schools to stick to the difficult process needed to re-create high-functioning environments when circumstances have eroded those qualities. As a research methodology, it holds the capability to address complex situations. Moreover, as schools are complex institutions, we suggest that the PAR process be taught as a mode of ongoing inquiry and included in teacher education programs, especially when teachers face issues related to educational disadvantage.

Higher education is challenged by the difficult task of preparing teachers for educational settings so diverse that not all potential situations and issues can be covered in classroom discussion. Likewise, as levels of immigration (Camarota, 2001) and technological advances rise, no teacher preparation program today can adequately prepare students for the schools that will evolve in the next decade. In facilitating the use of PAR in the study of homelessness and high mobility, two issues that are the most difficult educational environments, we know of its facility to aid educators who face stresses for which they were unprepared. Rather than continue with a system that, in our experience, consistently results in tenured professionals saying "no one taught us this," we propose that all educators become adept at this methodology. As Young, Petersen, and Short (2001) point out, all stakeholders in the development of new educational leadership need to do what they can to develop ways in which educators develop a mutual and complex understanding of the issues.

CONCLUSION

Educators work in complex environments. Many theorists believe that adaptive behaviors will help sustain school reform efforts. Utilizing PAR to guide the process of small and large-scale projects within schools, educators can develop adaptive environments. Two mind-sets are useful: both/and attitudes (as opposed to either/or) increase flexibility, and outliers carry messages to the whole system that are worth noting.

PAR is in its infancy as an adaptive tool implemented in schools. Nevertheless, it has proven results as a method of professional development and an aid to both formal and informal leadership. Optimally, informal leaders employ PAR to maintain a single focus on an issue while gathering data. Simultaneously, formal authority uses PAR to create an environment that holds tensions down so that adaptive work may move forward. The study of complex systems illustrates how processes such as PAR, which keep information flowing through multiple parts of systems, allow leaders to avoid failure and to implement small, steady steps toward their goals.

Finally, PAR synchronizes well with other school improvement efforts. In environments that are driven by inquiry, it augments professional development, PLCs, CoPs, distributed leadership, and organizational development strategies. For educational leaders at any level, PAR should help them maintain (a) solid group dynamics within supportive contexts, (b) a focus on the holistic nature of education, and (c) an overall atmosphere of partnership within schools and communities.

Glossary

Action research (AR) A multistage type of research designed to yield practical results and capable of improving a specific aspect of practice and made public to enable scrutiny and testing.

Adaptive problems The distance between the real and the ideal is great enough to cause distress in individuals trying to solve the problem.

Bias Influences that distort the results of a research study.

Code A label put on data that summarizes its content or highlights a primary idea. The purpose of coding is to segment sections of data for ease of recall and comparison. Later data are reread, grouped in sections with like or similar codes, and larger theories or understandings emerge.

Cognitive dissonance A condition of conflict or anxiety resulting from inconsistency between one's beliefs and one's actions.

Community of practice A group of people who share a concern, interest, or passion for an issue, topic, or activity. Through regular interaction, the group gains knowledge and skills.

Correlation The strength and direction of the relationship between two variables.

Credible The degree to which the person reading a report thinks the conclusions make sense. This is a subjective

	judgment and requires PAR researchers to be cognizant of their audience and context.
Critical friend	In a 1993 article, Costa and Kallick defined *critical friend* as "a trusted person who asks provocative questions, provides data to be examined through another lens, and offers critique of a person's work as a friend. A critical friend takes the time to fully understand the context of the work presented and the outcomes that the person or group is working toward. The friend is the advocate for the success of that work"(p. 50).
Descriptive statistics	Describe what data demonstrate by providing simple summaries about the sample and the measures. As such they are commonly used by PAR researchers when describing their outcomes to their stakeholders.
Disclaimer	A statement that explains a potential flaw in the findings because of research methodology issues that can be construed to weaken results. Disclaimers allow other researchers to avoid similar problems.
Do no harm	Not to cause injury or damage to an individual; in research, caused by misuse of research subjects, and often related to "informed consent" protocols in educational studies.
Fallacy	An idea that is believed to be truth but is based on erroneous logic or reasoning whereby the conclusion does not follow the premises.
Families	As data are sorted into codes, they are separated from the root document. As PAR researchers reread their data, they focus on one code at a time. This action encourages researchers to see new overarching themes under which the ideas held by codes and memos congregate.
Field notes	Written explanations or data taken, often by multiple observers at a single event, capturing interactions of interest related to the larger topic under study.

Final report A document that researchers develop at the conclusion of a research project that typically includes a summary of the methodology used, a review of the key findings, and conclusions or interpretations of what the findings mean.

Focus group An interview conducted with a small group of people, all at one time, to explore ideas on a particular topic. The goal of a focus group is to uncover additional information through the exchange of participants' ideas.

Formative evaluation Focuses on the process and judges the value of an activity or program while the activity or program is in progress.

Grounded theory Developed originally by Barney Glaser and Anselm Strauss, this systematic methodology uncovers meaning from a systematic analysis of and the generation of theoretical understanding from qualitative data.

Holding environment A situation set up by a leader of a group facing a difficult and complex set of issues in order to diminish discouragement of participants who work together to address the situation.

Inferential statistics Used for looking at a small sample of data from which the PAR researcher draws some conclusions (makes inferences).

Informed consent An agreement between concerned parties related to the data-gathering process and/or the disclosure, reporting, and/or use of data, information, and/or results from a research experiment.

Iteration An instance or the act of doing something again; a core element of PAR.

Ladder of inference A problem-solving strategy in systems thinking used to help understand the development of inferences.

Likert scale A scale on which survey respondents indicate their level of agreement or disagreement with a series of statements. The responses are often scaled and summed to give a composite measure of attitudes about a topic.

Logic model Developed in the 1980s for use in program evaluation, logic models are employed in PAR to help practitioners focus on their purpose and find related literature to solidify their diagnosis of the problem when working through each cycle.

Mean The average score of all the data for one variable. It is determined by dividing the sum of the numbers by the size of the population captured in the data.

Meta-analysis A method designed to increase the reliability of research by combining and analyzing the results of all known trials of the same object or experiments on the same subject.

Observation A research technique in which direct questions are not asked, but individuals in public locations (e.g., shoppers and drivers) are observed and their behavior recorded.

Open code Single words or short phrases that capture the emerging patterns of ideas as researchers repeatedly read qualitative data.

Outliers Cases within a sample that are in some way extreme, often aggravating the chaos in their surrounding environments.

Participatory action research (PAR) A participatory group of equal stakeholders gather, investigate an issue, analyze their data using standard research methodology, take action, measure their results, reflect on their learning, and work to improve their local educational settings.

Participatory research Research conducted in circumstances where diverse practitioners work together to achieve reliable results. In local context, this implies groups of citizens who have an equal say in all the parts of the study.

Population A group of persons who one wants to describe or about which one wants to generalize. To generalize about a population, one often studies a sample that is meant to be representative of the population.

Positivist A theoretical doctrine that denies the validity of any notion of reality that is not measurable.

Purpose statement One or two sentences that convey the motivation behind the PAR project, to help researchers keep focused on the goals of the study.

Qualitative research Data collected as words or pictures and report findings as words. In its most common form, qualitative data quote people as a form of evidence, using the interview, or one of its variants, to gather evidence.

Quantitative research Reports findings as numbers primarily using the survey or questionnaire, with all its variants, to gather evidence.

Random control trial Basically understood as the comparison between two identical or very similar groups of subjects. In the typical random control trial, one group receives an intervention while the other group does not, and the results are compared.

Reflective practice To consciously review one's work on a daily or regular basis to influence future work and action steps.

Reliable The consistency and dependability of the research findings in general to ascertain whether and to what degree the findings would transfer to another context.

Research design The plan to be followed to answer the research objectives; the structure or framework to solve a specific problem or to investigate a particular issue.

Research methods Defined as a series of steps taken to complete a certain task, such as learning the answer to a question or to reach a certain objective, such as finding a solution to a problem or analyzing the effectiveness of a current solution.

Research question The focus of the study, which is stated in an inquiry format.

Review of literature A survey of research already written on a topic. Generally, researchers present the literature review at the beginning of a research paper to support how the researchers arrived at their research questions.

Rubric	Written guidelines that articulate specific standards for how student work is judged.
Sample	A representative selection of a population that is examined to gain statistical information about the whole; a group of subjects selected from a larger group in the hope that studying this smaller group (the sample) will reveal pertinent information about the larger group.
Scale	A group of related measures for a particular variable that can be sorted along a continuum according to some weight or opinion.
Selective coding	The reader starts with specific themes or ideas and subsequently sorts the data by assigning the themes or ideas as codes to the data according to preselected categories.
Semistructured interview	A type of interview when researchers know what the literature says about their topic and map out pertinent questions with possible probing subquestions. Semistructured interviews allow the opportunity to digress from primary question and to probe a response to understand more clearly what is seen as a provocative remark on the part of the interviewee.
Stages of change	As presented in the stages of change model, a change in behavior does not happen in one step. In the process of successful change, people tend to move through different stages and progress at their own rate.
Standard deviation from the mean	A statistic used to characterize the distribution among the measures in a given population.
Statistics	Mathematical tests with the purpose of clarifying the relative position and meaning of data.
Structured interview	Researchers decide upon a series of questions and read this exact selection to establish an understanding of respondents' ideas on a topic.
Summative evaluation	Evaluation focused on determining the overall effectiveness and usefulness of the evaluation object.

Survey An exercise to measure people's opinions on a subject. The survey is not to be confused with the questionnaire. (When people say, "The interviewer did 50 surveys," they generally mean 50 interviews for one survey.)

Tenet A system or code of beliefs upon which solid practice is built. Although similar to values, tenets are defined and subscribed to on an individual basis and are confirmed through increasing capacity.

Trend analysis Measures taken over time as a means of demonstrating growth.

Triangulation Using a variety of research methods to compare diverse sources of data pertaining to a specific research problem or question. This process helps to enhance the validity of results, since the results do not overly rely on any particular method of study.

Unstructured interview Starts with general ideas or areas of concern. The specific questions asked are likely to change depending on the subject's responses and interests. Unstructured questions may be open-ended, such as, "Tell us about your experience of this topic."

Valid The degree to which data and results are accurate reflections of reality. Validity refers to the concepts that are investigated, the people or objects that are studied, the methods by which data are collected, and the findings that are produced.

Variable An attribute or characteristic of a person or an object that varies within the population under investigation (e.g., age, weight, IQ, test scores, attendance).

References

Allers, D. (2004). *The use of extrinsic motivators to increase English output in the ELL classroom.* Retrieved July 5, 2006, from http://www.madison.k12.wi.us/sod/car/abstracts/4.pdf

Altrichter, H. (2005). The role of the professional community in action research. *Educational Action Research, 13*(1), 11–26.

Anderson, G. L., Herr, K., & Nihlen, A. S. (1994). *Studying your own school: An educator's guide to qualitative practitioner research.* Thousand Oaks, CA: Corwin Press.

Angelides, P., Evangelou, M., & Leigh, J. (2005). Implementing a collaborative model of action research for teacher development. *Educational Action Research, 13*(2), 275–290.

Argyris, C., Putnam, R., & Smith, D. M. (1985). *Action science.* San Francisco: Jossey-Bass.

Argyris, C., & Schön, D. A. (1974). *Theory in practice: Increasing professional effectiveness.* San Francisco: Jossey-Bass.

Bagin, C. B., & Rudner, L. M. (1994, February). *What should parents know about standardized testing in schools?* Retrieved July 6, 2006, from http://www.kidsource.com/kidsource/content/standardized.testing.html

Baker, K. (1997). To study learning, study learning. *Phi Delta Kappan, 79*(3), 246–248.

Barell, J. (2003). *Developing more curious minds.* Alexandria, VA: Association for Supervision and Curriculum Development.

Basile, C. (2004). *A good little school.* Albany: State University of New York.

Bassoff, T. C. (2004). How can I improve reading achievement among my highly mobile and homeless fifth grade student population? In *Colorado educators study homeless and highly mobile students* (pp. 83–97). Retrieved December 1, 2006, from http://www.crsllc.org/pdfs/COPAR%20Book%20Final.pdf

Bennett, N., Wise, C., & Woods, P. (2003). *Distributed leadership.* Retrieved August 11, 2006, from http://www.ncsl.org.uk/media/3C4/A2/distributed-leadership-literature-review.pdf

Bernhardt, V. (2004). *Data analysis for continuous school improvement* (2nd ed.). Larchmont, NY: Eye on Education.

Blakley-Reid, A. (2001). Action research: The alchemy of change. *Adult Learning, 11*(3), 25–26.

Blessing, B. (1996). *Writing workshop: An outlet for success.* Retrieved July 20, 2006, from http://www.madison.k12.wi.us/sod/car/abstracts.htm#Blessing

Booth, W. C., Colomb, G. G., & Williams, J. M. (2003). *The craft of research.* Chicago: University of Chicago Press.

Bransford, J. D., National Research Council (U.S.), Committee on Developments in the Science of Learning, & National Research Council (U.S.), Committee on Learning Research and Educational Practice. (2000). *How people learn: Brain, mind, experience, and school* (Expanded ed.). Washington, DC: National Academy Press.

Brause, R. S. (2000). *Writing your doctoral dissertation.* London: Routledge Falmer.

Braxton, J., & Caboni, T. (2005). Using student norms to create positive learning environments. *About Campus, 9*(6), 2–7.

Bray, J. N., Lee, J., Smith, L. L., & Yorks, L. (2000). *Collaborative inquiry in practice: Action, reflection, and making meaning.* Thousand Oaks, CA: Sage.

Brodhagen, B. (1994). *Assessing and reporting student progress in an integrative curriculum.* Retrieved July 20, 2006, from http://www.madison.k12.wi.us/sod/car/abstracts.htm#Brodhagen

Bucknam, A. (2005). *Drawings for web-based professional development.* Denver, CO: Center for Research Strategies and the Colorado Department of Education. Retrieved July 1, 2006, from http://wbpd.org

Byrne-Armstrong, H., Higgs, J., & Horsfall, D. (Eds.). (2001). *Critical moments in qualitative research.* Boston: Butterworth-Heinemann.

Calhoun, E. (1994). *How to use action research in the self-renewing school.* Alexandria, VA: Association for Supervision and Curriculum Development.

Camarota, S. A. (2001). *Census releases immigrant numbers for year 2000: Analysis by CIS finds size, growth unprecedented in American history.* Washington, DC: Center for Immigration Studies.

Caro-Bruce, C. (2000). *Action research facilitator's handbook.* Oxford, OH: National Staff Development Council.

Caro-Bruce, C., & Zeichner, K. (1998). *The nature and impact of an action research professional development program in one urban school district.* Retrieved July 22, 2006, from http://www.madison.k12.wi.us/sod/car/descriptors.htm#BEHAVIOR_CLASSROOM_MANAGEMENT

Chrislip, D. D. (2002). *The collaborative leadership fieldbook: A guide for citizens and civic leaders.* San Francisco: Jossey-Bass.

Clements, D., & Chao, R. (2004). Studying homeless and highly mobile students at Westminister Elementary School: Raising awareness and building relationships. *COPAR reports.* Retrieved July 21, 2006, from http://www.crsllc.org/resources/html

Coghlan, D., & Brannick, T. (2001). *Doing action research in your own organization.* London: Sage.

Coghlan, D., & Brannick, T. (2005). *Doing action research in your own organization* (2nd ed.). London: Sage.

Coghlan, D., & Coughlan, P. (2003). Acquiring the capacity for operational improvement: An action research opportunity. *Journal of the Human Resource Planning Society, 26*(2), 30–38.

Cook, D., Heintzman, L., & McVicker, J. (2004). Three elementary schools' experiences with access to services, welcoming culture and thoughtful placement of students. In E. A. James & M. Milenkiewicz (Eds.), *Colorado educators study homeless and highly mobile students* (pp. 53–62). Denver, CO: Center for Research Strategies.

Costa, A. L., & Kallick, B. (1993). Through the lens of a critical friend. *Educational Leadership, 51*(2), 49–51.

Creswell, J. W. (2002). *Educational research: Planning, conducting, and evaluating quantitative and qualitative research.* London: Pearson Education.

Creswell, J. W. (2003). *Research design: Qualitative, quantitative, and mixed method approaches* (2nd ed.). Thousand Oaks, CA: Sage.

Dana, N. F., & Yendol-Silva, D. (2003). *The reflective educator's guide to classroom research.* Thousand Oaks, CA: Corwin Press.

Dick, B. (1998a, September). *Action research and evaluation.* Paper presented at the Innovations in Evaluation and Program Development online conference.

Dick, B. (1998b). *Cycles within cycles: Occasional pieces in action research methodology, #8.* Retrieved July 23, 2006, from http://www.scu.edu.au/schools/gcm/ar/arm/op008.html

Dörner, D. (1996). *The logic of failure.* Cambridge, MA: Perseus Books.

Eaker, R., DuFour, R., & Burnette, R. (2002). *Getting started: Reculturing schools to become professional learning communities.* Bloomington, IN: National Education Service.

Earl, L., & Katz, S. (2006). *Leading schools in a data-rich world.* Thousand Oaks, CA: Corwin Press.

Early, M. (2001). Language and content in social practice: A case study. *Canadian Modern Language Review, 58*(1), 156–179.

Ecord, E. (2006). *Ongoing reports of community teams studying the education of homeless children and youth.* WBPD report. Retrieved October 2006, from http://www.crsllc.org/resources.html

Elliott, J. (1991). *Action research for educational change.* Milton Keynes, UK: Open University Press.

Encarta Dictionary. (n.d.). Emancipation. Retrieved from http://encarta.msn.com/dictionary_/emancipation.html

Epstein, J. L. (2001). *School, family, and community partnerships: Preparing educators, and improving schools.* Boulder, CO: Westview Press.

Essex, M. (1967). *New concepts in teacher utilization.* Columbus: Ohio State Department of Education.

Fiester, L. (2001). *Putting the pieces together: Comprehensive school-linked strategies for children and families.* Retrieved July 21, 2006, from http://www.nwrel.org/cfc/frc/ncrel/putting.htm

Fitz-Gibbon, C. T., & Morris, L. L. (1987). *How to design a program evaluation* (2nd ed.). Newbury Park, CA: Sage.

Fowler, F. J. (2002). *Survey research methods.* Thousand Oaks, CA: Sage.

Francis, D. J., Rivera, M., Leseaux, N., Kieffer, M., & Rivera, H. (2006). *Practical guidelines for the education of English Language Learners: Research-based recommendations for instruction and academic interventions.* Retrieved November 7, 2006, from http://www.centeroninstruction.org/files/ELL1-Interventions.pdf

Freire, P. (1986). *Pedagogy of the oppressed.* New York: Continuum.

Freire, P. (1993). *Pedagogy of the oppressed* (Rev. ed.). New York: Continuum.

Fullan, M. (2001a). *Leading in a culture of change.* San Francisco: Jossey-Bass.

Fullan, M. (2001b). *The new meaning of educational change* (3rd ed.). New York: Teachers College Press.

Garmston, R., & Wellman, B. (1992). *How to make presentations that teach and transform.* Alexandria, VA: Association for Supervision and Curriculum Development.

Garmston, R., & Wellman, B. (1995). Adaptive schools in a quantum universe [Electronic version]. *Educational Leadership, 52,* 6–12. Retrieved July 15, 2006, from http://www.eric.ed.gov/sitemap/html_0900000b8003f7b3.html

Garson, G. D. (2002). *Guide to writing empirical papers, theses, and dissertations.* New York: Marcel Dekker.

Gladwell, M. (2002). *The tipping point: How little things can make a big difference.* Boston: Back Bay Books.

Glanz, J. (2003). *Action research: An educational leader's guide to school improvement* (2nd ed.). Norwood, MA: Christopher-Gordon.

Gorard, S. (2003). *Quantitative methods in social science.* New York: Continuum.

Goree, K., Pyle, M. D., Baker, E., & Hopkins, J. V. (Eds.). (2004). *Ethics applied* (4th ed.). Boston: Pearson.

Gough, A., & Sharpley, B. (2005). Toward effective teaching and learning: Stories of primary schools' environmental science interest and action. *Educational Action Research, 13*(2), 191–209.

Greenwood, D. J., & Levin, M. (1998). *Introduction to action research: Social research for social change.* Thousand Oaks, CA: Sage.

Hand, D. (2002). Elementary statistics. In T. Greenfield (Ed.), *Research methods for postgraduates* (2nd ed., pp. 239–252). London: Arnold.

Hargreaves, A., & Fullan, M. (1998). *What's worth fighting for out there?* New York: Teachers College Press.

Hart, C. (1998). *Doing a literature review: Releasing social science research imagination.* Thousand Oaks, CA: Sage.

Harvey, S., & Goudvis, A. (2000). *Strategies that work: Teaching comprehensively to enhance understanding.* York, ME: Stenhouse.

Heifetz, R. A. (2000). *Leadership without easy answers* (2nd ed.). Cambridge, MA: Harvard University, Belnap Press.

Heifetz, R. A., Kania, J. V., & Kramer, M. R. (2005). The dilemma of foundation leadership. Retrieved July 15, 2006, from http://www.cambridge-leadership.com/publications/pdfs/FoundationLeadership.pdf

Herman, J. L., Morris, L. L., & Fitz-Gibbon, C. T. (1987). *Evaluator's handbook*. Newbury Park, CA: Sage.

Herr, K., & Anderson, G. L. (2005). *The action research dissertation*. Thousand Oaks, CA: Sage.

Higgs, J. (2001). Charting standpoints in qualitative research. In H. Byrne-Armstrong, J. Higgs, & D. Horsfall (Eds.), *Critical moments in qualitative research* (pp. 44–67). Thousand Oaks, CA: Corwin Press.

Hollingsworth, S. (Ed.). (1997). *International action research*. London: Falmer Press.

Houghton, S. (2003). *Barnsley education development plan: 2003–2007*. Retrieved July 20, 2006, from http://www.barnsley.gov.uk/Documents/InformationPerformanceandFinance/Education%20-%20Policies,%20Plans%20and%20Service%20Information/edp-2003-2007.pdf

Hoyle, R. H., Harris, M. J., & Judd, C. M. (2002). *Research methods in social relations* (7th ed.). Fort Worth, TX: Wadsworth.

Hubbard, R. S., & Power, B. M. (1993). *The art of classroom inquiry*. Portsmouth, NH: Heinemann.

Hughes, I., & William, R. (2001). *Planning your action research project*. Retrieved July 24, 2006, from http://www2.fhs.usyd.edu.au/arow/o/m01/reader.htm

Jackson, S. L. (2003). *Research methods and statistics: A critical thinking approach*. Belmont, CA: Thomson Wadsworth.

James, E. A. (2004). Unpublished data from CO PAR educators. Denver, CO: Center for Research Strategies.

James, E. A. (2005a). Prospects for the future: Use of participatory action research to study issues of educational disadvantage. *Journal of Irish Educational Research, 24*(2–3), 199–206.

James, E. A. (2005b). *The use of participatory action research to create new educational practices for homeless and highly mobile students*. Unpublished dissertation, Teachers College, Columbia University, New York.

James, E. A. (2006a, September). *Implementing a national program for educators to use PAR to study disadvantage: What works?* Paper presented at the ECER 2006, Geneva, Switzerland.

James, E. A. (2006b). A study of PAR for educators developing new practise in areas of educational disadvantage. *Educational Action Research, 14*(4) 525–534.

James, E. A. (2006c). Unpublished data from WBPD.1. Denver, CO: National Center for School Engagement.

Kalinosky, K. (1997). Action research and learner participation in a homeless shelter. *New Directions for Adult and Continuing Education, 73*, 52–55.

Keene, E. O., & Zimmermann, S. (1997). *Mosaic of thought*. Portsmouth, NH: Heinemann.

Kemmis, S., & McTaggart, R. (1988). *The action research planner* (3rd ed.). Geelong, Australia: Deakin University.

Kemmis, S., & McTaggart, R. (Eds.). (1990). *The action research reader*. Victoria, Australia: Deakin University.

Kent, R. (2001). *Data construction and data analysis for survey research*. New York: Palgrave.

Kock, N. F., Jr., McQueen, R. J., & Scott, J. L. (1997). *Can action research be made more rigorous in a positivist sense? The contribution of an iterative approach.* Retrieved July 24, 2006, from http://www.scu.edu.au/schools/gcm/ar/arr/arow/kms.html

Kolb, D. A. (1984). *Experiential learning: Experience as the source of learning and development.* Englewood Cliffs, NJ: Prentice-Hall.

Kurosawa, A. (Director). (1950). *Rashomon* [Motion picture]. Japan: Daiei Studios.

Leedy, P. D., & Ormrod, J. E. (2005). *Practical research: Planning and design* (8th ed.). Upper Saddle River, NJ: Pearson.

Legard, R., Keegan, J., & Ward, K. (2003). In-depth interviews. In J. Richie & J. Lewis (Eds.), *Qualitative research practice* (pp. 138–169). Thousand Oaks, CA: Sage.

Levy, P. (2002a). Graphical presentation. In T. Greenfield (Ed.), *Research methods for postgraduates* (pp. 334–352). London: Arnold.

Levy, P. (2002b). Presenting your research: Reports and talks. In T. Greenfield (Ed.), *Research methods for postgraduates* (pp. 317–333). London: Arnold.

Lewin, K. (1951). *Field theory in social science.* New York: Harper & Row.

Lewis, J. (2003). Design issues. In J. Richie & J. Lewis (Eds.), *Qualitative research practice* (pp. 47–76). Thousand Oaks, CA: Sage.

Lewis, J., & Ritchie, J. (2003). Generalizing from qualitative research. In J. Ritchie & J. Lewis (Eds.), *Qualitative research practice* (pp. 263–286). Thousand Oaks, CA: Sage.

Lexico Publishing. (2006). Assumption. Retrieved from Dictionary.com.

Loerke, K., & Oberg, D. (1997). Working together to improve junior high research instruction: An action research approach. *School Libraries Worldwide, 3*(2), 56–67.

Lohner, R. M. (2006). *Summary of the movie* Rashômon. Retrieved November 11, 2006, from http://www.imdb.com/title/tt0042876/plotsummary

Lopez, G. R., & Mapp, K. L. (2002). *On whose terms? Understanding involvement through the eyes of migrant parents.* Available from National Center for Family and Community Connections With Schools, Southwest Educational Development Laboratory, 211 East 7th St., Austin, TX 78701-3281.

Maxwell, J. A. (1996). *Qualitative research design: An interactive approach* (Vol. 41). Thousand Oaks, CA: Sage.

Mayer, M. (2003). Living at the border between multiculturality, complexity and action research. *Educational Action Research, 11*(2), 213–231.

McKay, J. (1992, Winter). Professional development through action research. *Journal of Staff Development,* 28–31.

McKernan, J. (1996). *Curriculum action research: A handbook of methods and resources for the reflective practitioner* (2nd ed.). London: Kogan Page.

McNiff, J. (1993). *Teaching as learning: An action research approach.* New York: Routledge.

McNiff, J., Lomax, P., & Whitehead, J. (1996). *You and your action-research project.* London: Routledge.

McTaggart, R. (1989, September). *Sixteen tenets of participatory action research.* Paper presented at the 3er Encuentro Mundial Investigacion Participatva (The Third World Encounter on Participatory Research), Managua, Nicaragua.

McTaggart, R. (1997). *Participatory action research: International contexts and consequences.* Albany: State University of New York Press.

Mills, G. E. (2003). *Action research: A guide for the teacher researcher.* Columbus, OH: Merrill Prentice Hall.

National Institutes of Health. (1979). *Ethical principles and guidelines for the protection of human subjects of research.* Retrieved June 1, 2006, from http://www.hhs.gov/ohrp/humansubjects/guidance/belmont.htm

Nelson, S. L. (2002). *Excel data analysis for dummies.* Hoboken, NJ: Wiley.

Noddings, N. (2003). *Happiness and education.* Cambridge, UK: Cambridge University Press.

Noffke, S. E., & Brennan, M. (1997). Reconstructing the politics of action in action research. In S. Hollingsworth (Ed.), *International action research: A casebook for educational reform* (pp. 63–69). London: Falmer.

Noffke, S. E., & Stevenson, R. B. (Eds.). (1995). *Education action research: Becoming practically critical.* New York: Teachers College Press.

O'Kelly, D. (2006, July). *Creating and performing your own material.* Paper presented at the Kinsale Arts Festival, Municipal Hall, Kinsale, County Cork, Ireland.

Patton, M. Q., & Patton, M. Q. (2002). *Qualitative research and evaluation methods* (3rd ed.). Thousand Oaks, CA: Sage.

Payne, R. K., & Evans, C. A. (1995). *A framework: Understanding and working with students and adults from poverty* (Rev. ed.). Baytown, TX: RFT.

Pflug, R., & Watson, P. (2004). Planning for the impact of high mobility. In E. A. James & M. Milenkiewicz (Eds.), *Colorado educators study homeless and highly mobile students* (pp. 23–38). Denver: Colorado Department of Education, Center for Research Strategies.

Piantanida, M., & Garman, N. B. (1999). *The qualitative dissertation: A guide for students and faculty.* Thousand Oaks, CA: Corwin Press.

Prochaska, J. O., Norcross, J. C., & DiClemente, C. C. (1994). *Changing for good: The revolutionary program that explains the six stages of change and teaches you how to free yourself from bad habits.* New York: W. Morrow.

Rabenstine, A. (2002). *Bully-proofing our school.* Retrieved July 22, 2006, from http://www.madison.k12.wi.us/sod/car/descriptors.htm#BEHAVIOR_CLASSROOM_MANAGEMENT

Rahn, J., & Skrobela, J. (2004). To what extent are we meeting the needs of highly mobile students? In E. A. James & M. Milenkiewicz (Eds.), *Colorado educators study homeless and highly mobile students* (pp. 127–139). Denver: Colorado Department of Education, Center for Research Strategies.

Ramsey, F. L., & Schafer, D. W. (2002). *Statistical sleuth.* Pacific Grove, CA: Duxbury.

Reverby, S. M. (Ed.). (2000). *Tuskegee's truths: Rethinking the Tuskegee Syphilis Study.* Chapel Hill: University of North Carolina Press.

Reynolds, J. (2005). *CO PAR paper.* Denver: Colorado Department of Education, Center for Research Strategies.

Ritchie, J. (2003). The applications of qualitative methods to social research. In J. Richie & J. Lewis (Eds.), *Qualitative research practice: A guide for social science students and researchers* (pp. 24–46). Thousand Oaks, CA: Sage.

Roberts, C. M. (2004). *The dissertation journey.* Thousand Oaks, CA: Corwin Press.

Robertson, J. M. (2004). Coaching in learning networks. *NLG International Perspectives, 2*, 39–46. Retrieved August 11, 2006, from http://www.ncsl.org.uk/mediastore/image2/nlg/nlg_IPNL_7.pdf

Rosas, L. O. (1997). Using participatory action research for the reconceptualization of educational practice. In S. Hollingsworth (Ed.), *International action research: A casebook for educational reform* (pp. 219–224). London: Falmer.

Rudestam, K. E., & Newton, R. R. (2001). *Surviving your dissertation: A comprehensive guide to content and process* (2nd ed.). Thousand Oaks, CA: Sage.

Sagor, R. (1992). *How to conduct collaborative action research.* Alexandria, VA: Association for Supervision and Curriculum Development.

Sagor, R. (2000). *Guiding school improvement with action research.* Alexandria, VA: Association for Supervision and Curriculum Development.

Sagor, R. (2005). *The action research guidebook: A four-step process for educators and school teams.* Thousand Oaks, CA: Corwin Press.

Saurino, D. R., Crawford, L. W., Cornelius, C. C., Dillard, V., McSwain, M. G., Murray, M. S., et al. (1996, October & November). *Teacher team collaborative action research as staff development.* Paper presented at the 23rd Annual Meeting of the National Middle School Association, Baltimore.

Schön, D. A. (1983). *The reflective practitioner: How professionals think in action.* New York: Basic Books.

Schostak, J. F. (2002). *Understanding, designing, and conducting qualitative research in education.* Buckingham, UK: Open University Press.

Senge, P. M. (1990). *The fifth discipline: The art and practice of the learning organization.* New York: Doubleday/Currency.

Senge, P. M. (1994). *The fifth discipline fieldbook: Strategies and tools for building a learning organization.* New York: Doubleday/Currency.

Senge, P. M., Cambron-McCabe, N., Lucas, T., Smith, B., Dutton, J., & Kleiner, A. (2000). *Schools that learn.* New York: Doubleday.

Sergiovanni, T. J. (1994). *Building community in schools.* San Francisco: Wiley.

Shapiro, N. S., & Levine, J. H. (1999). *Creating learning communities: A practical guide to winning support, organizing for change, and implementing programs.* San Francisco: Jossey-Bass.

Smith, S. E., Willms, D. G., & Johnson, N. A. (Eds.). (1997). *Nurtured by knowledge: Learning to do participatory action-research.* New York: Apex Press.

Snape, D., & Spencer, L. (2003). The foundations of qualitative research. In J. Ritchie & J. Lewis (Eds.), *Qualitative research practice* (pp. 1–23). Thousand Oaks, CA: Sage.

Soffer, E. (1995). The principal as action researcher. In S. E. Noffke & R. B. Stevenson (Eds.), *Educational action research: Becoming practically critical* (pp. 115–126). New York: Teachers College Press.

Sommers, C., & Sommers, F. (Eds.). (2004). *Vice and virtue in everyday life.* Belmont, CA: Thomson Wadsworth.

Spencer, L., Ritchie, J., & O'Connor, W. (2003). Analysis: Practices, principles and processes. In J. Richie & J. Lewis (Eds.), *Qualitative research practice: A guide for social science students and researchers* (pp. 199–218). Thousand Oaks, CA: Sage.

Stanton-Salazar, R. D. (2001). Defensive network orientations as internalized oppression: How schools mediate the influence of social class on adolescent development. In B. Biddle (Ed.), *Social class, poverty, and education: Policy and practice* (pp. 101–131). New York: Routledge Falmer.

Stecher, B. M., Davis, W. A., & Morris, L. L. (1987). *How to focus an evaluation.* Newbury Park, CA: Sage.

Stenhouse, L. (1983). *Authority, education, and emancipation.* London: Heinemann.

Stevenson, R. B. (1995). Action research and supportive school contexts: Exploring the possibility for transformation. In S. E. Noffke & R. B. Stevenson (Eds.), *Educational action research: Becoming practically critical* (pp. 197–210). New York: Teachers College Press.

Strauss, A., & Corbin, J. (1998). *Basics of qualitative research: Techniques and procedures for developing grounded theory* (2nd ed.). Thousand Oaks, CA: Sage.

Stringer, E. T. (1999). *Action research* (2nd ed.). Thousand Oaks, CA: Sage.

Stringer, E. T. (2004). *Action research in education.* Upper Saddle River, NJ: Pearson/Merrill/Prentice Hall.

Sumara, D., & Carson, T. (1997). Reconceptualizing action research as a living practice. In D. Sumara & T. Carson (Eds.), *Action research as a living practice* (Vol. 67, pp. xiii–xxxii). New York: Peter Lang.

Thomas, R. M. (2003). *Blending qualitative and quantitative research methods in theses and dissertations.* Thousand Oaks, CA: Corwin Press.

Timmerman, M. A. (2003). Perceptions of professional growth: A mathematics teacher educator in transition. *School Science and Mathematics, 103*(3), 155–167.

Tomal, D. R. (2005). *Action research for educators.* Lanham, MD: Rowman & Littlefield Education.

U.S. Department of Health and Human Services. (2005). *Code of federal regulations: Title part 46, Protection of human subjects* (Rev. ed.). Retrieved July 15, 2006, from http://www.hhs.gov/ohrp/humansubjects/guidance/45cfr46.htm

Valentine, T. (1997). Understanding quantitative research about adult literacy [Electronic version]. *Focus on Basics: Connecting Research to Practice, 1.* Retrieved July 6, 2006, from http://www.ncsall.net/?id=470

Waldrop, M. M. (1992). *Complexity: The emerging science at the edge of order and chaos.* New York: Simon & Schuster.

Wampold, B. E., Ahn, H.-N., & Kim, D.-M. (2000). Meta-analysis in the social sciences: A useful way to make sense of a series of findings from a large number of studies. *Asia Pacific Education Review, 1*(1), 67–74.

Watling, R. (2002). The analysis of qualitative data. In M. Coleman & A. R. Briggs (Eds.), *Research methods in educational management and leadership* (pp. 262–278). London: Paul Chapman.

Watson-Peterson, M. (2000). *A principal's role in supporting elementary team planning.* Retrieved July 22, 2006, from http://www.madison.k12.wi.us/sod/car/descriptors.htm#BEHAVIOR_CLASSROOM_MANAGEMENT

Waxman, H., Gray, J. P., & Padron, Y. N. (2004). Promoting educational resilience for students at-risk of failure. In H. Waxman, Y. N. Padron, & J. P. Gray (Eds.),

Educational resiliency: Student, teacher and school perspectives (pp. 37–62). Greenwich, CT: Information Age.

Wenger, E. (1998). *Communities of practice: Learning, meaning, and identity.* Cambridge, UK: Cambridge University Press.

Wenger, E. (2004). *Communities of practice: A brief introduction.* Retrieved May 7, 2005, from http://www.ewenger.com/theory/communities_of_practice_intro.htm

Wenger, E., McDermott, R. A., & Snyder, W. (2002). *Cultivating communities of practice: A guide to managing knowledge.* Boston: Harvard Business School Press.

Wenger, E., & Snyder, W. (2000, January–February). Communities of practice: The organizational frontier. *Harvard Business Review*, pp. 139–145.

Wheatley, M. J. (1992). *Leadership and the new science: Learning about organization from an orderly universe.* San Francisco: Berrett-Koehler.

Wheatley, M. J. (1999). *Leadership and the new science: Discovering order in a chaotic world* (2nd ed.). San Francisco: Berrett-Koehler.

Whitehead, J., & McNiff, J. (2006). *Action research: Living theory.* London: Sage.

Wolk, E. (2001). *Pio Pico Student Researchers participatory action research: From classroom to community: Transforming teaching and learning* [Electronic version]. Retrieved July 21, 2006, from http://www.goingpublicwithteaching.org/ewolk/

Woolhouse, M. (2005). You can't do it on your own: Gardening as an analogy for personal learning from a collaborative action research group. *Educational Action Research, 13*(1), 27–42.

World Bank Participation Sourcebook. (1996). *Participation in the education and training sector.* Retrieved July 22, 2006, from http://www.worldbank.org/wbi/sourcebook/sba207.htm#F

Young, M., Petersen, G., & Short, P. (2001). *The complexity of substantive reform: A call for interdependence among key stakeholders.* Paper presented at the Meeting of the National Commission for the Advancement of Educational Leadership Preparation, Racine, WI, September 19–21.

Zeichner, K. (2003). Teacher research as professional development for P–12 educators in the USA. *Educational Action Research, 11*(2), 301–326.

Zenisky, A. L., Keller, L. A., & Sireci, G. (2004). A basic primer for understanding standardized tests and using test scores [Electronic version]. *Adventures in Assessment, 16.* Retrieved July 6, 2006, from http://www.sabes.org/resources/adventures/v0116/16zenisky.htm

Zohar, D., & Marshall, I. (1994). *The quantum society: Mind, physics, and a new social vision.* New York: Quill, William Morrow.

Zuber-Skerritt, O. (1992). *Professional development in higher education: A theoretical framework for action research.* London: Kogan Page.

Index

About the Authors

E. Alana James, MNM, EdD, is the associate chairperson of the Jones International University (JIU) EdD program. She has worked in education for two decades, often using community-based resources to aid educational activities in developing programs for high-risk youth. She serves as coordinator of professional development for the School of Education at JIU, where she provokes substantive conversation about the similarities and differences of teaching online rather than in a face-to-face venue. She designed and serves as the primary facilitator for the Web-Based Professional Development (WBPD) project, sponsored by the National Center for School Engagement. Participants in this project are school administrators, teachers, and community members using participatory action research as professional development to study and develop programs for students experiencing homelessness and high mobility. Originating during 2003 from a face-to-face participatory action research environment in Colorado with 18 educators, the WBPD project evolved into a blended but primarily online activity that serves educators across the United States. To date, project this project has included 90 participants in 34 communities in eight states across the United States. She completed her doctoral work at Teachers College, Columbia University, in educational leadership.

Margaret T. Milenkiewicz is an educational consultant working in Ireland and in the United States. Her work centers on professional development for educators and on the furthering of community and school partnerships to benefit the highest risk students. During the 2003–2004 school year, in partnership with a private foundation while working for the Colorado Department of Education, her office sponsored participatory action research for the development of educational practices for homeless and highly mobile students. She authored multiple publications and presented at numerous national and state conferences on the development of programs for students experiencing homelessness.

Alan Bucknam, AIGA, is the owner and principal of Notchcode Creative, a visual communications studio in Colorado. He has over 13 years' experience in graphic design, branding, and integrated marketing. Graduating with a BFA in photography from the Savannah College of Art and Design in 1993, his background includes small boutique design studios and a large private university. Since opening Notchcode for business in 1999, he has created award-winning campaigns for local and national clients in the nonprofit, small business, corporate, and government sectors.